New Heaven, New Earth

New Heaven, New Earth

Shakespeare's Antony and Cleopatra

Jan H. Blits

LEXINGTON BOOKS

A DIVISION OF
ROWMAN & LITTLEFIELD PUBLISHERS, INC.
Lanham • Boulder • New York • Toronto • Plymouth, UK

Published by Lexington Books
A division of Rowman & Littlefield Publishers, Inc.
A wholly owned subsidiary of The Rowman & Littlefield Publishing Group, Inc.
4501 Forbes Boulevard, Suite 200, Lanham, Maryland 20706
www.lexingtonbooks.com

Estover Road, Plymouth PL6 7PY, United Kingdom

British Library Cataloguing in Publication Information Available

The hardback edition of this book was previously cataloged by the Library of Congress
as follows:

Blits, Jan H.
  New heaven, new earth : Shakespeare's Antony and Cleopatra / Jan H. Blits.
    p. cm.
  1. Shakespeare, William, 1564–1616. Antony and Cleopatra. 2. Cleopatra, Queen of
Egypt, d. 30 B.C.—In literature. 3. Antonius, Marcus, 83?–30 B.C.—In literature.
I. Title. II. Title: Shakespeare's Antony and Cleopatra.
PR2802.B65 2009
822.3'3—dc22   2009006532

ISBN 978-0-7391-3823-6 (cloth : alk. paper)
ISBN 978-0-7391-3824-3 (pbk : alk. paper)
ISBN 978-0-7391-3825-0 (electronic)

Printed in the United States of America

~

Contents

~

Preface

Like much of the humanities in general, the study of Shakespeare has been plagued in recent years by countless literary theories. The theories include Structuralism, Poststructuralism, Historicism, New Historicism, Postmodernism, Postcolonialism, Feminism, Pragmatism, Cultural Materialism, Deconstruction, Queer Theory, Marxist Theory, and many more. Whatever their differences, the theories take for granted that Shakespeare (or any writer) is a product or a prisoner of the prejudices of his own day. Shakespeare, in this diminishing view, is simply an Elizabethan Englishman whose plays and poems are fully determined by the narrow perspective of his immediate locale and time. And as they reduce the author to his culture, so too, in turn, these theories reduce his culture to prejudice, persecution, paranoia, power relations, oppression and state ideology. The author becomes merely the spokesman for—the slave of—his culture's ignorance, bigotry, social exploitation and injustice.

Rather than intrude any theory upon the play, I try to draw out of *Antony and Cleopatra* the substance that Shakespeare deliberately put into it. My study of the play is meant to be a work of philosophy, not of theory. Taking the play on its own terms, I try to be true to Shakespeare's text. I approach Shakespeare as a thinker of the first order, who, a master of his own thought and writing, wrote poetry with an infinitely conscious art. Instead of being organized thematically, my book, like my previous books on *Macbeth*, *Hamlet*, *A Midsummer Night's Dream* and *Coriolanus*, begins at the beginning and follows the play through to the end. Treating *Antony and*

Cleopatra as a coherent whole, it reaches its conclusions by closely examining Shakespeare's plot, characters, language, structure, digressions, allusions and other devices. I try to show that, as with any great work of art, the play's whole cannot be understood apart from all its parts and the parts cannot be understood apart from the whole. Since each presupposes the other, the whole and the parts must considered in the light of each other.

Once again, I wish to thank Harvey Flaumenhaft, Mera Flaumenhaft and Linda Gottfredson for their thoughtful comments on the manuscript and their innumerable discussions of the play.

~

Introduction

Antony and Cleopatra, as much a history play as a love story, depicts the transition from the pagan to the Christian world—from the aftermath of the collapse of the Roman Republic and the decline of the pagan gods to the emergence of the Roman Empire and the conditions giving rise to Christianity.[1] Under the Republic, Rome conquered nearly the entire known world. Its empire ranged from Britain, Spain and Gaul to North Africa, Asia and the Middle East. At the start of the play, only the Parthians remain a serious foreign threat to Rome, and Ventidius soon crushes them ("The ne'er-yet-beaten horse of Parthia / We have jaded out o'th' field" [3.1.34–35]).[2] With the Parthians' defeat, Rome's centuries of foreign wars come to a triumphant conclusion. But in conquering the world, Rome has also destroyed its republican regime and its distinctive way of life. By the time of *Antony and Cleopatra*, Rome's greatness has destroyed what made Rome great.

Life in republican Rome had been rooted in the soil of its territory, the traditions of its people and the worship of its gods. Rome's conquests, however, have extended Rome's boundaries to the boundaries of the world—"from edge to edge / O'th' world" (2.2.122–23). "All other lands have certain limits given," Ovid writes. "Our Rome with all the world's wide room is even" (Ovid, *Fasti*, 2.683–84).[3] The early Romans built the city's walls wider than they needed in order "to provide . . . for a future multitude in time to come" (Livy, *History of Rome*, 1.8.4).[4] Now its walls encompass virtually all the enemies that Rome has conquered. With its enormous expansion, Rome's republican traditions, although often persisting in name, have fallen into utter

1

disuse. Sextus Pompey, the only character in the play claiming to champion the republican cause, addresses Antony, Caesar and Lepidus as "[t]he senators alone of this great world" (2.6.9). He greets "the triumvirate" (3.6.29) with the title of the office which they have, in practice, displaced. And because Rome is now a worldwide empire, the gods which for centuries were thought to protect the city as a separate political community, and which inspired its martial way of life, lose their significance and strength. "[T]he god Hercules whom Antony loved / Now leaves him" (4.2.21–22). After Cleopatra wishfully and woefully invokes Juno, Mercury and Jove as Antony lies dying (4.15.35–37), only two pagan gods are named. Cleopatra in her next breath rails against Fortune for Antony's death (4.15.45–47). And Charmian, bidding the dead Cleopatra farewell, sees her death as dimming Phoebus's visible splendor: "Downy windows, close, / And golden Phoebus, never be beheld / Of eyes so royal again" (5.2.315–17). A world in which one man has become "[t]he universal landlord," "[s]ole sir o'th' world" (3.13.76; 5.2.119), has no need for gods who support political freedom, warlike action or earthly glory. Such a world, ruled largely by Fortune, needs a universal god of peace—a god supporting the habits of humility, submission and patience, not of pride, strength and action.

Rome's republican regime rested on the subordination of private goods to the public good. As Shakespeare shows in *Coriolanus*, Rome's early republicans thought a citizen's highest private good is attached to the city's public good. "If my son were my husband," Volumnia declares, "I should freelier rejoice in that absence wherein he won honour, than in the embracements of his bed, where he would show most love" (*Cor.*, 1.3.2–5).[5] Cominius goes further. "I do love / My country's good," he affirms,

> with a respect more tender,
> More holy and profound, than mine own life,
> My dear wife's estimate, her womb's increase
> And treasure of my loins.

> (*Cor.*, 3.3.111–15)

Where the Roman mother finds the city's honor superior to a lover's embrace, the one-time consul places no private good whatever above the city's good. The public good is superior to even the most precious private goods.

Rome's vast empire, however, has liberated private interests in Rome. The more spacious Rome's empire has grown, the more narrow the Romans' concerns have become. Universalism frees the private. Unlike in *Coriolanus* and even in *Julius Caesar*, in *Antony and Cleopatra* the word "Rome" always refers simply to a location, never to a political regime or a way of life.[6] It lacks political or moral connotations.[7] Reversing the superiority of the public to the private, patriotism is replaced by private interests and personal honor. Romans now think most of all of their own advantage and seldom, if at all, of Rome's.

The absence of public spirit is perhaps nowhere more salient or significant than in the army. During the Republic, Rome's soldiers were its citizens who served their country. They had a country to love, property to protect and a share of political power to preserve. But with Rome's continual expansion, military campaigns became more prolonged and more remote from Rome. Rome's citizen army could no longer maintain or extend its empire. Noncitizens and even freed slaves needed to be recruited in the most distant provinces. Rome's soldiers thus ceased to be Romans.[8] Nor could Rome's commanders be rotated annually, one consul succeeding another, as had previously been done. Fighting far from home, the generals commanded their armies for extended periods of time—Caesar for ten years in Gaul, for example, and Pompey for six years in Spain and another five in the East.[9] The commanders consequently conquered their own armies as well as their foreign enemies. Recruited and rewarded directly by their commanders, the armies ceased being the armies of Rome and became the private armies of their generals.[10] Rather than conscripted citizens fighting for their country, the soldiers were now mercenaries fighting for plunder and pay, recognizing no authority but that of their commander (see 3.1.31–35). "[N]o man [is] rich," Crassus famously boasted, ". . . that [can] not maintain a whole army with his own proper goods" (Plutarch, *Crassus*, 2.7–8).[11] And just as the soldiers' ties to their commanders became purely private, so did the commanders' own aims. The generals now fought "for Rome" only in a quibbling sense. Instead of fighting to protect or to augment Rome, they now fought to obtain it. Rome itself became the prize of civil wars rather than the beneficiary of foreign wars.

Desertions are quite common in *Antony and Cleopatra*. Among others, Menas deserts Pompey; Canidius, Enobarbus, Alexas and Dercetus desert Antony, as do his sailors, foot soldiers and cavalry. Romans behave not like fellow citizens, but like foreigners pursuing their own interests: "To Caesar will I render / My legions and my horse. Six kings already / Show me the way of yielding" (3.10.33–35). With all command now purely personal and the only links between a commander and his troops ones of personal interest, loyalty has become a matter of the soldier's own choice. Just as men are no longer obliged to be soldiers, soldiers can switch their loyalties as they choose.[12] Because all causes are alike and everyone is fighting only for himself and only for the sake of his commander's private inducements, the moral difference between loyalty and desertion largely disappears. Rather than abandoning friend for foe, desertion now amounts to changing like for like. Indeed, where desertion was formerly unpardonable in Rome, it not only has lost its deep opprobrium, but is now handsomely rewarded.[13]

The structure of Antony and Cleopatra reflects the joint ascendancy of the universal and the private. Scenes are set not just in Italy and Egypt, but in Greece and Syria, and the play's most famous speech describes Cleopatra in Asia Minor (2.2.201ff.). In almost every scene, messengers arrive or leave, criss-crossing "all the world," "the whole world," "this great world" (2.6.9; 2.7.62, 63, 66; 4.14.87; 5.1.39; 5.2.133).[14] On the other hand, none of the scenes in Rome occurs in public. In sharp contrast to Coriolanus and Julius Caesar, both of which begin with scenes of civil strife in the streets of Rome,[15] the Roman scenes take place indoors and in private rather than in the streets, the Capitol or any other public setting.[16] With a single exception (which confirms the rule), the only streets mentioned are in Egypt.[17] The Capitol, the only public building in Rome named, is spoken of only in the context of Rome's historic past (2.6.18).

The people are, likewise, mostly missing from Antony and Cleopatra. They are mentioned, but never seen or directly heard. Only Pompey counts on them for support ("The people love me" [2.1.9]), and he is disappointed. All the leaders, including Pompey himself, have nothing but contempt for or bitter indignation at the people's fickleness. And all, but Pompey, seem more concerned about avoiding their opposition or directing it against others than gaining their backing.[18] The people have lost their great political importance, not because they are fickle—they have always been a "many-headed multitude" (Cor., 2.3.16–17)—but because Rome's centuries-old clash between plebeians and patricians is now over, succeeded by armed conflict among its victorious generals. Paradoxically, the people lost their political power with their victory over their traditional enemies. Once the people defeated the nobles, their champions—the party of Caesar—no longer needed them and therefore dispensed with them.

As the people are missing, so, consequently, is political oratory. Political oratory, critical to events in Coriolanus and Julius Caesar,[19] comes to an end in Rome with the end of the Republic. Where there is no political freedom or public deliberations, there is no use for political oratory. It surely is no accident that Shakespeare makes Antony's funeral oration, which leads directly to the ouster of the republicans from Rome ("Brutus and Cassius / Are rid like madmen through the gates of Rome" [JC, 3.2.270–71]), the final political oration in Rome. With the end of the Republic, "a hush fell upon [political] eloquence" (Tacitus, *Dialogue on Orators*, 38).[20] While the leaders are fighting for who should be the people's master, the people, if engaged at all, are now fighting for whose slaves they should be.[21]

The reduction of the public to the private deprives political action of an ennobling spirit. Actions are only as noble as the cause they serve. Courage alone does not make a deed noble. When an action serves no good higher than one's own private good, it can be considered noble only in a diminished sense. This seems especially true in Rome. The Romans have always associated the word "noble" with the decorous. To the Romans, the noble implies the suitable and the seemly—what is appropriate and how one appears to others. "[The noble] may be named decorum in Latin, for in Greek it is called *prepon* [seemliness]" (Cicero, *De officiis*, 1.93).[22] To a traditional Roman, the noble befits a life of public duty, lived in constant public view. A noble act presupposes a public good.[23] But, just as the word "decorum" is spoken in the play only by Egyptians and only in un-Roman contexts (1.2.75–76; 5.2.17–18), the word "noble" is used mostly in an un-Roman fashion. While characters are frequently described or addressed as "noble," often by servants, subordinates and the obsequious Lepidus, few deeds are called "noble." Antony defiantly describes his and Cleopatra's loving embrace as "[t]he nobleness of life" (1.1.37–38). Lepidus fawningly characterizes Antony's apology to Caesar as "noble spoken" (2.2.104). And Thidias, reducing the noble to the expedient, cynically advises Cleopatra that surrendering to Caesar would be her "noblest course" (3.13.82). Apart from these instances of eros, softness and surrender, nearly the only deeds that anyone calls "noble" are suicides (4.14.61, 96–100; 4.15.90; 5.2.191, 236, 284, 343).[24] Pointing up the problem of performing noble actions in post-republican Rome, Enobarbus and Menas jokingly acknowledge that while one of them is "a great thief by sea," the other is a great thief "by land." The men are indistinguishably "two thieves" (2.6.93–98). In the absence of a public good, the moral difference between a Roman officer and a notorious pirate vanishes.

Throughout the play, we hear of Fortune rather than virtue ruling human affairs.[25] As Caesar and Antony win victories through their subordinates ("Caesar and Antony have ever won / More in their officer than person" [3.1.16–17]), their subordinates, in turn, win advancement through flattery and favor. Fortune's supremacy lessens even the greatest political achievement. "'Tis paltry to be Caesar," Cleopatra contemptuously declares. "Not being Fortune, he's but Fortune's knave, / A minister of her will" (5.2.2–4). Even supreme political glory deserves being despised, for it depends not on the victor but on Fortune. Owing to the increased role of Fortune and the reduced possibility of noble action, some Romans surrender themselves to luxury and sensual pleasure, while others withdraw from the world through philosophy. Eastern debauchery and Roman Stoicism take deep root in late- and post-republican Rome. The one turns men to pleasures of the body; the other, to a virtue of the mind. While neither necessarily precludes a political life, as Antony on the one hand and Brutus on the other show,[26] both pursuits, by placing happiness in the private realm, tend to detach a man from the activities and outcomes of political life. As Antony dismisses Rome and its empire ("Let Rome into Tiber melt, and the wide arch / Of the ranged empire fall!") while declaring that "[t]he nobleness of life" is for the world's greatest lovers to embrace (1.1.34–35, 37), the defeated Brutus can claim at Philippi that he will "have glory by this losing day / More than Octavius and Mark Antony / By this vile conquest shall attain unto" (JC, 5.5.36–38). For both men, their own private self-satisfaction eclipses the well-being of their country.

Yet, the self-satisfaction of private life soon turns against itself. Again and again, characters in *Antony and Cleopatra* express their deep dissatisfaction at gaining what they had long sought. "And what they undid did" applies not only to the pretty dimpled boys fanning Cleopatra's checks (2.2.215), but to nearly everyone in the play. Actions continually undermine and defeat themselves. Caesar complains that the people love the man they do not have until they have him and then no longer want him. "[H]e which is," he says, "was wished until he were, / And the ebbed man, ne'er loved till ne'er worth love, / Comes deared by being lacked" (1.4.42–44). Ventidius chooses not to pursue the Parthians back to Mesopotamia, for fear of offending Antony, in whose name he would win the great victory. "[A]mbition, / The soldier's virtue," he explains,

> rather makes choice of loss
> Than gain which darkens him.
> I could do more to do Antony good,
> But 'twould offend him, and in his offence
> Should my performance perish.

> (3.1.22–27)

For Ventidius to accomplish more in order to do his commander good would be to harm his own good and destroy his action. His doing would be his undoing. And Antony, who, much like Caesar, claims that the people's "love is never linked to the deserver / Till his deserts are past" (1.2.193–94), says the same about his own love: "What our contempts doth often hurl from us, / We wish it ours again" (1.2.130–31). Hence, Fulvia, whose death he had wished ("Thus did I desire it"), is "good, being gone. / The hand could pluck her back that shoved her on" (1.2.129, 133–34). We desire what we do not have until we have it, and reject what we have until we no longer have it. Our desires resist satisfaction: "What willingly he did confound he wailed"; "And strange it is / That nature must compel us to lament / Our most persisted deeds" (3.2.58; 5.2.28–30). Thus Antony, although declaring that "not a minute of our lives should stretch / Without some pleasure now" (1.1.47–48), finds that constant pleasure naturally turns into displeasure. "The present pleasure, / By revolution lowering, does become / The opposite of itself" (1.2.130–33). A constant pleasure, by becoming cloying or palling, becomes its own opponent ("[t]he opposite of itself") in the sense both of turning unpleasant and of causing us to desire something else. "[B]y revolution lowering," it is lowered in our estimation and replaced in our desire. Self-satisfaction, canceling itself, becomes self-dissatisfaction.[27]

The prospects regarding death are even more disturbing. Citizens of the Republic thought of themselves, first and foremost, as Romans. They were born, lived and died as Romans, not simply as human beings. Related to the city as parts to whole, they depended on the city for their being, while the city depended on them and their conduct for its continued existence and excellence. A Roman's desire for immortality could therefore find satisfaction in the continuation of Rome, for Rome bore the traces of his deeds and would retain his memory as long as it existed: ". . . our renown Rome, whose gratitude / Towards her deserved children is enroll'd / In Jove's own book" (Cor., 3.1.288–90). In dying for his country, a Roman gained his immortality. Seeing himself fundamentally as a member of the city's community, he needed no immortality other than his city's continued existence.[28]

Worldwide empire puts an end to this hope. Rome has ceased to be a city or a community. As Shakespeare shows, Romans now include men with such non-Roman names as Demetrius, Philo, Alexas, Eros and Dercetus. "Roman," no longer a term of distinction, has become a term of inclusion. If men are still parts of a whole, that whole is now the entire world or even the cosmos itself. Men are therefore forced to think differently of death. As the supremacy of the public gives way to the ubiquity of the private, men become unable to think of themselves as living on through their city. Their concern for immortality remains. If anything, it becomes more troubling. But men are now compelled to seek their immortality as individuals rather than as citizens. Having become atomized subjects of a universal empire, they must find their immortality within themselves. Immortality, like everything else, becomes radically private. If formerly a Roman's immortality lay in the immortality of

his country, it now comes to lie in that of his soul. Reversing the classical relation of a man and his country, the personal supplants the political. The salvation of one's soul replaces the salvation of one's country. The next world
replaces this one.

Antony concludes his initial exchange with Cleopatra by saying that she
would need to find "new heaven, new earth" to contain his love (1.1.17). His
remark is the first of the play's numerous allusions to the New Testament and,
particularly, to the Book of Revelation: "And I saw a new heaven and a new
earth: for the first heaven and the first earth were passed away" (Rev. 21:1).[29]
Rome's universal empire brings forth a new heaven as it establishes a new
earth.[30] While the empire does away with the need for gods who work
through the city and provide for men by providing for their city, Christianity, speaking to all men everywhere, teaches that God has a direct, immediate relation with every person in the world individually. Related to private
individuals rather than to political communities, the new religion is at once
particular and universal. Its new heaven mirrors the new earth.[31]

By conquering the world, Rome's principle of war produces a religion of
peace. The principle of war teaches men to love their fellow citizens and hate
their country's enemies. But now that all of Rome's enemies have become Romans, there are no enemies left to hate and so all of mankind must be loved.

> God . . . requires and rewards benevolence that makes no distinctions among
> persons. . . . It is equally forbidden to us to wish evil, to do evil, and to speak
> evil of our neighbors, yea, to think evil of whoever it be.
>
> (Tertullian, Apology, 36.3–4)

Dolabella will thus speak of swearing by a "command," which his "love makes
religion to obey" (5.2.197–98). An empire won by arms, paradoxically, ush-
ers in a religion based on peace, whose "first and great commandment" is love
(Matthew 22:37–39).

Antony, bored with Roman life, is drawn to the East: "I'th' East my pleasure lies" (2.3.39). Egypt is an exotic world of extravagance and sensuality. It
is the opposite of what austere republican Rome had been. The East is also
the source of Christianity: "Let me have a child . . . to whom Herod of Jewry
may do homage" (1.2.29–30; see Matt. 2:8). The East combines sensuality
and spirituality. Charmian hails the dying Cleopatra, "O eastern star!"
(5.2.307). The eastern star is, at once, Venus, the morning star, named for
the goddess of love, and the star signifying the birth of Jesus: "[W]e have seen
his star in the East, and are come to worship him" (Matt. 2:1–2). While capturing the sensuality and spirituality of the East, the star's double nature also

reflects Christianity's double treatment of the body. Christianity incarnates God as a man ("And the word was made flesh" [John 1:14]) and at the same time decarnalizes man's life. While the son of God not only lives but dies, man is promised an eternal life in death ("[T]he gift of God is eternal life" [Romans 6:23]). While Jesus accepts all the sufferings of death in the flesh, man's life becomes wholly spiritualized. Cleopatra, the "eastern star," thus faces death possessing "[i]mmortal longings" (5.2.280), believing that she will find "[a] better life" in death (5.2.2). Indeed, where John saw "the holy city, new Jerusalem, come . . . out of heaven, prepared as a bride trimmed for her husband" (Rev. 21:2), both Antony and Cleopatra echo his vision in envisioning their own deaths, he as the groom ("I will be / A bridegroom in my death and run into't / As to a lover's bed" [4.14.100–2]), she as the bride or the holy city itself ("Husband, I come!" [5.2.286]). As death seems to offer a better life, Roman spiritedness turns against itself and becomes spiritualized. "I am fire and air; my other elements / I give to baser life" (5.2.289–90). Replacing pride, honor and victory with humility, abjectness and suffering as the highest good, pagan spirit, directed inward and against man's worldly nature, becomes Christian spirituality.

Notes

1. "Of all Shakespeare's historical plays, 'Antony and Cleopatra' is by far the most wonderful. There is not one in which he has followed history so minutely." Samuel Taylor Coleridge, *Lectures and Notes on Shakespeare* (London: George Bell and Sons, 1908), 316.

2. All references to *Antony and Cleopatra* are to the Arden Shakespeare, ed. John Wilders (London: Routledge, 1995). I have occasionally revised quotations, based on the New Variorum Edition, ed. Horace Howard Furness (Philadelphia: J.B. Lippincott, 1907). References are to act, scene, and line.

3. Ovid, *Ovid's Festivals or Roman Calendar*, trans. John Gower (London: University of Cambridge, 1640), 41. See also, e.g., Polybius, *The Histories*, 3.1.4, 6.50.6, 15.9.5; Cicero, *Philippics*, 6.19; Livy, *Roman History*, 1.16.7; Virgil, *Aeneid*, 1.277ff., 6.780ff., 850–54, *Georgics*, 3.25.33; Appian, *Civil Wars*, 5.130. "[T]he greatest glory of all glories in [Pompey the Great] was . . . (as himself delivered openly in a full assembly, at what time he discoursed of his own exploits) that whereas Asia when he received it was the utmost frontier province and limit of the Roman Empire, he left the same in the very heart and minds thereof." Pliny the Elder, *Natural History*, 7.99; trans. Philemon Holland (London: Adam Islip, 1601), 169.

4. *The Roman History*, trans. Philemon Holland (1600) (London: Gabriel Bedell, 1659), 6. Where needed, the spelling and punctuation of early translations have been modernized, including some titles.

5. All references to *Coriolanus* are to the Arden Shakespeare, ed. Philip Brock-bank (London: Methuen, 2001).

6. Twenty-four of the thirty times the word appears in the play, "Rome" is pre-ceded by prepositions expressing a local relation ("in," twelve times; "to," six; "from," three; "at," two; and "of," one). Although the word "city" appears five times, it never refers to Rome. Enobarbus tells of "[t]he city" (Tarsus) casting its people out to see Cleopatra on her barge (2.2.223), Antony thrice refers to Alexandria as "the city" (4.8.8, 36; 4.10.5), and, looking back ruefully on his life, he boasts that he had once "made cities" (4.14.60). Cp. *Julius Caesar*, 1.2.149–55, 170–73; 1.3.108–11; 2.1.47–58, 321; 3.1.170; 3.2.22–35, 45–46; 5.3.63. All references to *Julius Caesar* are to the Arden Shakespeare, ed. T. S. Dorsch (London: Methuen, 1955).

7. "Roman," on the other hand, still retains its traditional significance. See, e.g., 1.2.88; 1.3.85; 1.5.45; 2.6.16; 4.15.59 [twice], 90.

8. See, e.g., Cicero, *Pro Balbo*, 24; Sallust, *Jugurthine War*, 86.2; Valerius Max-imus, *Memorable Deeds and Sayings*, 2.3.3; Plutarch, *Marius*, 9.1; Suetonius, *Augustus*, 16.1; Florus, *Epitome of Roman History*, 1.36.13; Gellius, *Attic Nights*, 16.10.10–15. See also Appian, *The Spanish Wars*, 84. For the earlier, republican practice, see, e.g., Polybius, 6.19.

9. Velleius Paterculus, *Compendium of Roman History*, 2.44.5, 46.1–2; Livy, *Peri-ochae*, 105; Plutarch, *Pompey*, 17ff., 31–42, 48.3, 51–52, 55.7, *Caesar*, 14.6, 15.3, 21.3, 28.5, *Crassus*, 15.5; Suetonius, *Divus Julius*, 24.1; Appian, *The Civil Wars*, 2.13, 17–18; Dio Cassius, *Roman History*, 38.8.5, 39.33.2–3, 40.56.2.

10. See, e.g., Cicero, *Philippics*, 10.12; Appian, *Civil Wars*, 4.93, 98. It was from Gaul that Caesar set out to cross the Rubicon; see, e.g., Caesar, *The Civil War*, 1.7–8.

11. *North's Plutarch*, trans. Thomas North, 8 vols. (1579; rpt. London: David Nutt, 1895), 4:46.

12. 2.7.82–85; 3.10.33–35; 3.13.205–6; 4.1.13–15; 4.5.4–6; 4.6.13–15; 4.12.11–13. See, e.g., Caesar, *Gallic War*, 1.39–41; Livy, *Periochae*, 98; Plutarch, *Sulla*, 25.1, 28.1–3, *Lucullus*, 7.1–2, 33–35; Appian, *The Mithridatic Wars*, 51–53, 59–60, 72, *Civil Wars*, 1.85, 89–90, 112; 2.47; Dio, 36.14–16, 47.2, 41.26.1.

13. Appian, *Civil Wars*, 5.17. Cp., e.g., Polybius, 11.25–30; Livy, *History*, 28.24–29; also Vegetius, *Epitome of Military Science*, 3.4.

14. The word "world" occurs forty-four times in the play, far more often than in any other Shakespeare play (*King John* is second with twenty-eight).

15. Likewise, in *The Rape of Lucrece* Brutus carries Lucrece's body through the streets of Rome to replace the kings with consuls (*Lucrece*, 1828–55).

16. The one Roman scene set (apparently) out of doors (2.4) is a private meeting. The scene's stage-designation of "*a street*," which can be found in some editions, comes not from the Folio, but from Edward Capell, *Comedies, Histories, & Tragedies*, 10 vols. (London: J. and R. Tonson, 1768; rpt. New York: AMS Press, 1968), 8:35.

17. 1.1.54; 1.4.20; 2.2.239; 4.3.3. The exception, whose location is universal or indefinite, is that Caesar, hearing of Antony's death, speaks of the failure of "[t]he round world" to shake lions "into civil streets / And citizens to their dens"

(5.1.15–17). That is also the play's sole mention of "citizen." Although Caesar's complaint about Octavia's unobtrusive return to Rome (3.6.43–51), and Antony's and Cleopatra's warning descriptions of Caesar's triumph in Rome, clearly allude to Rome's streets (4.12.33–37; 5.2.54–56, 208–14), they do not mention them.

    18. E.g., 1.2.192–99; 1.3.50–53; 1.4.36–37; 3.6.20–23.

    19. See also *Lucrece*, Argument, 31–36, 1818–55.

    20. Political speech is replaced by personal encomium, delivered in private (e.g., 1.4.56–72; 2.2.200–250; 5.2.75–99).

    21. Dio, 46.34.4.

    22. Cicero, *Marcus Tullius Cicero's Three Books of Duties*, trans. Nicholas Grimald (1556; rpt. Washington: Folger Books, 1990), 86.

    23. See, further, Jan H. Blits, *Spirit, Soul, and City: Shakespeare's "Coriolanus"* (Lanham: Lexington Books, 2006), 36.

    24. Antony describes his defeated army as having "nobly held" (3.13.175), and Proculeius, trying to prevent her suicide so Caesar can parade Cleopatra in Rome, speaks of her letting the world see Caesar's "nobleness well acted" (5.2.44). Although "noble" and its derivatives appear forty-five times in the play, Caesar and his subordinates seldom mention them and almost always disingenuously. Apart from his exclaiming "O noble weakness!" at the suicides of Cleopatra and Charmian (5.2.343), Caesar mentions "noble" only once, saying farewell to Antony and Octavia ("Most noble Antony" [3.2.27]), Agrippa once, sarcastically, describing Lepidus ("'Tis a noble Lepidus" [3.2.6]), and Thidias and Proculeius once each, trying to convince Cleopatra to surrender (3.13.82; 5.2.44). Octavia, on the other hand, lovingly calls Caesar "My noble brother" (3.2.42), and Dolabella similarly calls Cleopatra "Most noble empress" (5.2.70).

    25. The word "fortune" appears forty-five times in the play, more than twice as often as in any other Shakespeare play: twenty-five as "fortune" or "Fortune," nineteen as "fortunes," and once as "fortuned" (*The Merchant of Venice* ranks second with twenty-five mentions of all). "Fortunate" also appears once, "chance" seven times, and "luck[y]" thrice. With the single exception of Cleopatra's holding back money from Caesar (5.2.149), the word "deed" always refers to a deed one is unable or unwilling to perform (1.5.16–17; 3.1.14), a deed one hopes another will take or the gods will assist (1.1.63; 2.1.2), an act of mollifying speech (2.2.1) or an act of suicide (5.1.30; 5.2.5, 236). The words "act," "action" and "actor" are more varied. In addition to often playing on the theatrical sense, their meanings range from military plans, victories and defeats, to private complaints, specious offers and personal conduct, from murder and betrayal, to marriage, sexual intercourse and suicide (1.2.151; 2.2.27, 51, 121, 155; 2.5.9; 2.7.79; 3.1.13; 3.5.8; 3.7.68; 3.10.22; 3.12.35; 4.8.12; 5.1.22; 5.2.44). The play's only "noble act," like its only "noble deed," is Cleopatra's suicide (5.2.236, 284).

    26. JC, 2.2.116–17; 4.3.143–46; 5.1.62. Cassius similarly becomes an Epicurean (JC, 5.1.77–79).

    27. See also 4.14.48–50.

28. See, e.g., Cicero, *De senectute*, 6.18–19.

29. All quotations from the Bible are from *The Geneva Bible* (Geneva: Rovland Hall, 1560; rpt. Madison: University of Wisconsin Press, 1969). See Ethel Seaton, "*Antony and Cleopatra* and the *Book of Revelation*," *The Review of English Studies*, 22 (1946), 219–24.

30. Augustine, *The City of God*, 5.12.15ff.; Orosius, *Seven Books of History against the Pagans*, 3.8; 6.22; Dante, *Convivio*, 4.5.

31. 1 Corinthians 15:22; 1 Timothy 2:4–6.

~

Act One

Act One, Scene One

1.

The play opens in Egypt with two Roman officers discussing or disputing Antony's infatuation for Cleopatra and her influence on him as a soldier. Correcting Demetrius, who has evidently been defending Antony's indulgence as tolerable, Philo answers, "Nay, but this dotage of our general's / O'erflows the measure" (1.1.1–2). Virtually everything associated with Egypt will, both literally and figuratively, "o'erflow the measure." The land in which life depends on "the o'erflowing Nilus" (1.2.51) is a land of excess— of extravagance, exorbitance, luxuriance, prurience, indolence and magnificence.[1] Nothing in Egypt stays within the measure.

Philo underscores what Antony has become by contrasting him to his former glory. "Those his goodly eyes, / That o'er the files and musters of the war / Have glowed like plated Mars," he begins, "now bend, now turn / The office and devotion of their view / Upon a tawny front" (1.1.2–6). As Philo emphasizes with a pun on "front," Antony's eyes have turned from the face of war (see 1.4.80; 2.2.66; 3.13.5) to the face of a woman. The duty and devotion that he used to give to battle Antony now gives to Cleopatra. As a result, his heart has lost its temper. "His captain's heart," Philo continues,

> Which in the scuffles of great fights hath burst
> The buckles on his breast, reneges all temper

13

> And is become the bellows and the fan
> To cool a gipsy's lust.

> (1.1.6–10)

In Philo's view, Antony's heart was both self-restrained ("temper[ed]") and hard as steel ("temper[ed]"). To this Roman soldier, there can be no immoderate degree of martial hardness or virtue. While excess in love is immoderate, excess in war is moderate. Indeed, according to Philo, the more like Mars, the more moderate. Though bursting the buckles of his armor, Antony's heart was "temper[ed]."

Throughout the play, characters, including Antony himself, contrast him now to what he once had been. Virtually every time, the comparison is unfavorable. What Antony had been is seen as better. It is the standard by which his martial greatness is measured. Philo, however, magnifies and simplifies the contrast. Disregarding Antony's well-known earlier sensual life in Rome, he speaks as though Antony had never been "given to sports [and] wildness," never "revel[ed] long a-nights," never was "a masker and a reveller" (JC, 2.1.189; 2.2.116; 5.1.62), until he met Cleopatra. Indignant at, or repelled by, what he sees, he ignores a characteristic part of Antony's past in order to increase his indictment of his present life.

Philo stresses that Cleopatra is Egyptian ("a tawny front"; "a gipsy's lust"). Since to be a man is to be stronger than pleasure and pain, to surrender to sensuality is to cease to be a man. Antony has thrown away his Roman greatness not only for a woman, however, but for an Egyptian woman. Compounding his disgrace by enslaving himself to a foreigner, he has degraded his great heart by devoting himself to arousing and satisfying an Egyptian's lust.[2] Shakespeare will later identify Cleopatra as a Ptolemy and hence of pure Macedonian blood (1.4.6, 17; 2.7.34; 3.6.15; 3.12.18).[3] Yet, to Philo and other Romans, not least of all Antony, Cleopatra is emphatically Egyptian ("'my serpent of old Nile' / . . . he calls me" [1.5.26–27]).[4] Even as Rome has conquered the world and made many foreigners Romans—"Rome received [men of all nations] as slaves and sent them out as Romans" (Montesquieu, Considerations on . . . the Romans, 13)[5]—Romans, whether in fascination or disgust, emphasize and even exaggerate the difference between themselves and foreigners. This seems the reason why Shakespeare, although leaving many other characters nameless, puts the description of Cleopatra as a "tawny . . . gipsy" in the mouth of a Roman bearing a famous Alexandrian name, talking to another Roman with a famous Macedonian name—names which, moreover, are never mentioned in the play's dialogue or in Plutarch's Antony.[6] Philo ignores Cleopatra's Greekness and enlarges his own Romanness. He turns himself, a Greco-Roman, into a Roman, and Cleopatra, a Greco-Egyptian, into an Egyptian. While brought together by Rome's sweeping empire, he is Roman owing to Rome's conquest of Greece, and she is Egyptian owing to Alexander's conquest of Egypt.

Philo seems to consider himself a traditional Roman. *Virtus*, to him, is virtue. Valor, standing before all and in place of many other virtues, outshines them all. But unlike a traditional Roman, Philo tacitly grants that some dotage or infatuation is acceptable. The only question for him is whether Antony has gone too far. Nothing that Philo says suggests the republican contempt for sensuality that characterized Cassius ("Yond Cassius has a lean and hungry look" [*JC*, 1.2.191]), let alone the heroic admiration for austerity, even severity, that marked Coriolanus ("The moon of Rome, chaste as the icicle / That's curdied by the frost from purest snow . . ." [*Cor.*, 5.3.65–66]). Philo is not alone. Enobarbus, Maecenas, Agrippa, Lepidus, Pompey and Demetrius are all at least as tolerant of sensuality as he. Caesar is the only exception. Yet, his objection to Alexandrian revelry will be a utilitarian calculation of, rather than a spirited contempt for, the body's demands. The weakness of his body, not the strength of his soul, will spur his disapproval. Fear rather than pride animates his virtue (2.7.98–100, 119–26).[7]

Philo also fails to mention Rome. The closest he comes is to call Antony "[t]he triple pillar of the world," an allusion to him as a member of the ruling triumvirate. Instead of being concerned with the effect of Antony's conduct on Rome, Philo is concerned with the change in Antony himself. "Look where they come," he says of the arriving entourage, "Take but good note, and you shall see in him / The triple pillar of the world transformed / Into a strumpet's fool" (1.1.10–13). Unlike the citizen-soldiers of the Republic, Philo and Demetrius serve Antony, not Rome. They fight for their commander rather than for their country. In one important way, however, the loyalty of at least some of Antony's men will prove different from that of the other leaders' men. Like that of the others, their loyalty will be their own choice. Antony's men will stay loyal only so long as they wish. But while the others' will rest on promised payments, the loyalty of many of Antony's men will rest in large part on their respect and admiration—indeed, their love— for him. When, after Actium, Antony offers them gold and tells them to leave him ("I have a ship / Laden with gold. Take that, divide it. Fly / And make your peace with Caesar"), many will refuse: "Fly? Not we" (3.11.4–6). Worthiness will mean something to them that it does not mean to the others.[8] Thus, the only issue for Philo and Demetrius is whether Antony is still worthy of their loyalty.

Ironically, Philo's speech, like what it indicts, is itself marked by excess. Plutarch says that Antony "used a manner of phrase in his speech, called Asiatic, which . . . was like to his manners and life" (Plutarch, *Antony*, 2.5; North, 6:2).[9] Philo's speech is similar. Asiatic speech is characterized by long sentences amplifying thoughts and words, including the use of redundancy, expansiveness, ornateness, histrionics, listings and periphrasis for what might have been said directly.[10] After initially stating his conclusion, Philo has two long sentences, each five lines with strong mid-stops and parallel structure. Both sentences contain the subject (in half a line), modified by a personal possessive pronoun and an admiring adjective ("his goodly eyes," "His captain's heart"), a subordinate clause (a line-and-a-half, with a mid-stop), describing how Antony used to be ("That o'er . . ."; "Which in . . ."), a double verb, telling the change in his eyes and heart and hence, metonymically, in Antony himself ("now bend, now turn"; "reneges / And is become"), and a final pejorative phrase describing the tawdry Cleopatra ("a tawny front"; "a gipsy's lust"), whom Philo never mentions by name. In addition also to using alliteration,[11] Philo speaks, throughout, in hyperbole and pleonasm. Besides comparing Antony's eyes to the bright and shining Mars clad in his armor and describing his heart in battle as bursting the armor on his chest, he uses a double genitive ("this dotage of our general's"), collocates a demonstrative and a personal pronoun ("Those his . . . eyes"), pairs terms differing, at most, only slightly ("the files and musters," "now bend, now turn," "The office and devotion," "the scuffles of great fights," "the bellows and the fan"), transforms a part into the whole ("The triple pillar of the world"), and emphatically repeats himself ("Look . . . / Take but good note, and you shall see . . . / Behold and see").[12]

Philo, at once Antony's critic and mimic, simultaneously stresses and obscures the difference between West and East, Rome and Egypt. Fittingly, both words in his opening phrase, the dissenting "Nay, but . . ." are stated as negatives; yet, in context, "Nay," which reproves as well as denies,[13] means "yes," while "but" is a qualification strong enough to cancel the agreement. The words speak against themselves as they affirm themselves. Equally affirming and denying traditional Roman standards, they epitomize the tension within many of the characters' Egyptianized Roman taste, and point, more broadly, to the frequent tendency in the play for something to become its own opposite and for stark opposites to become interchangeable. The play's opening words foreshadow Antony's and Cleopatra's final words (4.15.61; 5.2.312).

2.

Antony and Cleopatra enter, accompanied by "*her Ladies . . . with Eunuchs fanning her*" (s.d. 1.1.10). If Egypt is given to licentiousness on the one hand, it is given to effeminacy and emasculation on the other. Egypt's extraordinarily long history is one of continual enslavement. Besides having lived for the last half millennium subservient to foreign (Persian and Macedonian) monarchs, the Egyptians have lived since time immemorial under the absolute rule of divine kings and queens, incarnations of the gods' majesty.[14] Cleopatra is only the latest of countless Egyptian monarchs who have claimed divine status.[15] As a result, Egypt is a country whose people devote themselves entirely to private concerns and pay no attention whatever to political matters. Their lives are completely apolitical. In fact, meddling in politics is a punishable crime. "[A]mong the Egyptians," Diodorus Siculus writes, "if any artificer were so hardy to meddle with matters of the law . . . he should be grievously amerced and punished utterly therefore."[16] And as divine pretension follows from the monarchs' unlimited power over their subjects, so, too, does slothful effeminacy. Where Roman freedom always rested on the Romans' sense of their manliness,[17] Egyptian submission and passivity are equally a cause and a consequence of Egyptian emasculation. The Egyptians are political eunuchs. Thus, while the only Egyptians she listens to are women, Cleopatra surrounds herself with eunuchs as well as with a female court.[18] Trusted as personal servants because of their need for protection and hence their capacity for loyalty,[19] and displayed as royal ornaments because of their absolute submission to the monarch,[20] the eunuchs, viewed by Romans with horror,[21] are a synecdoche for the effeminacy, docility, servility and impotence of the Egyptian way of life. Their emasculation exalts their monarchs as it denatures and degrades the eunuchs themselves.

Antony and Cleopatra seem to place their private love above their public duties, yet they make their private love completely public. They not only display it in public; they put it on display. Just as Philo introduces their appearance as though he were introducing a theatrical performance ("Look . . . / Take but good note, and you shall see . . . / Behold and see"), the lovers treat their love as though it were a stage show which an admiring audience is watching them perform. Although everything seems personal, nothing is private for Antony and Cleopatra. Except for a brief moment when he is furious at her (3.13.110–36), they are never "all alone" (1.1.53) on stage.[22] They are always before others, always noted, and always discussed.

Cleopatra begins their exchange with a test and a tease: "If it be love indeed, tell me how much" (1.1.14). Unless Antony can tell her how much he loves her, he does not love her "indeed," but only in words (see 1.5.15–17). Yet, although making it necessary for Antony to tell her, Cleopatra also makes it impossible, for he cannot tell her how much he loves her without limiting his love. To tell how much is to say that he could love her still more.

Antony tries to escape Cleopatra's teasing trap by denying its first principle: "There's beggary in the love that can be reckoned" (1.1.15). No great love can be measured. Cleopatra, taking Antony at his word, suddenly reverses her tease. Instead of forcing him to prove his love by telling how much it is, she confidently assumes his love, but seeks to set a limit on it: "I'll set a bourn how far to be beloved" (1.1.16). Like any limit, Cleopatra's would imply that Antony could love her still more, more than she allows. As with her first tease, his love would not be as great as it might be. Antony, with a mixture of surrender and persistence, grants Cleopatra's premise but denies that she could find such a limit in the world: "Then thou must needs find out new heaven, new earth" (1.1.17). If she were to set a limit to his love, it would have to exceed any limit in the world.

Antony's answer alludes to the Apocalypse: "And I saw a new heaven and a new earth: for the first heaven and the first earth were passed away" (Rev. 21:1). Antony's unwitting allusion is apt not only because it points generally to the rise of Christianity, but also because it points specifically to a new, immeasurable, spiritual heaven beyond the natural heavens of fixed proportions and the fixed stars (cp. 2.7.14–16; 3.13.150–52; 5.2.82–83; also 3.6.50). "The pure in heart ascends to the region of the air until he reaches the kingdom of the Heavens, passing through those mansions which the Greeks called spheres and the Scriptures Heavens" (Origen, *On First Principles*, 2.11.6).[23] The new heaven is limitless.

As will be their wont, Cleopatra takes the initiative in their first exchange and Antony responds. She acts; he reacts. She opposes, cleverly tests and thwarts him, and he does his best to match her. Cleopatra begins with the conditional "If," a word she will often use to challenge, contrive, threaten or promise.[24] Antony will soon boast that he and Cleopatra are a peerless pair of lovers (1.1.38–41). But however great their love may be, to the very end— even when Cleopatra imagines their lives in death (5.2.300–302)—it will be shadowed by their mutual uncertainties and jealousies. It will always be, in some important sense, conditional.

A messenger arrives from Rome. Antony, annoyed by the intrusion, wants to hear only a brief summary of his report ("Grates me! The sum" [1.1.19]). Cleopatra, however, suddenly jealous, taunts him. No longer playful, she countermands him ("Nay, hear them, Antony" [1.1.20]) and then accuses Antony of unmanliness. Where Philo criticized him for unmanly sensuality, Cleopatra accuses him of unmanly submission. "Fulvia perchance is angry," she mocks;

or who knows
If the scarce-bearded Caesar have not sent

His powerful mandate to you: "Do this, or this;
Take in that kingdom or enfranchise that.
Perform't, or else we damn thee."

(1.1.21–25)

A manly man neither fears a woman's anger nor obeys a boy's command.[25] Philo complained of Antony's enslavement to Cleopatra and of his abandonment of Rome and war. Cleopatra proves him right precisely by her insistence that he is wrong. In addition, she does exactly what she accuses Fulvia of doing. By accusing Antony of being unmanly for obeying Fulvia, she proves him unmanly for obeying her. She shows his fear of a woman by shaming him for his fear of a woman.

Antony blushes, and Cleopatra, claiming that the blush confesses that she is correct, shames him further. "As I am Egypt's Queen," she chides, "Thou blushest, Antony, and that blood of thine / Is Caesar's homager; else so thy cheek pays shame / When shrill-tongued Fulvia scolds" (1.1.30–33). Shame often shows on the face—in a blush, an averted gaze, lowered eyes, a lowered head (e.g., 3.11.51–54; 4.14.74–77). While shame judges the sort of person one is, the whole of one's being,[26] the face represents the person himself ("The face is the image of the soul" [Cicero, *Orator*, 18.60]).[27] Cleopatra, while ignoring that his blush might be for his submission to her—for his shame at allowing her to shame him—not only shames Antony with her taunt, but adds to his shame by drawing attention to his blush. She compounds his shame by causing him to feel ashamed of his shame and does so, moreover, in the sight of others. While shame, involving a sense of having been seen uncovered,[28] prompts a strong desire not to be seen, Cleopatra publicly directs everyone's eyes to Antony's face. She adds to his loss of face by drawing attention to his face.

Rather than defending himself by reminding Cleopatra of his responsibilities as one of the world's rulers, Antony, responding in her terms, renounces Rome and political life altogether. "Let Rome in Tiber melt, and the wide arch / Of the ranged empire fall!" he declares. "Here is my space. / Kingdoms are clay; our dungy earth alike / Feeds beast as man" (1.1.34–37). The glory of an empire at once wide-ranging and well-ordered ("the wide arch / Of the ranged empire") offers no distinction. On the contrary, even the peak of political greatness, reducing politics to earth and earth to dung, reduces man to the level of a beast.

Despite what Philo seems to believe, however, Antony does not reject politics for mere sensuality. As his denigration of the body suggests, Antony seeks what is noble or splendid. The realm of noble activity, however, has radically shifted. Nobility has taken on a new meaning. "The nobleness of life / Is to do thus," Antony exults, embracing Cleopatra,

> when such a mutual pair
> And such a twain can do't, in which I bind,
> On pain of punishment, the world to weet
> We stand up peerless.

(1.1.37–41)

From the earliest days of the Republic, Romans vied with one another for the highest public honors. Spiritedness ruled their souls. Hungry for glory and greedy for praise, the Romans strove to surpass one another in war in order to win the city's highest renown.[29] "[I]t is incredible to report," Sallust writes, "in how short a time, the city, having obtained . . . liberty in government, increased and prospered, so infinite a desire for glory had possessed the minds of all sorts" (Sallust, *Catiline Conspiracy*, 7.3).[30] Spirited ambition for unrivaled distinction still governs Antony's soul, but its object has changed. The noblest activity, he declares, is to be found not in public but private pursuits, not in political but amorous activity. And as the activity has changed, so has the glory. Where an earlier Roman sought his individual glory (". . . get the start of the majestic world, / And bear the palm alone" [*JC*, 1.2.130]), Antony claims the greatest glory for himself and Cleopatra as a couple. Stressing both their reciprocity and high station ("such a mutual pair / And such a twain"), he emphasizes the intimacy and the greatness of their love. Not he alone, but they as a royal pair, are peerless.

However much Antony repudiates politics, his antipolitical claim to glory is fundamentally political. His and Cleopatra's complete devotion to each other does not imply an indifference to the rest of the world. Philo suggested that he has eyes only for Cleopatra, but Antony has eyes for how their love appears to the whole world. He wants public recognition for what is essentially private and even threatens to punish the world if it fails to acknowledge ("weet")[31] Cleopatra and himself as supreme lovers.[32] His reevaluation of what constitutes nobility thus has a distinctive Roman ring. It uses the traditional, spirited Roman locution for ambition and honor. Rome may "melt" and the empire may "fall," but Antony and Cleopatra will "stand up" unequaled for their love. The low will sink and fall; the high will stand up and stand out.[33] Cleopatra disbelieves what she hears, but likes it all the same. "Excellent falsehood!" (1.1.41). Because love speaks in perpetual hyperbole, a certain kind of falsehood is an essential part of love-speech. A lover says things which both the lover and the beloved know are untrue, but which the beloved still welcomes, for the words express what the lover wishes were true. The indicative is really the optative ("Eternity was in our lips" [1.3.36]). Cleopatra twice calls something excellent: "Excellent falsehood," here; "excellent dissembling," later (1.3.80). Both times, she sharply distinguishes excellence from truthfulness in love. "Excellent," for her, describes what eminently pleases or flatters her.

Cleopatra's proof that Antony is speaking falsely is that he married and therefore loved and still loves Fulvia. "Why did he marry Fulvia and not love her?" she asks rhetorically (1.1.42). Cleopatra will frequently ask rhetorical questions. She has already asked two to mock Antony (1.1.26, 29). While using them nearly whenever she speaks of Fulvia, she will ask them throughout the play to accuse, command, confirm, threaten and silence as well as to express amazement, contempt, desire, impatience, self-pity, incredulity and indignation, among other things. Her dying words and her words when Antony dies will be rhetorical questions.[34] Cleopatra will soon say that she keeps Antony's love by continually opposing him (1.3.4–11). A rhetorical question is of a piece with her tactic. In the guise of an inquiry, it forcefully asserts the opposite of what it ostensibly asks, and it is calculated entirely for effect.[35] Here, Cleopatra asks a rhetorical question to emphasize that her implicit accusation cannot be denied. In making her point, she overlooks that Antony's marriage to Fulvia might have been a loveless political marriage, which, as we shall see, is common in Rome, or that he could love a later love more than an earlier one, as she will protest is true of herself (1.5.76–78). Despite enjoying Antony's superlative claim for their love, she speaks both jealously and tauntingly of Fulvia, as she always will.

Cleopatra says she will pretend to believe Antony ("I'll seem the fool I am not"), while "Antony / Will be himself" (1.1.43–44). Always an actress, she will play the part of foolishly believing Antony's excessive vows of love. And, in pretending to be fooled, she will fool Antony, who, being himself, will be both the (would-be) deceiver and the (unwitting) deceived. She will deceive him with his own deception, fool him by playing the fool, as she will later do in her only meeting with Caesar (5.2.110–89). As though on cue, Antony turns Cleopatra's description of him into his flattery of her: "But stirred by Cleopatra" (1.1.44). Antony will be himself—Cleopatra's noble lover—inspired by her.

Antony, trying to end the argument ("conference harsh" [1.1.46]), appeals to "the love of Love and her soft hours" (1.1.45). Love, he says, goes together with softness, not with harshness. It is contrary to war. In speaking of "the love of Love," Antony conflates the passion and the object of love as well as the human experience and the goddess of love (Venus). Love, he suggests, beautifies itself as well as the beloved.[36] While tending to flatter the beloved, it also flatters itself. The lover's belief that love itself is beautiful seems to point to an element of self-love which is manifest in jealousy, but otherwise often hidden in love. "The love of Love" may be essentially as well as literally self-love.

Rejecting the quarreling, Antony says that every minute of their lives should be pleasurable: "There's not a minute of our lives should stretch / Without some pleasure now" (1.1.47–48). Their lives should have constant pleasure. Constant pleasure, however, requires constantly changing pleasures. "[S]ome pleasure now" means "some pleasure new."[37] To avoid satiety or boredom, every minute must have a new pleasure. The life of constant pleasure thus requires Cleopatra's "infinite variety" (2.2.246) of pleasures. Whether "in sport or in matter of earnest," Plutarch reports, Cleopatra "[always] devised sundry new delights" for Antony (Plutarch, Antony, 29.1; North, 6:29). Without the constant variety, the constant pleasure would end.[38]

Cleopatra, however, does not quit goading. Continuing to cross him ("Hear the ambassadors" [1.1.49]), she once again demands that Antony do what she blames him for doing. As before, she makes it impossible for him to answer. Initially, Antony could not show that he loves her in deed without showing that he does not love her enough. Now, he cannot do what she wants without not doing what she says, or do what she says without not doing what she wants. He must defy either her words or her wishes. Yet, although beginning to become impatient, Antony quickly turns the cause of his impatience into Cleopatra's beauty: "Fie, wrangling queen, / Whom everything becomes—to chide, to laugh, / To weep; whose every passion fully strives / To make itself, in thee, fair and admired!" (1.1.49–52). Nothing lacks beauty in Cleopatra. Everything that she does—everything that she becomes—becomes her. Every passion, however much a wanting, a needing, a longing, a scolding, makes itself beautiful in her.

Refusing to hear any messenger except from her, Antony, evidently trying to indulge Cleopatra, proposes that they wander through the streets tonight and note the peoples' characteristics.[39] "Come, my queen, / Last night you did desire it" (1.1.55–56). Despite the continual changes in their pleasures, last night's whim might still be tonight's desire. Antony might be indulging himself as well, however. Cleopatra's whim promises to exhibit the exotic to him. In the same way that it requires fresh pleasures, the life of pleasure relishes the exotic. The pursuit of different pleasures includes the pursuit of pleasures of difference. This is all the more so in an age of universalism. Universalism, by itself, places a premium on the exotic, as Antony's love of the

Egyptian queen ("'my serpent of old Nile' / . . . he calls me" [1.5.26–27])
seems to show.[40] Sameness makes strangeness enchanting.

3.
Antony has proved Philo correct. Philo urged Demetrius to watch Antony
and see him transformed into a strumpet's fool. And Demetrius, no longer defending him, reluctantly agrees. "Is Caesar with Antonius prized so slight?"
he asks or remarks, using Antony's name in Latin, for emphasis (1.1.57).
Philo, perhaps surprisingly, softens his criticism and now partly defends
Antony. "Sir, sometimes, when he is not Antony," he explains, "He comes
too short of that great property / Which still should go with Antony"
(1.1.58–60). Philo manages to avoid blaming Antony while nevertheless acknowledging his failing. He distinguishes Antony from Antony. When
Antony behaves in an infatuated fashion, he is not Antony. He is Antony
only when he measures up to the great quality proper to him. What is proper
to Antony—"that great property" which makes Antony Antony—is somehow separable from him. The separation of "Antony" from "[h]e" allows
Philo to identify only the noble Antony as Antony—the only Antony he
identifies (twice) by name[41]—and thus to shield Antony from blame.
Antony and Enobarbus will similarly divide themselves in order to preserve
their noble selves (e.g., 3.10.35–37; 3.11.7ff.; 3.13.42).

Demetrius says he is sorry that Antony "approves the common liar who /
Thus speaks of him at Rome" (1.1.61–62). The common talk in Rome, typ-
ically malicious, turns out to be correct this time. Neither Philo nor
Demetrius states whether Antony is still worthy of their loyalty. All
Demetrius says is that he "will hope / Of better deeds tomorrow" (1.1.62–63).
While Shakespeare leaves their judgments uncertain or implicit, all of the
other characters in the play who speak of their hopes are greatly disappointed
(2.1.10, 39; 2.6.57; 3.13.181; 4.2.42; 4.3.10; 4.12.8).

Act One, Scene Two

1.
The scene's opening section, set in the serving room for an Alexandrian banquet, combines sensuality and spirituality, levity and gravity, sexuality and
mortality. Charmian, who guides the conversation, begins by flattering
Alexas ("Lord Alexas, sweet Alexas, most anything Alexas, almost most absolute Alexas" [1.2.1–2]), pretending to be unable to find the words to praise
him sufficiently, and asking him for the Soothsayer whom he praised so highly
to Cleopatra. "O, that I knew this husband which you say must charge his

horns with garlands" (1.2.3–5). It is hard to be certain what the Soothsayer had said. As we shall see in a moment, he, like soothsayers generally, is ambiguous and enigmatic, and Charmian, wanting to hear what she considers favorable prophecies, is disposed to willfully misunderstand him at every chance. Whatever he might have said, Charmian understands him to have promised that her husband will be a cuckold whose horns will be garlanded in triumph. He will be the champion cuckold—the cuckold laureate—of Egypt.[42]

When Alexas produces the Soothsayer and Charmian asks whether he knows things, the man replies, "In nature's infinite book of secrecy / A little I can read" (1.2.10–11). He can know a little of the future, which other people cannot. Charmian seems to think this means that the Soothsayer can cause the future which he prophesies. Offering her hand, she bids, "Good sir, give me a good fortune" (1.2.14–15). The Soothsayer, however, corrects her: "I make not, but foresee" (1.2.16). Powerless and passive, the Egyptians, as Charmian exemplifies here, place their trust not in themselves, but in fortune.

Ever since the time of Romulus and Numa, the Romans have practiced augury or divination.[43] Believing that the gods take part in human affairs, they hold that the gods send meaningful signs to men, solicited or unsolicited, through thunderstorms, comets, shooting stars, entrails, dreams and other forms of omens and auspices. The interpretation of portents and prodigies is thus central to Roman religion and Roman life. One might therefore think that Roman divination and Egyptian soothsaying are similar. The former reads the flights of birds; the latter, the palms of humans. Traditionally, however, Roman augurs have not told fortunes. Rather than providing foresight or knowledge of future events, they have ascertained divine approval or disapproval of courses of action already proposed.[44] Instead of foretelling what the future holds, they have encouraged or discouraged men in actions already decided upon. Thus, while the Egyptians use soothsaying to ascertain their fate, the Romans have used augury to test their decisions. Their traditional understanding of divination has allowed and even encouraged them to act in such a way as to make the gods' signs come true.[45] While the Romans' trust in divination is therefore entirely compatible with freedom, action and self-governance, the Egyptians' trust in soothsaying is, reciprocally, cause and effect of their submission, passivity and royal despotism. The one supports, the other thwarts, human freedom and action.[46]

Charmian, with increasingly bawdy banter, intentionally misunderstands the Soothsayer's prophecies. When the Soothsayer first prophesies that she will be "yet far fairer" than she is (1.2.18), Charmian understands "fairer" not as nobler or even as more fortunate, but as better looking ("He means in flesh" [1.2.19]). And when he next prophesies that she "shall be more belov- ing than beloved" (1.2.24), Charmian, wanting pleasant prophecies, rejects this one: "I had rather heat my liver with drinking" (1.2.25). She would rather arouse her sexual desire by drinking than by unrequited love.[47] Eager to hear "some excellent fortune" (1.2.27), Charmian proposes her own:

> Let me be married to three kings in a forenoon and widow
> them all. Let me have a child at fifty to whom Herod of Jewry may
> do homage. Find me to marry me with Octavius Caesar and
> companion me with my mistress.

> (1.2.27–31)

Charmian, unwittingly and irreverently alluding to the advent of Christian- ity, combines the hedonistic and the holy. She aspires to be the wife and widow of the Magi, the mother of Jesus,[48] the wife of Caesar, and hence the equal of Cleopatra (via Caesar's fellow triumvir, Antony).[49] She would com- bine the new heaven and the new earth, the religion of Christianity and the politics of triumviral Rome.

While the women understand them in a sexual sense, the Soothsayer's prophecies will turn out to be true in an unexpected and untoward sense with Cleopatra's death. "[Y]et far fairer" and "more beloving than beloved," Charmian will kill herself for love of Cleopatra (5.2.321). "You shall outlive the lady whom you serve," the Soothsayer continues (1.2.32). Charmian quite naturally mistakes the prophecy for the promise of a long life: "O ex- cellent, I love a long life better than figs" (1.2.33–34). The prophecy will prove true, however, only when she outlives Cleopatra by a few moments. And while Charmian's declared love of figs seems meant, in context, to hint at her love of male genitals ("The fig leaf . . . seemeth naturally to resemble the member of generation" [Plutarch, *Isis and Osiris*, 36 (365B)]),[50] a basket of figs will provide the instrument of their deaths (5.2.233, 321, 350).

The Soothsayer offers another prophecy, which will also come true with Cleopatra's death: "You have seen and proved a fairer former fortune / Than that which is to approach" (1.2.35–36). Charmian understands the prophecy to refer to her moral reputation: Her reputation will not be as fair in the fu- ture as it has been in the past. Untroubled by what others might consider a shameful prospect, Charmian construes the prophecy to signify that she will have bastard children: "Then belike my children shall have no names" (1.2.37–38). Her only question is how many she will have: "Prithee, how many boys and wenches must I have?" (1.2.38–39). The Soothsayer answers,

"If every of your wishes had a womb, / And fertile every wish, a million" (1.2.40–41). Charmian's sexual wishes are boundless. Charmian, evidently embarrassed by the Soothsayer's accurate answer, dismisses him as a sham: "Out, fool! I forgive thee for a witch" (1.2.42). Wanting to hear a pleasing, not a truthful, fortune, she rejects the truth teller as a foolish fraud. Alexas, joining in, suggests that what the Soothsayer said is known to all. "You think none but your sheets are privy to your wishes" (1.2.43–44). Everyone knows Charmian's desires. They are an open secret.

When Charmian wants to hear Iras's fortune and Alexas wants to hear everyone's ("We'll know all our fortunes" [1.2.46]), Enobarbus, whose only previous words ordered the servants to serve the banquet quickly and keep the wine flowing (1.2.12–13), answers Alexas's request with joking candor: "Mine, and most of our fortunes tonight, shall be drunk to bed" (1.2.47–48). Enobarbus is quite at home in Cleopatra's court. At least as much as any of Antony's other officers, he enjoys Egypt's voluptuous pleasures, especially those of heavy drink ("Shall we dance . . . the Egyptian Bacchanals / And celebrate our drink?" [2.7.104–5]). Yet, Enobarbus also has a certain Roman contempt for his Egyptian indulgence.[51] A man of both Roman and Egyptian tastes, he often distances himself from his enjoyment, as he does here, by speaking of it half as spectator and half as participant, with the former bluntly if comically candid about the latter. His characteristic ironic detachment, frequently mistaken for a choric function,[52] allows him to have things both ways. It permits him to be, and not be, superior to his Eastern pleasures.

Iras, holding out her oily palm to be read, proudly declares, "There's a palm presages chastity, if nothing else" (1.2.50). Charmian, not allowing Iras to have a claim, however bogus, to any kind of superiority, tries to refute her while ostensibly strengthening her claim. "E'en as the o'erflowing Nilus presageth famine," she sarcastically replies (1.2.51–52), reversing a principle of palmistry. The hand corresponding to the heart, "an oily palm" signifies not a chaste but a lecherous disposition ("a fruitful prognostication" [1.2.54–55]).[53]

In contrast to the prophecy she proposed for herself, Charmian wants Iras to have "but a workaday fortune" (1.2.56). When the Soothsayer, however, says that their fortunes are alike, Iras presses him for details: "But how? But how? Give me particulars" (1.2.58). The Soothsayer, refusing to say more, ends his fortune-telling with a Latinism gravely suggesting finality: "I have said" (1.2.59).[54] Charmian and Iras will indeed have fortunes that "are alike." As the Soothsayer's Latinism underscores, both women, devoted to Cleopatra, will die with her.

Iras, wanting the Soothsayer to tell more, asks, or complains, "Am I not an inch of fortune better than she?" (1.2.60). Each woman wants a better fortune than the other. And when Charmian asks where she would choose to have it if she had an inch of better fortune, Iras answers, "Not in my husband's nose" (1.2.63), to which Charmian responds with mock pious reproval: "Our worser thoughts heavens mend!" (1.2.64). Charmian now wants to hear Alexas's fortune. But rather than wait to hear it, she offers a pretended prayer. Entreating the goddess Isis, she prays that Alexas is to marry a woman who is never sexually satisfied ("... that cannot go" [1.2.66]),[55] the woman is to die, Alexas is then to marry a worse wife, "and let worse follow worse, till the worse of all follow him laughing to his grave, fiftyfold a cuckold!" (1.2.66, 67–69). Much as Charmian imagined for herself (1.2.3–5), Alexas's last wife would glory in her unfaithfulness and her husband's humiliation. Twice beseeching "Good Isis" (1.2.69, 71), Charmian, with a sexual play on "weight" (see 1.5.22), asks for her prayer even if the goddess denies her the lovers she craves ("... though thou deny me a matter of more weight" [1.2.70–71]).[56] Iras, seconding the prayer, imagines that it comes from the whole nation: "Amen. Dear goddess, hear that prayer of the people! For as it is a heartbreaking to see a handsome man loose-wived, so it is a deadly sorrow to behold a foul knave uncuckolded" (1.2.73–75). In the view of the Egyptians, Iras says, handsome men deserve faithful wives; ugly men deserve unfaithful wives. And since lapses of this proper order cause Egyptians deep pain ("a heartbreaking," "a deadly sorrow"), Isis should defend it: "Therefore, dear Isis, keep decorum and fortune him accordingly" (1.2.75–76). By the lights of Iras's Egyptian notion of decorum, the goddess should reward handsome men with chaste wives and punish ugly men with wanton wives. Just as Iras seconded Charmian's mock prayer, Charmian seconds hers ("Amen" [1.2.77]). Alexas recognizes the implication of the women's prayers. The women would make themselves whores just to cuckold him: "Lo now, if it lay in their hands to make me a cuckold, they would make themselves whores, but they'd do't" (1.2.78–80). The women would do anything, however indecent or immoral, to deceive and demean him. Love for them is a form of war, whose victory lies in their humiliating a man.

2.
Cleopatra enters. Whether facetiously or otherwise, Enobarbus identifies her as Antony ("Hush, here comes Antony" [1.2.81]). His joke or error seems to reflect not only Antony's boast of themselves as an unparalleled couple, but the strong criticism in Rome that they can scarcely be told apart (1.4.5–7).

So much under her influence, Antony is not merely seen with Cleopatra, but seen as her. He is as indistinguishable as inseparable from her.

Cleopatra, who is looking for Antony, describes a recent sudden change in his mood. "He was disposed to mirth," she reports, "but on the sudden / A Roman thought hath struck him" (1.2.87–88). The phrase "Roman thought," having both an active and a passive sense,[57] means a thought befitting as well as about Rome. It is, as Philo and Demetrius wished or hoped to see in Antony, a serious thought, not one of merriment or mirth. Antony seems to have reconsidered his renunciation of Rome and his refusal to hear the Messenger. His reversal causes Cleopatra great concern. Always jealous of his every thought of Rome, she becomes more fearful of losing him. But seeing Antony with a messenger, she quickly decides that the Messenger's presence is unfavorable for her purposes.[58] Announcing her withdrawal with the royal plural pronoun ("We will not look upon him. Go with us" [1.2.92]), she at once asserts her regal authority and retreats.

3.

Antony, entering, is listening to a messenger, presumably the one he had previously dismissed. The Messenger reports that Fulvia first fought against Antony's brother, Lucius, but when that war ended, circumstances forced them to join together to make war against Caesar, who drove them out of Italy in the first encounter.[59] Fulvia's war against Caesar, which was meant to draw Antony back to Italy but for which she used his grievances against Caesar as her justification, actually harmed his interests (2.2.72–74, 100–102).[60]

The Messenger has worse news, however, which he is afraid to tell. "The nature of bad news infects the teller" (1.2.101). Anger needs an object to punish, and so, if it cannot punish its true object, it will find another that it can punish. Although it seeks justice, it seeks satisfaction still more. Moreover, anger seeks to punish an animate object, for it wishes to punish (or think it is punishing) what caused or intended the harm. Thus, making no distinction between the messenger and his news, it is apt to punish the one for the other, as Cleopatra will expressly demonstrate (2.5.60ff.).

Antony indignantly claims to be above such base behavior. "When it concerns the fool or coward," he replies. "On!" he then commands, explaining, "Things that are past are done with me. 'Tis thus: / Who tells me true, though in his tale lie death, / I hear him as he flattered" (1.2.102–5). Antony juxtaposes hearing the truth and hearing flattery. He says he welcomes the former, no matter how bad, as much as the latter. Declaring that whatever is finished ("past") is finished ("done") for him, he says that he accepts the worst news as though it were flattery. The comparison of bad news and flattery, although intended for emphasis, seems to weaken rather than strengthen his protest, for it rests on the premise that Antony would welcome flattery. He would hear an unpleasant truth as he would hear an ingratiating falsehood. Antony, who, oddly, finds it necessary to explain himself to a messenger, in fact seems to flatter himself—or to force the Messenger to flatter him—by allowing himself to show or display his willingness to face bad news. If Antony is open to flattery in welcoming frankness from all,[61] he seems to illustrate that flattery rests on self-flattery, that flattery's root is vanity.

The worse news comes from the East. Labienus, who supported the republican cause in the civil wars following Julius Caesar's death, had been sent by Cassius to Parthia to enlist the Parthians' aid against Antony and Octavius. After the republicans' defeat at Philippi, he was stranded in Parthia. Now, with an army of Parthian cavalry under Pacorus, the king's son, Labienus is overrunning the Roman provinces "[f]rom Euphrates / . . . from Syria, / To Lydia, and to Ionia" (1.2.107–9).[62] This is the first time the Parthians, long considered a dangerous enemy, have reached further west than Syria.[63] And virtually all of the Roman provinces in Asia as far west as the Aegean have come under attack, "Whilst—", the Messenger begins to say, and Antony continues, "'Antony,' thou wouldst say—" (1.2.110). As he was willing to hear the worst news, Antony is willing to state it himself. Yet, as bad as it is, the "stiff news" (1.2.106) by itself is not enough to arouse him to action. Antony needs to be expressly told what he already knows that Romans, particularly Fulvia, are saying about him in Rome. "Speak to me home; mince not the general tongue," he orders the Messenger,

> Name Cleopatra as she is called in Rome;
> Rail thou in Fulvia's phrase, and taunt my faults
> With such full licence as both truth and malice
> Have power to utter.
>
> (1.2.111–15)

In order to act, Antony must be shamed by others—or imagine that he is. He must be spurred by what others say of him. Like many other Romans, as much as he loves honor and fame, he is moved more by the fear of ignominy than by the desire for praise. Shame is his paramount concern.[64] Thus, generalizing, Antony describes the opposite effects of idleness and of shaming. "Oh, then we bring forth weeds / When our quick minds lie still, and our ills told us / Is as our earing" (1.2.115–17). While our minds produce vices rather than virtues when left idle, when we are scolded for our vices we uproot them, as Antony stresses with his pun on "earing": giving ear to what is said of our vices leads to our plowing ("earing") them up.

Having just mentioned Fulvia's railing, Antony summons a messenger from Sicyon, a city in Greece where Fulvia has gone. "These strong Egyptian fetters I must break, / Or lose myself in dotage," he tells himself, echoing Philo (1.2.122–23; see 1.1.1, 58–60). Antony presumably hopes that the Messenger's report of Fulvia's fierce reproof will rouse him to action. But the Messenger reports something else: "Fulvia thy wife is dead" (1.2.124). The woman whose "shrill-tongue . . . scold[ing]" (1.1.33) might have stirred Antony to break his Egyptian fetters is now silent.

Antony, alone, reflects on Fulvia and the effect of her death on him. "There's a great spirit gone," he first admiringly observes (1.2.129). Fulvia, Plutarch writes, was a woman who took no interest in managing a household, nor was she content to rule her husband merely at home. Her desire was to rule a world ruler—to "command him that commanded legions and great armies" (Plutarch, *Antony*, 10.3; North, 6:11). The first woman to command a Roman army and the real authority in Rome during the year that Lucius fought Octavius,[65] Fulvia stirred up a war in Italy to force Antony to leave Cleopatra. Antony confesses that he desired her death ("Thus did I desire it" [1.2.129]). But then, generalizing again, as he frequently does,[66] he reflects on the inconstancy of human pleasure and desire: "What our contempts doth often hurl from us / We wish it ours again. The present pleasure, / By revolution lowering, does become / The opposite of itself" (1.2.130–33). Antony said that our lives should have constant pleasure (1.1.47–48). Here, he makes explicit that "the present pleasure" is an ever-changing pleasure, for it becomes "[t]he opposite of itself." As an unchanging pleasure becomes both cloying and palling, too much and too little, it becomes its own opponent— "[t]he opposite of itself"—both in becoming unpleasant and in leading us to desire something else. "By revolution lowering," the present pleasure becomes reduced in our appraisal and replaced in our desire, often by its reverse. Much of the pleasure of the present pleasure lies in its newness, in the change itself. "She's good, being gone," Antony thus says of Fulvia. "The hand could pluck her back that shoved her on" (1.2.133–34). He who wished her gone would now willingly bring her back because she is gone. He would now desire what he scorned, because he achieved being rid of it. Satisfaction, by its nature, turns into dissatisfaction.

4.

When Antony tells him that he must leave soon, Enobarbus, whose first words to Antony ask what his "pleasure" is (1.2.138), replies with bawdy misogyny. Voicing a soldier's scorn for women, he mocks women in general and Cleopatra in particular. Playing on the literal and the sexual senses of "die," "mettle" and "nothing," he combines ridicule for the women's suffering from love's disappointments with derision for their strong sexual desire and their swift and frequent pleasure. The news of their departure will kill all their women, he says. But "[u]nder a compelling occasion," he equivocally adds, "let women die. It were a pity to cast them away for nothing, though between them and a great cause they should be esteemed nothing" (1.2.144–47). Treating her not as the queen of Egypt but simply as any woman, Enobarbus is certain that "Cleopatra, catching but the least noise of this, dies instantly." In fact, he continues, "I have seen her die twenty times upon far poorer moment. I do think there is mettle in death which commits some loving act upon her, she hath such a celerity in dying" (1.2.147–51). As Cleopatra dies (has orgasm) quickly and often, death itself (sexual pleasure) is an ardent lover making love to her.

Antony, evidently understanding Enobarbus to be suggesting that she feigns her passion, replies that Cleopatra is extremely crafty (". . . cunning past man's thought" [1.2.152]). But Enobarbus, both praising and mocking her cunning, defends her passions as genuine. Quibbling on "made" and "cunning," he says that if her passions are not composed ("made" [1.2.153]) of the finest part of pure love and her tears are not the genuine effect of natural feeling, they are artificial ("made"). But even if they are artificial, "[t]his cannot be cunning" (1.2.157)—this cannot be artful—in her, he says, for her skill in rainmaking (". . . makes a shower of rain" [1.2.157–58]) equals Jove's.[67] Where "made" (or "makes") shifts from "composed" to "artificial," "cunning" shifts from "deceitful" to "skillful." Cleopatra is, and is not, cunning: She is clever but not deceitful in her passions.

When Antony, acknowledging his inability to resist her, says he wishes he had never seen Cleopatra, Enobarbus again corrects him. "O, sir, you had then left unseen a wonderful piece of work" (1.2.160–61). Enobarbus's compliment, once more, quibbles. Cleopatra is a masterpiece ("piece of work"), but also a difficult woman ("piece of work"). Enobarbus says that not to have seen her would have injured Antony's reputation as a traveler (". . . would have discredited your travel" [1.2.162]). As Cleopatra is a wonder of the world, Antony is an intelligent sightseer. Egypt—the land of the Nile, pyramids, eunuchs, revels, serpents, crocodiles and Cleopatra—is the land of exotic travel.[68]

Antony tells Enobarbus the news of Fulvia's death, which he greets with further dismissive, ribald wordplay. Advising Antony to thank the gods for her death, he says that the deities comfort men by replacing one wife with another, just as a tailor replaces worn-out clothes with new "members" (1.2.172). Were Fulvia the only woman in the world, then Antony would have suffered a "cut" and a lamentable "case," he says. But "[t]his grief is crowned with consolation: your old smock brings forth a new petticoat" (1.2.174–76). Something to welcome rather than lament, Fulvia's death should cause Antony to shed no tears other than those an onion would produce. Although different in tone, Enobarbus closely repeats Antony when he first heard the news. In order to maintain a man's pleasure, the gods remove his wife so that he can replace an old pleasure with a new one. Thus the gods solace ("comfort" [1.2.171]) men.

Enobarbus plainly demonstrates Plutarch's remark, echoed disapprovingly by Caesar (1.4.18–21), that Antony flattered himself by allowing his subordinates to be informal and forward as well as frank in speaking to him (Plutarch, *Antony*, 4.2; 24.7–8). Quibbling coarsely, Enobarbus disparages both Antony's royal lover and his Roman wife. He does so, moreover, explicitly in the name of erotic pleasure. It is perhaps no surprise that the conversation is one of only two in which Antony speaks in prose and that in the other he is drunk (2.7.24–53). Prose is appropriate to indecency. Antony, thus resuming verse, states a political necessity for him to leave. "The business she hath broached in the state," he says referring to Fulvia, "Cannot endure my absence" (1.2.178–79). And when Enobarbus puns bawdily on Antony's word ("And the business you have broached here cannot be without you, especially that of Cleopatra's, which wholly depends on your abode" [1.2.180–82]), Antony calls for an end to his "light answers" (1.2.183) and, stressing his authority by repeatedly using the royal plural pronoun, as he does nowhere else in addressing Enobarbus (1.2.183, 184, 188, 189, 190, 192, 201, 202, 203), gives "more urgent" (1.2.187) reasons for his return.

The reasons concern Sextus Pompey, who, having challenged Caesar, now commands the sea and enjoys strong popular support.[69] "Our slippery people, / Whose love is never linked to the deserver / Till his deserts are past," Antony says, "begin to throw / Pompey the Great and all his dignities / Upon his son" (1.2.192–96). According to Antony, the people, always vacillating and never showing good judgment in bestowing their favor, having failed to honor Pompey the Great when he deserved to be honored, now love the son as they never loved the father, though the father deserved their love and the son does not. Antony's indignation seems misplaced. Contrary to what Antony says, Pompey the Great was especially well loved by the Roman people. "[N]ever any other Roman but Pompey had the people's earnest goodwills so soon, nor that in prosperity and adversity continued longer constant, than unto Pompey" (Plutarch, *Pompey*, 1.2; North, 4:206).[70] Antony, vexed on all sides with his own situation, unwittingly mimics what he accuses the people of having foolishly done. Conflating the father and the son, he transforms the Romans' celebration of Julius Caesar's defeat of Pompey's sons into their lack of love for Pompey himself.[71] Now, one might say that the people's gratitude toward Pompey should have prevented their celebrating his sons' defeat, as the tribune Marullus says in *Julius Caesar* (*JC*, 1.1.35–51). But that is not what Antony says. Instead, he denies that the people ever loved Pompey, or any other worthy man, until he no longer deserved their love. His accusation is invariable and absolute: "Whose love is never linked to the deserver / Till his deserts are past." Antony's rebuking "never" reverses Plutarch's appreciating "never."

Antony, accordingly, considers Sextus both dangerous and not dangerous, since his strength lies at least partly in the people's confusion of him and his father. Sextus, Antony continues, "high in name and power, / Higher than both in blood and life, stands up / For the main soldier" (1.2.196–98). High in name and popular support, and still higher in courage and spirit ("blood and life"), Sextus presents himself as being or aspiring to become ("stands up / For . . .") the greatest soldier in the world. And if his growing power is not checked, he would endanger the triumvirs' empire ("The sides o'th' world may danger" [1.2.199]). Sextus's strength, though dangerous, is largely an appearance. "Much is breeding," Antony explains, "Which, like the courser's hair, hath yet but life / And not a serpent's poison" (1.2.199–201).[72] Sextus, whose power depends largely on what he has received from his father ("breeding"), and who will in fact see himself chiefly as his father's son, is potentially dangerous, but not yet poisonous. Only appearing to be a serpent, he can still be stopped, though speed ("Our quick removal from hence" [1.2.203]) is crucial.

Act One, Scene Three

1.

Cleopatra, never wanting Antony out of her sight,[73] asks Charmian where he is. Even before he says anything about going, Cleopatra, expecting him to try to leave, prepares to use her art to keep him. Charmian is to find out where Antony is, who is with him and what they are doing. Then, "[i]f you find him sad, / Say I am dancing; if in mirth, report / That I am sudden sick" (1.3.4–6). Cleopatra attempts to keep Antony, not by giving him what he wants, but by crossing whatever mood he is in. If he is serious ("sad"), he should think she is merry; if merry, he should think she is ill. Her erotic tactic consists in opposing him at every moment in word and deed.

Charmian, who, like Enobarbus with Antony, freely advises her queen on her private life, disapproves of the ploy: "[M]ethinks if you did love him dearly, / You do not hold the method to enforce / The like from him" (1.3.7–9). When Cleopatra asks what she should do, Charmian answers, "In each thing give him way; cross him in nothing" (1.3.10). Gratify Antony in everything; oppose him in nothing.[74] Cleopatra dismisses the suggestion out of hand: "Thou teachest like a fool: the way to lose him" (1.3.11). The way to hold Antony is to oppose him. Where Antony spoke of the intimate mutuality of their love (1.1.38–39), Cleopatra speaks of her calculated opposition. Where he emphasizes love that is freely given, she subjects love to an art. It is no accident that she will liken her winning and keeping Antony's love to her catching fish (2.5.11–15).

Charmian, still not convinced, offers a caution: "Tempt him not so too far; I wish, forbear. / In time we hate that which we often fear" (1.3.12–13). Opposition can draw, but can also repel. It can arouse fear, Charmian warns, and frequent fear can turn into hate, for we come to hate what we fear because we fear it. Constant contrariety can chase away the love that it is meant to hold.

2.

When Antony enters, Cleopatra immediately decides to appear in low spirits ("sick and sullen" [1.3.14]). Antony, however, is not in good spirits, but "sorry" to deliver his news (1.3.15). And as soon as he tells Cleopatra this, she magnifies her professed condition: "Help me away, dear Charmian, I shall fall. / It cannot be thus long; the sides of nature / Will not sustain it" (1.3.16–18). Antony's news will kill her. Rather than directly opposing his mood, Cleopatra matches or exaggerates it with her own. Yet, she does not ignore her stated tactic. Instead, she attributes a cheerful mood to Antony and then opposes it. "I know by that same eye there's some good news," she declares, guessing that the good news is that "the married woman," as she disparagingly but jealously calls Fulvia, says "you may go" (1.3.20–21). Cleopatra crosses Antony's mood by willfully misreading it and then opposing what, with bitter irony, she pretends it is. Making her opposition more overbearing, more vexing, more subtle and more elusive, she opposes his "Roman" mood by denying it.

Having asserted that Fulvia has given him permission to go, Cleopatra says that she wishes "she had never given [him] leave to come" (1.3.22). Much later, Antony will compare Cleopatra and himself in death to Dido and Aeneas in Elysium (4.14.51–55). Here, Cleopatra echoes Ovid's account of Dido's dismissal of Aeneas in life for leaving her: "But God doth force thee flee, / Would God had kept away" (Ovid, *Heroides*, 7.139–40).[75] Where the earlier North African queen blames the earlier Roman for his pious duty to his city, the later North African queen blames the later Roman for his hen-pecked obedience to his wife. "Let her not say 'tis I that keep you here. / I have no power upon you; hers you are" (1.3.23–24). Antony, sounding like Ovid's Aeneas, appeals to the authority of the gods ("The gods best know—" [1.3.24]). Cleopatra, however, not letting him speak, plaintively laments, "Oh, never was there queen / So mightily betrayed!" (1.3.25–26). And as Dido accuses Aeneas of having forsaken and betrayed not only her but his Trojan wife (Ovid, *Heroides*, 7.81–84), Cleopatra accuses Antony of having forsaken and betrayed not only her but his Roman wife: "Why should I think you can be mine and true— / Though you in swearing shake the thronèd gods— / Who have been false to Fulvia?" (1.3.28–30). Although she began by blaming Antony for being domineered by his wife, now, as if taking her rival's side, she blames him for being faithless to Fulvia. Thus, reproaching herself for trusting him, Cleopatra says that it was "[r]iotous madness" for her to believe his "mouth-made vows" (1.3.30, 31). Antony's vows, "[w]hich break themselves in swearing" (1.3.32), are broken even as they are being sworn. Although sworn to the gods with the utmost fervor, they are never more than empty words.

Cleopatra, nonetheless, wishes to believe Antony's words of love and even quotes them. Telling him to bid farewell and simply go, she says that when he begged to stay, "[t]hen was the time for words" (1.3.35). Then, "[e]ternity was in our lips and eyes, / Bliss in our brows' bent; none our parts so poor / But was a race of heaven" (1.3.36–38). Then, every feature of hers ("our parts"),[76] however poor or low, was said to be divine. Despite her accusation that Antony's words were empty, they not only were true then, Cleopatra insists, but are still true now. "They are so still," she concludes, referring to what Antony described as her godlike features, "Or thou, the greatest soldier of the world, / Art turned the greatest liar" (1.3.38–40).

While Antony can utter only his astonishment ("How now, lady?" [1.3.40]), Cleopatra taunts him with an explicitly unrealizable threat. "I would I had thy inches. / Thou shouldst know / There were a heart in Egypt" (1.3.41–42). Had Cleopatra his stature and manliness ("thy inches" [see 1.2.61–63]), Antony would know there was a lover willing to fight for love ("a heart") in Egypt. Claiming that as a woman she is unable to fight for love, she accuses Antony of being too unmanly to do so.

Despite numerous attempts, beginning with his first words, Antony has been unable to speak.[77] Finally, commanding to be heard ("Hear me, queen" [1.3.42]), he starts to explain his need to leave. Distinguishing between himself as one of Rome's triumvirs and as Cleopatra's lover, as he emphasizes by moving from the royal plural to the personal singular pronoun ("Our services . . . my full heart" [1.3.44]), he says that "[t]he strong necessity of time commands" his services awhile, but his full heart "[r]emains in use with [Cleopatra]" (1.3.43–45). He must depart, but his heart will stay. Elaborating what he told Enobarbus, Antony explains that Italy is suffering everywhere from civil war. While Sextus Pompey threatens Rome's port, the equality of power between him and the triumvirs has produced divisions among the Romans on even small matters ("[b]reed scrupulous faction" [1.3.49]). Those who were hated, having become powerful, are now loved. And the proscribed ("condemned" [1.3.50]) Pompey, rich in his father's honor as leader of the anti-triumvirate forces, quietly but quickly steals into the hearts of those who have not done well under the present order, whose large numbers threaten. Even peace itself, whose very restfulness has caused corruption ("grown sick of rest" [1.3.54]), has added to the difficulty, for it has produced excesses which can be cured only by violence. Antony cites only domestic dangers and says nothing about Labienus and his Parthian forces. He mentions the dangers that draw him back to Rome, but not the one that might keep him in the East. Finally, concluding with a more personal reason for Cleopatra to consider his departure safe for her, he tells of Fulvia's death.

Cleopatra, while silent about Antony's political difficulties, is incredulous at the news of Fulvia's death. "Though age from folly could not give me freedom, / It does from childishness. Can Fulvia die?" (1.3.58–59). Cleopatra distinguishes between the madness of love ("folly") and the gullibility of childhood ("childishness"). Although age does not free her from mad love, it does from childish naiveté. And so, with the experience of an adult, she can see right through Antony and recognize that he would fabricate any excuse— even Fulvia's death—in order to get away. Antony is no less extravagant in his excuses to leave than he was originally in his begging to stay.

When Antony, reassuring her, gives her letters describing the trouble Fulvia had caused in Italy and, "best" (1.3.62), the time and the place of her death, Cleopatra swiftly reverses herself. She now believes what she just doubted. Her reversal, however, is no less quarrelsome than quick: "O most false love!" (1.3.63). Turning her complaint that Antony is leaving her for Fulvia into her complaint that Antony did not love Fulvia enough, and returning to her earlier charge that he was as false to Fulvia as he has been to her, Cleopatra contends that Antony's lack of tears for Fulvia shows how he will take her own death: "Now I see, I see, / In Fulvia's death how mine received shall be" (1.3.65–66). If Antony does not weep for Fulvia, he will not weep for Cleopatra.

Cleopatra, earlier, characterized Fulvia as a shrill-tongued scold dominating Antony (1.1.33). Yet, ironically, Fulvia's domination prepared Antony for Cleopatra's. When remarking that Fulvia took no interest in managing a household and was not content to master her husband at home, but wanted also to command a commander and rule a ruler, Plutarch goes on to say, "so that Cleopatra was to give Fulvia thanks for that she had taught Antonius this obedience to women, [who] learned so well to be at their commandment" (Plutarch, *Antony*, 10.3; North, 6:11). By the time Antony met Cleopatra, Fulvia had already tamed him to obey a strong woman. She was Cleopatra's precursor as well as her rival. Cleopatra's success in taunting Antony about Fulvia demonstrates Cleopatra's great debt to her. Antony's obedience is Fulvia's gift to Cleopatra.

Antony, seeking to end her quarreling, assures Cleopatra that she will command him in everything he does. He will keep or abandon his purposes as she wishes. "By the fire / That quickens Nilus' slime," he swears, "I go from hence / Thy soldier, servant, making peace or war / As thou affects" (1.3.69–72). Swearing by the Egyptian understanding of what gives life to Egypt (see 2.7.26–28),[78] the Roman triumvir declares himself the soldier and servant of the Egyptian queen. He is ruled by her. Rome's interests are wholly subordinate to Egypt's, even to the whims of its queen.

Cleopatra feigns fainting and a rapid recovery: "I am quickly ill and well— / So Antony loves me" (1.3.73–74). Her words are ambiguous. "So" could mean "since" or "just as." Cleopatra may mean that she is ill or well depending on Antony's love. When he does not love her, she is ill; when he does, she is well. Or she may mean that Antony's love is as fickle as her condition. Just as she quickly changes from being well to being ill, he no less quickly changes from loving to not loving her. The former meaning would express her love; the latter, her accusation.

Again urging her to refrain, Antony asks Cleopatra to allow him bear true witness of his love, "which stands / An honourable trial" (1.3.75–76). But Cleopatra, repeating that he shed no tears for Fulvia, denies that his love could sustain an honorable test: "So Fulvia told me" (1.3.76). Antony's lack of tears for Fulvia proves his lack of love for Cleopatra. Antony can neither shed tears for Fulvia nor withhold them, for either course would seem to deny his love for Cleopatra. Cleopatra, seizing upon his difficulty, asks him to perform a deception. "[T]urn aside and weep for her," she tells him; "Then bid adieu to me, and say the tears / Belong to Egypt" (1.3.77–79). Antony is to weep for Fulvia but, saying good-bye to Cleopatra, pretend the tears are for her. He is to "play one scene / Of excellent dissembling, and let it look / Like perfect honour" (1.3.79–81). Where by "honourable trial" Antony meant a truthful test of love, by "perfect honour" Cleopatra means a gallant gesture. She turns truth into showy, staged flattery. She not only lies to Antony, but asks him to lie to her.

Cleopatra does not stop. When Antony warns that she is raising his anger and tells her to stop, she mocks his anger while pretending to praise him at least mildly: "You can do better yet, but this is meetly" (1.3.82). She no sooner says that he should playact his love than she taunts his anger as play-acting. Cleopatra, always a consummate actress, accuses Antony of feigning an appearance. Her criticism, however, is not that he is pretending, but that he is pretending only moderately well ("meetly"). He could do better. When Antony, shifting from an Egyptian to a Roman oath, swears angrily, "Now by my sword—," Cleopatra adds, "And target" (1.3.83). She turns a soldier's solemn oath into a swashbuckler's bluster.[79] Antony's anger is nothing but bravado. Then, describing him in the third person as though she were a dis-interested observer, Cleopatra continues her critique of his theatrical per-formance. "Still he mends," she says, crediting Antony with improvement; "But this is not the best" (1.3.83–84). A good actor would do better. Finally, Antony's rising fury evident, Cleopatra compliments his performance. "Look, prithee, Charmian, / How this Herculean Roman does become / The carriage of his chafe" (1.3.84–86). Antony very well plays the role of the furious hero. But while his Herculean anger, like his passionate love, may be good acting, it is nothing but histrionic swagger.

Antony, no longer seeking to reassure or to stop Cleopatra, tries simply to leave: "I'll leave you, lady" (1.3.87). But Cleopatra asks for "one word" (1.3.88). For the first time in the play, she addresses Antony politely ("Cour-teous lord" [1.3.88]). Yet her "one word" masks criticism of him as criticism of herself. Cleopatra starts as though she has something to say that she has never told him before: "Sir, you and I must part, but that's not it; / Sir, you and I have loved, but there's not it; / That you know well" (1.3.89–91). But after appearing to begin to say something new ("Something it is I would—" [1.3.91]), she claims or pretends to have forgotten what it was, crying out, "Oh, my oblivion is a very Antony, / And I am all forgotten" (1.3.92–93). Cleopatra, equating Antony with oblivion,[80] plays on the active and the pas-sive, the subjective and the objective, senses of "oblivion" and "forgotten": she forgets entirely and is entirely forgotten. Her memory abandons her, just as—or because—Antony does.

Antony, exasperated and yet admiring, distinguishes between Cleopatra and her playacting. "But that your royalty / Holds idleness your subject, I should take you / For idleness itself" (1.3.93–95). Antony, punning on "idle-ness" as both folly and feigning, uses the metaphor of monarchy to express

Cleopatra's command of the appearance of foolishness. If he did not know that she was entirely in command of her appearance, he would be taken in by her performance, he says. He would take her for the personification of foolishness itself. Her performance, which she ably commands for her own ends, would be perfect.

Cleopatra denies her theatrics. What Antony calls flawless playacting, she describes as painful childbirth. "'Tis sweating labour," she replies, "To bear such idleness so near the heart / As Cleopatra this" (1.3.95–97). Demonstrating precisely what she denies, Cleopatra claims that her suffering is entirely genuine and in no way sham. She cannot help the behavior that Antony dismisses as affected folly. Cleopatra, nevertheless, apologizes, not, however, for what causes her conduct, but for her conduct's effect on him. But just as she tries to transform what Antony calls her idleness into her life-giving, she turns his disapproval into the cause of her own death. "But, sir, forgive me," she says, as though contrite, "Since my becomings kill me when they do not / Eye well to you" (1.3.97–99). Cleopatra's "becomings" are at once her graces and her changes. While capturing the connection between her captivating charm and her constant changes, her pun tacitly acknowledges the playacting that she expressly denies.

Shifting suddenly, Cleopatra finally addresses Antony as he had originally hoped, telling him to do what his honor requires ("Your honour calls you hence" [1.3.99]), though not without a further self-pitying charge: "Therefore be deaf to my unpitied folly / . . . Upon your sword / Sit laurel victory, and smooth success / Be strewed before your feet!" (1.3.100–103). Antony can have his triumphal procession, but only by having no pity on Cleopatra. He may be leaving her for his glory rather than for Fulvia, but he is, nevertheless, still heartless in leaving her.

Cleopatra is unpredictable, unreasonable and untruthful, does not listen, often quarrels, taunts, exasperates, belittles and humiliates, is jealous and high-handed, self-pitying, self-indulgent and self-dramatizing, and always calculating an effect. Yet, afraid to lose him, she tries to keep Antony from doing what she most admires him for doing. She wants him to be a "Herculean Roman" (1.3.85), "the greatest soldier of the world" (1.3.39), but attempts to keep him by her side. She unmans him to keep him her man.

Earlier, able at last to speak, Antony said that he must go but his heart would remain with Cleopatra (1.3.43–45). Now, ending the quarrelsome scene (and again moving from the royal plural ["Let us go . . ."] to the personal singular pronoun), he declares that he and Cleopatra will be present to each other in their absence: "Our separation so abides and flies / That thou, residing here, goes yet with me, / And I, hence fleeting, here remain with thee" (1.3.103–6). Though separate, they remain together. Though apart, they remain paired. Their separation, as Antony paradoxically puts it, joining or switching opposites, "abides and flies." Antony's parting words are his last to Cleopatra until just before the battle of Actium (3.7.19).

Act One, Scene Four

1.

Caesar is reading a letter from Alexandria, describing Antony's conduct. Like scene 1, which began with Philo and Demetrius disputing Antony's infatuation for Cleopatra, scene 4 begins with Caesar and Lepidus disputing his behavior in Egypt. "You may see, Lepidus, and henceforth know," Caesar says, "It is not Caesar's natural vice to hate / Our great competitor" (1.4.1–3). Caesar's first words are about himself (to whom he refers in the third person and by the royal plural pronoun), negative (telling what is not natural to him), meant as an edifying lesson ("You may see . . . and henceforth know"), and a self-justification. The words are not so much a criticism of Antony as Caesar's defense of himself for criticizing him. They are intended to disclaim his own pettiness and defend his dignity, which Caesar is always eager to protect.[81] In reply to Lepidus, who has evidently been supporting Antony, Caesar denies that it is his "natural vice" to hate him. He presumably means that he does not choose to criticize Antony. Neither unprovoked nor mean-spirited, his criticisms, he tries to suggest, have been forced on him by Antony's shameful conduct.

Caesar quickly sketches that conduct, stressing Antony's adopted Eastern ways. Antony not only wastes his time, day and night, in frivolity and reveling. He is also "not more manlike / Than Cleopatra, nor the Queen of Ptolemy / More womanly than he" (1.4.5–7). Each taking on the character of the other's sex, Antony has been emasculated by Cleopatra, whom Caesar identifies by her royal incest ("the Queen of Ptolemy"),[82] and she masculinized by him. Antony, furthermore, has ignored Caesar's messengers and hardly acknowledged that he had partners. "You shall find there," Caesar concludes in summary, "A man who is the abstract of all faults / That all men follow" (1.4.8–10). Antony is the epitome of every fault ("all faults") that any man ("all men") possesses.

Lepidus attempts to defend Antony without offending Caesar. He does not deny Antony's faults, but he denies that there are enough to darken his virtues. Indeed, it is the contrast with his virtues, he argues, that makes his faults so apparent. Lepidus, however, seems to invert the saving contrast. He first associates Antony's faults with darkness and his virtues with light ("Evils enough to darken all his goodness"), but then in his next breath states, "His faults, in him, seem as the spots of heaven, / More fiery by night's blackness" (1.4.11–13). Antony's faults are fiery; his virtues, night's blackness. Lepidus's attempt to find a middle ground—the first of his many such attempts and his first words in the play—produces only confusion. He muddles the middle. Lepidus then tries to excuse Antony by saying that his faults are inherited, not acquired: "hereditary / Rather than purchased; what he cannot change / Than what he chooses" (1.4.13–15). A man should be blamed only for what he could have done (or not done) otherwise. As Caesar implicitly argued in his own defense in criticizing Antony, choice is essential. But since Antony's faults are innate, he cannot change them and so he ought not to be blamed for them. Necessity excuses.[83]

Caesar impatiently counters that Lepidus is too indulgent: He indulges Antony's self-indulgence. To make his point, Caesar distinguishes between two kinds of Antony's faults or their effects. One kind deprives Antony of dignity and perhaps even of health. The other throws weight upon Caesar and Lepidus. The former harms only Antony; the latter, the other triumvirs. Caesar, with a mixture of rhetorical concession, sarcasm, exaggeration and moral revulsion, grants for the sake of argument ("Let's grant it is not / Amiss . . ." [1.4.16–17]) that one sort of Antony's faults—his tumbling on the bed of Ptolemy, giving away a kingdom to reward a joke, taking turns drinking toasts with a slave, staggering through the streets during the middle of the day, and exchanging boxing blows with sweaty servants—may not really be faults or even may become him.[84] "Say this becomes him—," he allows, though quickly canceling his concession by strongly qualifying it: "As his composure must be rare indeed / Whom these things cannot blemish." "[Y]et," he continues, "must Antony / No way excuse his foils, when we do bear / So great a weight in his lightness" (1.4.21–25). Caesar could overlook Antony's frivolity and sensuality if they punished only Antony. "If he filled / His vacancy with his voluptuousness, / Full surfeits and the dryness of his bones / Call on him for't" (1.4.25–28). Antony's self-indulgence would be self-punishing, harming only himself with disease and debility. But his childish irresponsibility punishes the other triumvirs. Antony therefore deserves to be scolded, Caesar says severely, "As we rate boys who, being mature in knowledge, / Pawn their experience to their present pleasure / And so rebel to judgement" (1.4.31–33). If Cleopatra taunts Antony for taking orders from a boy ("the scarce-bearded Caesar" [1.1.22]), Caesar blames him for acting like one. To Cleopatra, Antony sacrifices his pleasure to his responsibility at the command of a boy; to Caesar, he sacrifices his responsibility to his pleasure at the whim of a boy. Lepidus, whether convinced or simply discreet, silently drops his defense of Antony and does not raise it again in the scene. In fact, he says very little, at all.

2.

The immediate reason for Caesar's anger becomes clear when a messenger, one of those arriving "every hour" (1.4.34), reports the latest news of events abroad. The Messenger tells Caesar that Pompey is strong at sea and gains at his (not Antony's) expense. "Pompey is strong at sea, / And . . . is beloved of those / That have only feared Caesar" (1.4.36–38). Caesar is feared because, always needing to pay his veterans, he takes land from his political enemies in Italy. The veterans' compensation comes from Caesar's confiscations as well as from his similarly unpopular taxes.[85] While wealth lies in the East, particularly in Egypt,[86] the breadbasket of the Mediterranean world, debts pile up in the West.[87] When Romans soldiers were citizens obliged to serve, their meager pay was supplemented by plunder and by gifts on the occasion of a general's triumph (see *Cor.*, 1.5.1–8; 1.9.39–40). At the end of their term of military service, they received no special rewards but simply returned to their civilian jobs. Beginning with Marius, however, men without property, including former slaves, were enlisted into the army,[88] and whenever a major war was finished, the veterans, who had no civilian jobs to return to, looked to their generals for gifts of land in Italy to settle on. The gifts served both to reward the troops and to punish the general's enemies—and contributed greatly to the soldiers' fighting for their commanders rather than for Rome.[89] Perhaps not surprisingly, the Messenger says that Caesar's enemies not only go over to Pompey's side, but declare him much wronged by Caesar ("To the ports / The discontents repair, and men's reports / Give him much wronged" [1.4.38–40]). Feeling wronged themselves, they see Pompey as also having been wronged. In their view, they share with him not only a common enemy, but a common cause. Caesar's enemies, moreover, may include not only the dispossessed landowners, but the veterans to whom he has given their land. For the veterans may be not so much grateful to Caesar for his favors as angry at him for refusing to make further concessions. While the one group is indignant at having been robbed of their property, the other may consider it no kindness to receive what they regard as their due. The one is angry at what it has lost; the other may be angry at what it has not gained.[90]

Caesar blames himself mildly for not having anticipated the people's disaffection for him and their new love for Pompey. He sees it as an instance of a universal truth. "It hath been taught us from the primal state," he says, referring to the earliest political society, "That he which is was wished until he were, / And the ebbed man, ne'er loved till ne'er worth love, / Comes deared by being lacked" (1.4.41–44). Caesar, largely repeating Antony's descriptions of pleasure and of the people (1.2.129–34, 192–94), says that the people always love the man they do not have until they have him and love the man who has lost the ability to help them, whom they did not love when he could benefit them. They love a man before he has come to power or after he has lost it, but not while he has it.[91] Except for blaming it on their subservience and emptiness ("lackeying"), Caesar does not say why the people love the man they lack and oppose the man they have. "This common body," he says in disgust, "Like to a vagabond flag upon the stream, / Goes to and back, lackeying the varying tide, / To rot itself with motion" (1.4.44–47). According to Caesar, the people "lackey" what they "lack" and dissolve themselves or make themselves putrid ("rot itself") with their ever-changing, ever-dissatisfied motion. Caesar, exonerating himself while justifying his indignation, seems to overlook that someone in power—he, in particular, as it turns out—must often harm those he rules. To benefit some, he must injure others. And his benefits as much as his injuries may arouse indignation.

Another messenger arrives with the news that the notorious ("famous" [1.4.49]) pirates, Menecrates and Menas, allies of Pompey, control much of the sea and are making incursions into Italy. According to his report, the pirates frighten the people along the coast, who turn pale at the thought of them ("Lack blood to think on't" [1.4.53]), inspire spirited ("flush" [1.4.53]) youth to revolt to them, and capture ships as soon as they are seen, preventing needed supplies, especially grain, from reaching Rome.[92] "[N]either in any other war . . . was [Caesar] in more and greater dangers," Suetonius writes (Suetonius, *Augustus*, 16.3; Holland, 1:92). Pompey and the pirates could easily starve Italy with a naval blockade.[93] Pompey's name alone causes great trouble. It "strikes more / Than could his war resisted" (1.4.55–56). As Antony had suggested (1.2.192–99), Pompey's name is more powerful than the man himself would be if the triumvirs actually fought him.

Caesar, apostrophizing Antony, urges him to leave his lascivious revels and reclaim his former virtue. Addressing him at length, he recalls Antony following the battle of Modena (Mutina). Antony is often described as a heroic warrior, especially by Cleopatra.[94] But, apart from the narrations of his battles at Actium and Alexandria, Caesar's depiction is the play's only extended description of him as a warrior, and it describes Antony after a battle (against Caesar's allies) which he lost.[95] Philo may liken Antony to Mars (1.1.4), but his virtue at Modena was shown by his arduous endurance of hardship in defeat and retreat, not by his noble display of courage in attack and victory.[96] While crossing the Alps in the winter's snow, Caesar recounts, Antony drank "[t]he stale of horses and the gilded puddle / Which beasts would cough at" and ate "[t]he roughest berry on the rudest hedge," "[t]he barks of trees" and "strange flesh / Which some did die to look on" (1.4.63–64, 65, 67, 68–69). "Though daintily brought up," he could endure the deprivation "with patience more / Than savages could suffer" (1.4.61–62). Able to astound others with his extraordinary feats of feasting (2.1.24–26; 2.2.186–93; 2.7.96, 103–5), Antony can do the same with his extraordinary feats of famine. If at his weakest in the face of pleasure, he is naturally at his best in adversity (Plutarch, *Antony*, 17.2).

Caesar tacitly distinguishes between Antony's motive for action and his own. For Antony, the motive is shame: "Let his shames quickly / Drive him to Rome" (1.4.73–74; also 1.4.70). For Caesar, it is political interest, for which he needs Antony's navy and money: "'Tis time we twain / Did show ourselves i'th' field. . . . / . . . Pompey / Thrives in our idleness" (1.4.74–77). When Caesar says that he will assemble an immediate war council, Lepidus, who has spoken only two brief interjections since Caesar accused him of being too indulgent (1.4.33, 73), promises to inform him, tomorrow, of the number of ships and troops that he can furnish. Caesar says he will make an estimate of his own strength ("Till which encounter, / It is my business too" [1.4.80–81]), but says nothing about informing Lepidus. Then, when Lepidus, addressing him deferentially as "my lord"[97] and "bessech[ing]" Caesar to "let" him take part (1.4.82–84), asks to be kept informed of any news from abroad, Caesar pledges to do so: "Doubt not, sir. / I knew it for my bond" (1.4.85). Where Lepidus's request is submissive and obsequious, Caesar's pledge is formal and surly. It solemnly pledges to do what Lepidus asks, but admonishes him for asking, since the request suggests that Caesar needed to be reminded of his bonded duty to his fellow triumvir. In trying hard not to offend, Lepidus only offends. Despite his ineptness, however, Lepidus's concern is not misplaced. Although Caesar ends the scene by speaking of "[his] bond," he will turn against Lepidus at his first chance (3.5.6–12). Tellingly, he speaks of his bond in the past tense ("I knew it for my bond").[98]

Act One, Scene Five

1.

Cleopatra, bored, idle and dejected, wants to sleep away the "great gap of time / My Antony is away" (1.5.5–6). By echoing his final word before leaving ("Away!" [1.3.107]), she seems to confirm his wishful thought that they remain together, even though parted. This is the only scene in which Cleopatra calls Antony "[m]y Antony" (also "my brave Mark Antony" [1.5.40]). When together, they are often quarreling,[99] and Antony is not "my

Antony," but usually the more formal "my lord"—a term she later uses for Caesar (e.g., 5.2.115, 135, 141, 189). Cleopatra reserves her strongest terms of endearment for the absent Antony.[100] He is "good, being gone" (1.2.133).

As we saw earlier, Cleopatra allows Charmian to be very forward with her. She permits her to ignore the vast difference between a queen and a maidservant. When Cleopatra commands a drink ("Give me to drink mandragora" [1.5.4]), Charmian forces her to explain herself ("Why, madam?" [1.5.4]). And when Cleopatra does, Charmian first admonishes her ("You think of [Antony] too much" [1.5.7]) and then contradicts her ("Madam, I trust not so" [1.5.8]). The servant corrects the queen.

When the "eunuch Mardian" (1.5.9), answering her command, asks what her pleasure is, Cleopatra says that she "take[s] no pleasure / In aught an eunuch has" (1.5.10–11). Mardian, the court singer, can sing (1.5.10; s.d. 2.5.2), but not have sex. Evidently feeling sorry for herself, Cleopatra ungraciously compliments the eunuch on his not having the strong sexual desire that makes her want to be elsewhere: "'Tis well for thee / That, being unseminared, thy freer thoughts / May not fly forth of Egypt" (1.5.11–13). Even his looser ("freer") thoughts do not range far. Cleopatra then asks whether Mardian has any sexual desire, at all. When he acknowledges that he does, she responds in surprise, "Indeed?" (1.5.15), by which she means "Really?" Mardian, however, plays on her word: "Not in deed madam, for I can do nothing / But what indeed is honest to be done" (1.5.16–17).[101] Mardian suggests that he is loyal to Cleopatra ("honest") for the same reason he is chaste ("honest"). While Cleopatra's desire knows no political boundary (". . . fly forth of Egypt"), Mardian's castration confines him to Egypt and to her. Mardian nevertheless claims to have strong desires: "Yet have I fierce affections, and think / What Venus did with Mars" (1.5.18–19).[102] Just as he is able only to sing, Mardian refers to a poetic representation of a sexual act rather than to the act itself. His acquaintance is mediated by literature.[103] Moreover, Mardian thinks of the act from Venus's point of view ("What Venus did with Mars"). He conceives of it from a woman's perspective rather than a man's.

Mardian's desirous mention of Venus and Mars further impassions Cleopatra, who now imagines Antony making love to her ("O happy horse, to bear the weight of Antony!" [1.5.22]), raises him to a demigod supporting half the world ("The demi-Atlas of this earth" [1.5.24]),[104] describes him as the perfect soldier, both leader and defender of men ("the arm / And burgonet of men" [1.5.24–25]), and finally imagines him calling to her, "'Where's my serpent of old Nile?'" (1.5.26). Antony's question turns the Egyptian reverence for serpents into his amorous name for Cleopatra. The Egyptians worship the serpent because it "does never age and wax old, but moves in all facility, ready ease and celerity, without the means of any instrument of motion" (Plutarch, *Isis and Osiris*, 74 [381a–b]; Holland, 1316). Antony's pet name, in addition to underscoring her exoticness, captures the crux of Cleopatra's charm for him—her agelessness and never-ending, easy changes ("Age cannot wither her, nor custom stale / Her infinite variety" [2.2.245–46]). All this thought of Antony, Cleopatra remarks, feeds her with "most delicious poison" (1.5.28). It is delicious, because it remembers Antony as she wishes her lover to be, but poison, because it reminds her that they are apart.

But, no sooner suggesting that he finds her beauty ageless, Cleopatra, exaggerating her age, playfully or perhaps anxiously wonders why she should suppose that Antony thinks of her.[105] "Think on me," she says or asks, "That am with Phoebus' amorous pinches black / And wrinkled deep in time" (1.5.28–30). As she exaggerates her age, Cleopatra magnifies or invents a past lover, turning her skin tanned by the sun into her skin darkened and wrinkled by the sun god's caresses. Cleopatra then boasts of two former Roman lovers. "Broad-fronted Caesar," she says, as though addressing Julius Caesar, "When thou wast here above the ground, I was / A morsel for a monarch; and great Pompey," she cheerfully continues, elevating by ambiguity the mostly undistinguished elder son of Pompey, Gnaeus Pompey, to Pompey the Great, "Would stand and make his eyes grow in my brow; / There would he anchor his aspect, and die / With looking on his life" (1.5.30–35). The Ptolemies, for generations, have used their influence in Rome to secure their rule in Egypt.[106] And ever since she was first on the throne, Cleopatra has used love for her own and for Egypt's political interests. While Caesar was conquering in Gaul, Pompey the Great became Egypt's patron and protector. And when Pompey, in return, appealed to her for help in his civil war with Caesar, Cleopatra received his son Gnaeus Pompey, who became her lover, and sent Pompey the Great ships loaded with grain. Then, after Pompey's defeat at Pharsalia, Cleopatra, seducing the man she had recently opposed, as Pompey's surviving son will remind Antony (2.6.67–70), won the love and much-needed support of Caesar in her own civil war with her brother.[107] While Cleopatra's political fortunes have helped determine her choice of lovers, her choice of lovers has helped determine her political fortunes.

Cleopatra's happy remembrance of Pompey's passion and pleasure plainly repeats Enobarbus's erotic wordplay about her own passion and pleasure, and brings out what his punning implied (1.2.144–51). To experience an orgasm is to "die," for it amounts to losing oneself in pleasure. Cleopatra, at the same time, introduces feasting as a metaphor for sex. "A morsel for a monarch," she satisfied Caesar's sexual appetite. Feasting will now become a frequent sexual metaphor: "[A] woman is a dish for the gods" (5.2.273). Enobarbus,

Pompey and Antony as well as Cleopatra herself will reduce her to sexual food—Enobarbus, appreciatively and crudely; Pompey, pruriently and curiously; Antony, angrily and contemptuously; and Cleopatra, boastfully and self-critically.[108] Sex, the metaphors suggest, consumes in different respects both the one receiving and the one giving pleasure.

2.

Alexas arrives from Antony. Although he does not look at all like Antony, just his coming from him, Cleopatra says, alters his looks, as though a base metal were transformed into gold. By virtue of his mere presence, Antony imparts some of his luster to lesser men (". . . that great medicine hath / With his tinct gilded thee" [1.5.38–39]). As a gift for her, Antony not only gives Cleopatra a lustrous ("orient" [1.5.43]) pearl, which he has kissed many times, but, depreciating the precious pearl as a "petty present," promises to lay at her feet "kingdoms" to add to her already "opulent throne." "All the East / . . . shall call her mistress" (1.5.47, 48–49). The lands which Antony has conquered or defends as a triumvir belong to him, not to Rome. They are his to give to whom he wishes as his personal gifts (see 1.4.18; 3.6.8–16).

Cleopatra, hearing of his profuse gifts, praises Antony for his moderation. She asks whether Antony was sad or merry when Alexas left him. Alexas, comparing Antony's mood to the time of the year "between the extremes / Of hot and cold," answers, "[H]e was nor sad nor merry" (1.5.54–55). The answer delights Cleopatra. Approving his "well-divided disposition" and describing him as having been "between both [extremes]" (1.5.56, 61), she joyfully explains that Antony was not sad because his men depend on his mood for their own and was not merry because he wanted them to know that his joy lay in Egypt. "O heavenly mingle!" she exclaims (1.5.62). This is the only time Cleopatra praises Antony (or anyone else) for moderation. Antony will later say that although she can guess what it should be, Cleopatra does not know what moderation is (3.13.126–27). Here, proving him right, she gets it wrong. Where Alexas, sounding like an old-fashioned Roman, explicitly spoke of Antony's avoiding extremes, Cleopatra, although initially claiming that he was "between both," quickly shifts and takes him to mean that Antony combined rather than avoided both ("mingle").[109] "[B]etween both" comes to mean not free from, but simultaneously subject to, both. Antony's disposition is "well-divided" only because it is torn by the power of conflicting extremes. Thus, Cleopatra goes on to conclude, "Be'st thou sad or merry, / The violence of either thee becomes, / So does it no man else" (1.5.62–64). What Cleopatra praises as Antony's moderation is the violence of clashing excesses in disguise.

A messenger spoke of Caesar's receiving reports on Antony every hour (1.4.34–36). Alexas speaks of his encountering on his way "twenty several" (1.5.65) of Cleopatra's messengers. Unable to keep Antony constantly in her eyes now that he is gone, Cleopatra tries to keep him in her sight as much as she can, as well as to tell him of her love for him. "Who's born that day / When I forget to send to Antony / Shall die a beggar" (1.5.66–68).[110] Yet, although imagining him as a demigod, the consummate soldier and the ruler of kingdoms, Cleopatra, again, shows no interest in Antony's political affairs. She is greatly concerned about his thoughts, but only those of her.

Preparing to send Antony more messages ("Ink and paper, Charmian!" [1.5.68]), Cleopatra asks Charmian whether she ever loved Julius Caesar so. She seems to have forgotten her repeated putative reproach that Antony cannot love her because he had loved Fulvia (1.1.42; 1.3.28–30, 63–66, 76–81). As before, Charmian is impudent, if only playfully. "O that brave Caesar!" she cries out (1.5.70). When Cleopatra demands that she praise Antony ("Be choked with such another emphasis! / Say, 'the brave Antony'"), Charmian, ignoring or defying her, again praises Caesar: "The valiant Caesar!" (1.5.70–73). And after Cleopatra threatens to beat her if she compares Caesar, once more, to her "man of men" (1.5.75), Charmian, asking for pardon, compounds her teasing criticism: "I sing but after you" (1.5.76). A good servant follows her mistress. Charmian is simply repeating what Cleopatra had said at an earlier time. It is not Charmian who contradicts Cleopatra. It is Cleopatra who contradicts herself. Charmian's only error is her timing.

Cleopatra blames her earlier praise of Caesar on her youth: "My salad days, / When I was green in judgement, cold in blood / To say as I said then" (1.5.73–75). She was just a child. Unlike now, neither her mind nor her passion was mature. Her error, too, was her timing. Calling again for ink and paper and linking her love with the number and frequency of her messages, Cleopatra threatens to "unpeople Egypt" (1.5.81) before letting a day go by without letters from her to Antony. No longer content to say it would be unlucky to be born on the day when she forgets to write to Antony, she now says no price is too high for her to show her love. If Antony can give her kingdoms as love gifts, she can empty her kingdom of people to deliver her love letters.

Notes

1. On the early introduction of luxury and extravagance in Egypt, see Diodorus Siculus, *The Library*, 1.45.1; on Egypt's unrivaled wealth, magnificence and lavishness, see, e.g., Diodorus, 1.45.4–49.6, 50.1.5–6, 57.4–58.3, 63.2–9, 71.5; on Alexandria, in particular, see Diodorus, 17.52.

2. "Gipsy" means both an Egyptian and a slut; see *Oxford English Dictionary*, s.v. Gipsy *n* 1a and 2b.

3. The first Ptolemy to rule Egypt, Ptolemy I Soter, was a Macedonian general, who, after the death of Alexander the Great, whose childhood friend and senior general he had been, seized power in Egypt (Pausanias, *Description of Greece*, 1.6.2–4). On the ten generations of Ptolemies ruling Egypt before Cleopatra, see Strabo, *The Geography*, 17.1.11. On the Ptolemies' liking to be called Macedonians, as in fact they were, see Pausanias, 10.7.8. On their keeping their blood line pure while at the same time legitimating themselves as Pharaohs by adopting the Egyptian royal practice of incest, see, Pausanias, 1.7.1, and note *A&C*, 1.4.6, 17; 2.1.38. On Cleopatra as only the first Ptolemy to speak the Egyptian language, see Plutarch, *Antony*, 27.4.

4. Also, e.g., 1.2.122; 2.1.38; 2.2.228; 2.6.128; 4.12.10; 5.2.207.

5. Montesquieu, *Considerations on the Causes of the Greatness of the Romans and Their Decline*, 13, trans. David Lowenthal (New York: Free Press, 1965), 125.

6. Philo is the name of the Hellenistic philosopher and political leader of Alexandria's large Jewish community, while Demetrius is the name of the Macedonian king, son of Antigonus, with whom Plutarch compares Antony's life and against whom Ptolemy I Soter fought for possession of Egypt (Plutarch, *Demetrius*, 5ff.). Demetrius is also the name of Theophrastus's student, Demetrius Phalereus, who was ousted as ruler of Athens by the former Demetrius and fled to Egypt, where he founded the Library of Alexandria under Ptolemy I (Cicero, *De finibus*, 5.54, *Laws*, 3.14; Diodorus Siculus, 20.45.2–4; Strabo, 9.1.20; Plutarch, *Demetrius*, 8.3–9.2; Diogenes Laertius, *The Lives and Opinions of Eminent Philosophers*, 5.75, 78).

7. See Suetonius, *Augustus*, 77.

8. Plutarch, *Antony*, 4.2.4, 43.2–3.

9. Also Suetonius, *Augustus*, 86.2–3.

10. Cicero, *Orator*, 25, *Brutus*, 51, 325, *De oratore*, 2.93–95; Quintilian, *Institutio oratoria*, 12.10.16ff.; Dionysius of Halicarnassus, *The Ancient Orators*, 1.

11. "[B]uckles . . . breast . . . / . . . become . . . bellows"; "Take . . . / . . . The triple pillar . . . transformed / . . . strumpet's fool."

12. Reuben A. Brower, *Hero and Saint: Shakespeare and the Graeco-Roman Heroic Tradition* (New York: Oxford University Press, 1971), 319–20.

13. Alexander Schmidt, *Shakespeare Lexicon and Quotation Dictionary*, 2 vols. (Berlin: 1902; rpt. New York: Dover Books, 1971), s.v. Nay. See, e.g., 3.4.1.

14. Herodotus says that there were 341 human generations—more than eleven thousand years—between the first king of Egypt and Sethos (Herodotus, *The Histories*, 2.142). Sethos lived more than six hundred years before Cleopatra. See also Diodorus, 1.44.1–4.

15. For Cleopatra as Isis, see 3.6.16–19; 3.13.158; 5.2.239–40; also Plutarch, *Antony*, 54.6.

16. Diodorus, 1.74.7, trans. John Skelton (c. 1489), *Bibliotheca Historica of Diodorus Siculus* (London: Early English Text Society, 1956), 102. See also Polybius, 34.14; Strabo, 17.1.12. According to Tacitus, the Egyptians knew nothing of laws and were unused to civil rule as late as Augustus's annexation (Tacitus, *History*, 1.11).

17. See, e.g., Cicero, *Against Catiline*, 4.21, *Philippics*, 4.13, *Verrine Orations*, 4.81; Sallust, *Catiline Conspiracy*, 51.42, 53.2–5. While the Romans traditionally identify valor as virtue, the word "virtue" comes from *vir*, the Latin word for man. See Plutarch, *Coriolanus*, 1.4; Cicero, *Tusculan Disputations*, 2.43, *Philippics*, 10.10.20, *Pro Milone*, 30.82; Varro, *On the Latin Language*, 7.73; *Cor.*, 2.2.83–85. See further Jan H. Blits, *Spirit, Soul and City*, 37, 92, 229–30, *The End of the Ancient Republic: Shakespeare's "Julius Caesar"* (Lanham: Rowman & Littlefield, 1993), 3–20.

18. On the prominence and political influence of eunuchs in Eastern courts, see Tacitus, *Annals*, 6.31; on their prominence and influence in Cleopatra's court, in particular, see Horace, *Ode*, 1.37.9–10; Seneca, *Letters*, 4.7, *Benefits*, 5.16.6; Dio, 50.5.2.

19. Xenophon, *The Education of Cyrus*, 7.5.58–64.

20. Herodotus, 6.9, 32.

21. See, e.g., Livy, *History*, 35.15.4; Horace, *Epode*, 9.13–14; Plutarch, *Antony*, 60.1; Seneca, *Letters*, 66.53; Valerius Maximus, 7.7.6; Tacitus, *History*, 2.71; for the loathing as late as Domitian, see Suetonius, *Domitian*, 7.1; see, further, Ammianus Maecellinus, *Res Gestae*, 14.6.17.

22. Harold Bloom, *Shakespeare: the Invention of the Human* (New York: Riverhead Books, 1998), 546.

23. Cp., e.g., Aristotle, *Physics*, 207b19–21, *On the Heavens*, 286b10–11; Cicero, *Republic*, 6.17, *De natura deorum*, 2.29–39, on the one hand, and Matt. 25:31–33; 2 Cor. 4:17–5:10; Rev. 7, 14, 21, on the other. See also Aquinas, *Summa Theologica*, 1a. 68,4; Dante, *Paradise*, 30.

24. 1.1.22; 1.3.4, 5; 1.5.74; 2.5.26, 28, 37, 39, 43, 91; 3.3.18; 4.15.26; 5.2.15, 18, 49; 5.2.294, 296, 300; see also 3.13.163; 5.2.95.

25. Cleopatra strengthens her charge by quoting Caesar using the royal plural pronoun "we" and addressing Antony with the insulting "thee."

26. E.g., Aristotle, *Art of Rhetoric*, 1383b11–85a15, *Nicomachean Ethics*, 1128b15–30; Livy, *History*, 6.38.11; 40.27.10; 45.39.8; Tacitus, *Annals*, 6.44.

27. Also Seneca, *Letters*, 11.10; Pliny the Elder, *Natural History*, 11.157; Plutarch, *On Shyness*, 1 (528e), *Alexander the Great*, 1.3; Juvenal, *Satires*, 9.18–20. See, e.g., 2.5.37; 3.11.12; 3.13.105; 4.9.12; 4.14.75–76, 86; 5.2.32, 78, 148.

28. A blush and the wish to hide one's shame reflect the common derivation of the English words *shame*, *skin* and *hide* from the Indo-European root *skam* or *skem*, meaning "to cover." On shame dwelling in the eyes, see, e.g., Aristotle, *Art of Rhetoric*, 1384b36; Cicero, *De officiis*, 1.127; Apollonius Rhodius, *Argonautica*, 3.92.

29. Cicero, *Concerning the Manilian Law*, 19–21.

30. *Heywood's Sallust*, trans. Thomas Heywood (1608; rpt. London: Constable and Co., 1924), 61–62.

31. "Weet," which Shakespeare uses only here, means to know something as the answer to a question; see *OED*, s.v. Weet.

32. Paul A. Cantor, *Shakespeare's Rome: Republic and Empire* (Ithaca: Cornell University Press, 1967), 185–86.

33. Contrary to Antony's proud boast, though in keeping with Philo's opening description of him, throughout the play, but especially in connection with Antony, Roman firmness bends, melts, sinks, falls and loses shape, Egyptian softness and sinuousness supplants Roman hardness and fixity, the solid gives way to the fluid, and the fluid finally becomes vaporized. See also, e.g., 1.1.34, 45; 1.2.197; 1.3.75; 1.5.26–27; 2.1.26, 45; 2.2.208; 2.3.15; 2.5.78–79, 94–95; 2.6.50; 2.7.20–27, 108; 3.7.65; 3.10.26; 3.13.45, 68, 95, 159; 4.1.9; 4.3.11; 4.4.20; 4.10.1–7; 4.12.22, 48; 4.14.1–14, 107; 4.15.65–70; 5.2.171, 176, 288–89. Also act 4, n. 40, below. For the Roman significance of standing up (etc.) and falling (etc.), see, further, Blits, *Ancient Republic*, 4–6.

34. E.g., 1.3.21, 59, 64–65; 1.5.20–21, 23, 26, 28–30, 69–70; 2.5.6, 18, 62; 3.7.5–6, 28; 3.13.19, 39, 120, 127, 157, 162; 4.15.61–64, 84–86, 87; 5.2.40–41, 45, 54–56, 73–74, 92–93, 146, 154, 169–70, 295, 308–9, 312.

35. Quintilian, 9.2.7–11.

36. For love's beautifying the beloved, see, e.g., 1.1.49–52; 1.3.34–38; 1.5.20–28, 56–64; 5.2.75–99.

37. See Warburton's emendation, William Warburton, *The Works of Shakespear*, 8 vols. (London: Knapton, Birt, Longman, et al., 1747; rpt.: New York: AMS Press, 1968), 7:99.

38. Polybius, 38.5.4–9; Cicero, *De oratore*, 3.98–100; Seneca, *On Benefits*, 7.2.2; Pliny, 12.81.

39. Plutarch, *Antony*, 29.1–2.

40. See also 1.5.45; 3.11.51, 56; 4.14.15; 4.15.19, 43.

41. Philo, who did not mention Antony by name in his opening indictment, further emphasizes the identification of Antony with the noble Antony by ending the first and final lines with Antony's name.

42. John Dover Wilson, ed., *Antony and Cleopatra* (Cambridge: Cambridge University Press, 1964), 145; Ann Slater, *Notes on "Antony and Cleopatra,"* (London: Ginn and Co., 1971), 46.

43. See, e.g., Cicero, *De natura deorum*, 2.7ff., 162–63, 166; 3.5, *Republic*, 2.26; Dionysius of Halicarnassus, *Roman Antiquities*, 1.86, 2.5–6; Livy, *History*, 1.7, 19–21; Plutarch, *Romulus*, 9.4–5.

44. Cicero, *Divination*, 2.33, 70.

45. See, e.g., Dionysius of Halicarnassus, *Roman Antiquities*, 6.17.3; also Suetonius, *Divus Julius*, 59, 77.

46. The orientalizing of Roman augury, which Antony will illustrate (2.3.9ff.), is already evident in Julius Caesar's Rome; cp. the Soothsayer's prophecy with Caesar's and Cassius's treatment of auspices (JC, 1.2.12–24; 1.3.42ff., 2.2.37–48; 3.1.1–2).

47. On the connection between the liver and desire, see Galen, *On the Doctrines of Hippocrates and Plato*, 6 (506.6–80.6).

48. "Then Herod privately called the Wisemen . . . [a]nd sent them to Bethlehem, saying, 'Go and search diligently for the babe . . . that I may come also, and worship him.'" Matt. 2:7–8.

49. Thaddäus Zielinski, "Marginalien," *Philologus* 64 (1905), 19. See Matt. 2:1–12. As for the connection between Charmian's having a child at fifty and the birth of Jesus, "This play opens in B.C. 40 . . . ; if Charmian be now eighteen or twenty, she will be fifty in the year when Christ was born." Horace Howard Furness, Jr., ed., *Antony and Cleopatra*, New Variorum Edition (Philadelphia: J.B. Lippincott Co., 1907), 27. See also Luke 2:1.

50. Plutarch, *The Philosophy Commonly Called the Morals* (1603), trans. Philemon Holland (London: J. Kirton, 1657), 1301.

51. Mungo MacCallum, *Shakespeare's Roman Plays and Their Background* (London: Macmillan, 1967), 352.

52. The long-standing error traces back at least to Maurice Morgann, *An Essay on the Dramatic Character of Sir John Falstaff* (London: T. Davies, 1777; rpt. New York: AMS Press, 1970), 78.

53. "In the palm of the hand is placed the sign of the bodily desires." A. R. Craig, *The Book of the Hand* (London: Sampson, Low, Son, and Marston, 1867), 23.

54. "Spoken with grave emphasis. Compare the use of *dixi* ['I have spoken'] in Latin." George Lyman Kittredge, *Sixteen Plays of Shakespeare* (Boston: Ginn and Company, 1941), 1363.

55. The specific meaning of the verb "go," here, is uncertain. It could mean "to copulate" or "to achieve pleasure." See Eric Partridge, *Shakespeare's Bawdy* (New York: Dutton, 1960), s.v. Go; E. A. M. Colman, *The Dramatic Use of Bawdy in Shakespeare* (London: Longman, 1974), 196. The context, however, suggests that the woman is never satisfied.

56. David Bevington, ed., *Antony and Cleopatra* (Cambridge: Cambridge University Press, 1990), 86.

57. E. A. Abbott, *A Shakespearean Grammar* (London: Macmillian, and Co. 1870; rpt. New York: Dover Publications, 1966), §3.

58. Bevington, 87.

59. Plutarch, *Antony*, 30.1; Appian, *Civil Wars*, 5.19, 32–50; Dio, 48.5ff.

60. Plutarch, *Antony*, 28.1; 30.2; Appian, *Civil Wars*, 5.14, 19, 59, 66.

61. Plutarch, *Antony*, 24.7–8; 29.1; 53.4, *How to Tell a Flatterer from a Friend*, 5 (51 c–d), 17–19 (59a–61b). On the flattery of Antony's vices as corrupting the character of the Romans, see Plutarch, *How to Tell a Flatterer from a Friend*, 12 (56e).

62. Plutarch, *Antony*, 30.1; Dio, 48.24.4–26.5; Livy, *Periochae*, 127; Velleius Paterculus, 2.78.1; Florus, 2.19.3–5.

63. On the Romans' long-standing (if intermittent) fear of the Parthians, see Cicero, *Letters to Friends*, 1.17.1; on the Romans' previously stopping the Parthians in Syria, see Cicero, *Letters to Friends*, 15.4.7, *Letters to Atticus*, 5.21.2.

64. Cicero, *De partitione oratoria*, 91. Hence the combined intensive and locational use of the adverb "home" (1.2.11; see also 4.7.5).

65. Velleius Paterculus, 2.74.2–3; Appian, *Civil Wars*, 5.33; Dio, 48.4.1–4, 10.1–14.6.

66. E.g., 1.1.15 (his first words), 36–39, 47–48; 1.2.102, 115–17, 199–201; 2.2.91–92; 2.6.50; 2.7.20–23, 42–46, 48, 50, 101; 3.2.43–44, 48–50; 3.7.26–27; 3.11.19–20, 74–75; 3.13.117–20; 4.14.1–11, 137–40.

67. Kittredge, 1363. See Ovid, *Metamorphoses*, 1.262ff.

68. Herodotus, 2.35.

69. Plutarch, *Antony*, 32.1; Appian, *Civil Wars*, 5.143; Dio, 48.17.3–6.

70. See also Plutarch, *Pompey*, 1.1; 14.6; 15.1; 22.3, 6; 43.3; 57; 61.4; 65.1, *Fortune of the Romans*, 7 (319e–f).

71. Appian, *Civil Wars*, 2.103–5.

72. "[I]t is believed . . . that an horse hair laid in a pail full of . . . [stagnant] water will in short time stir and become a living creature." William Harrison, *Description of England*, in Raphael Holinshed's *Chronicles* (1586), 6 vols., (rpt. New York: AMS Press, 1976), 1:3.3, 376.

73. Plutarch, *Antony*, 29.1.

74. See Ovid, *The Art of Love*, 1.755–70; Plutarch, *Conjugal Precepts*, 14 (139f–40a).

75. Ovid, *The Heroical Epistles of the Learned Poet Publius Ovidus Naso*, trans. George Turberville (London: Henry Denham, 1567), 45; Zielinski, 17.

76. Since she is quoting Antony's vows, Cleopatra's repeated "our" seems to be the royal plural, though it also might refer to them as the peerless "mutual pair" (1.1.38).

77. Cleopatra's seven interruptions form a ring-pattern: 1) her bodily weakness (1.3.16–18); 2) Antony should stand farther from her (1.3.19); 3) Fulvia (1.3.20–24); 4) never was a queen so mightily betrayed as she (1.3.25–27); 5) Fulvia (1.3.28–32); 6) Antony should bid farewell and go (1.3.33–40); and 7) her bodily weakness (1.3.41–42).

78. Also Ovid, *Metamorphoses*, 1.416ff.; Golding, 1.495ff.

79. Wilson, 153.

80. On "very" placed before a noun to indicate that the noun must be understood in its full and unrestricted meaning, see Schmidt, s.v. Very.

81. Suetonius, *Augustus*, 25.1.

82. As he will soon repeat ("the bed of Ptolemy" [1.4.17]). See Act 1, n. 3, above.

83. See, e.g., Aristotle, *Nicomachean Ethics*, 1109b30–32; Anonymous, *Ad herennium*, 1.24, 2.23; Cicero, *De inventione*, 1.15, 2.98ff.

84. On Antony's taste for low company, see 1.1.53–65; also, e.g., Cicero, *Philippics*, 2.15, 67, 101; Plutarch, *Antony*, 4.2; 6.5; 43.3.

85. 2.1.13–14. See also, e.g., Virgil, *Ecologues*, 1, 9; Plutarch, *Antony*, 58.1; Suetonius, *Augustus*, 13.3; Appian, *Civil Wars*, 5.12ff.; Dio, 50.10.4–5.

86. Hence the wordplay on "orient" (1.5.43).

87. Following their victory at Philippi, Antony and Caesar divided the military and political functions. Antony kept for himself the wealthy and more promising East, to which he was to restore order, while the younger Caesar was given the West and the opprobrious task of settling the veterans in Italy; see Appian, *Civil Wars*, 5.3;

Dio, 48.1–2; Suetonius, *Augustus*, 13.3. Lepidus, who did not fight at Philippi and was much weaker than either of the other triumvirs, was given a share of power because Caesar feared that he might lead senatorial opposition to him; see Appian, *Civil Wars*, 5.12; Dio, 48.3.6.

88. See Introduction, n. 8, above.

89. See, e.g., Sallust, *Jugurthine War*, 86; *Catiline Conspiracy*, 11.5–7; Plutarch, *Marius*, 9.1; Appian, *Civil Wars*, 1.49, 100; 5.12–13; Suetonius, *Augustus*, 13.3.

90. See Suetonius, *Augustus*, 13.3; Dio, 48.8.2–4.

91. Caesar emphasizes the shift by referring to the past with a progression of pithy past participles ("wished," "ebbed," "loved," "deared," "lacked"), the subjunctive ("until he were") and the repeated "ne'er." On his use of the subjunctive, here, see, Abbott, §302.

92. Plutarch, *Antony*, 32.1; Appian, *Civil Wars*, 5.25.

93. Appian, *Civil Wars*, 5.15, 18, 67; Dio, 48.18.1.

94. E.g., 1.1.2–8; 1.3.39, 85; 1.5.24–25; 2.5.117; 3.10.26–27; 3.11.36–38; 4.8.16–18; 4.15.66–67.

95. Plutarch, *Antony*, 17; Appian, *Civil Wars*, 3.65–76; Dio, 46.35–38.2. At 3.11.35–38, Antony describes briefly, and with great exaggeration and distortion, his fighting at Philippi.

96. "*Antony and Cleopatra* is the only one of Shakespeare's three principal Roman plays where the battles are narrated, not represented. Shakespeare confines battles to reports of action, and thus intensifies the feeling that the Roman concept of Antony's *virtus* belongs to the past, while in the present he subverts the Roman concept of *virtus* by his behaviour." Krystyna Kujawinska-Courtney, *"Th' Interpretation of the Time": The Dramatury of Shakespeare's Roman Plays* (Victoria: English Literary Studies, 1993), 73.

97. This is the only time a triumvir addresses another as "my lord." Antony, lost in remorse, will use the term addressing no one present (3.11.35); Caesar, trying to bring the drinking party aboard Pompey's ship to an end, will address all the other guests as "Gentle lords" (2.7.121).

98. Note also the ambiguity of "we twain," "ourselves," "[a]ssemble we," "our idleness" (1.4.74, 75, 76, 77). The plural pronouns may or may not include Lepidus.

99. They appear together in ten of the play's forty-two scenes and quarrel in five of them.

100. Cleopatra calls Antony "dear" when trying to end his most bitter accusations (3.13.163) and twice when refusing to leave the monument when he is dying (4.15.22, 23). She uses the term also for Charmian (1.3.16). Cleopatra asks or tells Antony of his love for her (1.1.14; 1.3.63, 74; 4.12.31), but tells him of her own love for him only once and only in the past perfect tense ("Sir, you and I have loved . . ." [1.3.90]).

101. The verb "do," the most frequent non-auxiliary verb in the play, is often used as a euphemism for sex, war (or killing), or both. For the former, besides the present lines, see, e.g., 1.1.38–39; 2.2.215; for the latter, see, e.g., 1.1.23; 2.1.8; 2.6.87, 90–91;

2.7.74, 79–80; 3.1.12, 14, 25; 3.7.53; 3.8.3; 3.13.154; 4.6.37; 4.7.5; 4.12.17; 4.14.28–29, 50, 68; 5.2.5, 43, 236, 289, 325, 334; for both, see 1.5.23; 4.14.103; 5.2.262.

102. On the sexual desire of eunuchs, see Philostratus, *Life of Apollonius of Tyana*, 1.33, 36. 37.1.

103. For the story of Venus and Mars, see Homer, *Odyssey*, 8.266–328; Ovid, *Art of Love*, 2.561–92, *Metamorphoses*, 4.171–89.

104. In calling Antony "[t]he demi-Atlas of this earth," Cleopatra seems to disregard Lepidus.

105. Bevington, 107.

106. See, e.g., Cicero, *Pro Rabirio Postumo*, 6; Polybius, *Histories*, 31.10, 20; Diodorus, 31.18.1–2; 33.28; Strabo, 17.1.11; Plutarch, *Pompey*, 49.6; Suetonius, *Divus Julius*, 11; 54.3; Dio, 39.12–14, 43.27.3; Valerius Maximus, 5.1.1f.

107. *Caesar, Civil War*, 3.5, 105–12; Plutarch, *Caesar*, 48–49, *Antony*, 25.3; Appian, *Civil Wars*, 2.71, 5.8; Florus, 2.13.56–60; see also Act 3, n. 19.

108. E.g., 1.5.76–78; 2.1.22–27; 2.2.235–36, 246–48; 2.6.63–65, 128; 3.13.121–22.

109. Neill, 176.

110. On the Egyptian belief that one's birthday determines one's fate, see Herodotus, 2.82.

~

Act Two

Act Two, Scene One

Although his father, Pompey the Great, drove from the sea the pirates who had been threatening Rome,[1] Pompey, having found himself proscribed by the Senate (1.3.50), has allied himself with pirates, including former slaves, and is now threatening Rome.[2] Evidently answering Menecrates, Pompey complains of the gods' failure to help his cause. "If the great gods be just, they shall assist / The deeds of justest men," he says, confident of his own justice (2.1.1–2). Menecrates, a peculiarly pious pirate, assures Pompey that what the gods delay they do not deny. When Pompey replies that what he and the others pray for steadily loses value while they continue to pray for it, Menecrates, shifting the substance but not the spirit of his assurance, now admits that the gods deny our prayers, but only for our own good. "We, ignorant of ourselves, / Beg often our own harms," he tells Pompey, "which the wise powers / Deny us for our own good; so we find profit / By losing of our prayers" (2.1.5–8). The gods protect us from ourselves as well as from our enemies. Their wisdom corrects our ignorance. We wish for what is good for us; the gods know what is good for us. Their denial is their blessing in disguise.[3]

Pompey turns to his present political advantage. "I shall do well," he flatly states (2.1.8), explaining that the people love him, the sea is his, his powers are increasing ("crescent"), and, he adds, "my auguring hope / Says [my fortunes] will come to th' full" (2.1.10–11). His hope is his augur. That hope appears well founded. Reviewing each of the triumvirs, Pompey says that

57

Antony will fight only wars of love (". . . will make / No wars without doors" [2.1.12–13]), Caesar raises needed money only by making enemies (". . . gets money where / He loses hearts" [2.1.13–14]), and Lepidus flatters and is flattered by both, while he loves neither and neither cares for him. The first will not fight, the second is hated, and the third is useless. Menas quickly corrects Pompey. "Caesar and Lepidus / Are in the field. A mighty strength they carry" (2.1.16–17). The last we heard, Caesar was going to call an immediate council to prepare for war (1.4.74–76). Now, Menas reports that he and Lepidus are already in the field with a large army. Pompey, however, does not believe the report ("'Tis false" [2.1.18]). While sure that the man who informed Menas "dreams" (2.1.19), he is certain—"I know" (2.1.19)—that Caesar and Lepidus are still in Rome, hoping for Antony. Instead of explaining how he knows, Pompey calls for Cleopatra to "[t]ie up the libertine in a field of feasts; / Keep his brain fuming," and for Epicurean cooks to sharpen his insatiable appetite so that sleep and feeding may postpone all thought of his honor until he has slipped into utter indifference and oblivion ("a Lethe'd dullness" [2.1.23–24, 27]). Pompey's auguring hope seems to lie crucially in Antony's continued sybarite indulgence. As Caesar had indicated (1.4.56ff.), the addition of Antony's army, not those of Caesar and Lepidus alone, is the danger.

Varrius enters with the "most certain" report (2.1.28) that "Mark Antony is every hour in Rome / Expected," saying that "[s]ince he went from Egypt 'tis / A space for further travel" (2.1.29–31). Varrius's report contradicts Pompey's confident hope, Caesar's contemptuous criticism (1.4.1ff.) and Menas's mistaken report. Yet, despite his unexpected activity, Antony is late. He could easily have arrived in Rome by now. Even when he acts, he is tardy.

Pompey does not doubt the new report. And although the news is unwelcome ("I could have given less matter / A better ear" [2.1.32–33]), it raises his estimation of himself. Pompey says that he and his allies present only "a petty" (2.1.35) threat to the triumvirs, hardly enough to arouse the "amorous surfeiter" (2.1.34). But, impressed that they have done so, he concludes that this should cause them to have a higher opinion of themselves. The danger to them is now greater, for Antony's "soldiership / Is twice the other twain."

> But let us rear
> The higher our opinion, that our stirring
> Can from the lap of Egypt's widow pluck
> The ne'er-lust-wearied Antony.

>   (2.1.35–39)

Act Two ～ 59

The principal basis for his hope has been dashed, and the danger of his enemy has been increased, yet Pompey's hopes rise even higher than they had been, for Antony's unlikely action shows just how seriously the triumvirs take Pompey's threat to them.

When Menas doubts that Caesar and Antony can come to an agreement after Fulvia's and Lucius Antonius's wars on Caesar, Pompey now fully expects their reconciliation. Arguing that "lesser enmities . . . give way to greater" (2.1.44), he concludes that the opposition between himself and the triumvirs exceeds that between Antony and Caesar. But for him, he declares, they would fight each other: "Were't not that we stand up against them all, / 'Twere pregnant they should square between themselves, / For they have entertained cause enough / To draw their swords" (2.1.45–48). Only "the fear of us" (2.1.48), Pompey says, permits Caesar and Antony to patch up their "petty difference" (2.1.50). Pompey originally thought Antony would not leave Egypt for "such a petty war" (2.1.35). But, now that he has done so, he thinks Antony and Octavius consider him the "greater" enemy and their own enmity a "petty difference." The "petty" has become the "greater."

Where Pompey began the scene impatiently awaiting the gods' support, he ends it by denying that their support is decisive: "Be't as our gods will have't! It only stands / Our lives upon to use our strongest hands" (2.1.51–52). The gods' support may be welcome, but when it is a matter of life or death, Pompey suggests, men's lives depend on their using their utmost strength. Men's courage, not the gods' justice, will determine the outcome. As it will turn out, however, neither the gods' support nor his own strength will bring Pompey victory. Easily allayed and flattered, he will fail to take advantage of his powerful position. Antony will have considerably overestimated his "blood and life" (1.2.197).

Act Two, Scene Two

1.

Varrius told of Caesar and Lepidus awaiting Antony in Rome. We now see their meeting. Lepidus, afraid of a quarrel between Antony and Caesar, urges "[g]ood Enobarbus" (2.2.1), as he unctuously addresses him, to "entreat" Antony to use "soft and gentle speech" (2.2.2, 3). Enobarbus, throwing Lepidus's verb back at him, says that he will "entreat him / To answer like himself. If Caesar move him, / Let Antony look over Caesar's head / And speak as loud as Mars" (2.2.3–6).[4] If Caesar provokes him, manly honor would demand that Antony answered the offense openly and strongly: "Were I the wearer of Antonio's beard, / I would not shave't today" (2.2.7–8). For Antony to "answer like himself" is for him to answer like a man.

Lepidus, trying to maintain peace, admonishes Enobarbus that this is no time for private resentment: "'Tis not a time / For private stomaching" (2.2.8–9). Lepidus does not mean that there is a public reason for overlooking private affronts. Neither here nor anywhere else does he ever mention Rome, let alone anything public. His concern is with the "stomaching," not that it is "private." Lepidus is afraid that Antony's private offense will endanger Lepidus's own private interests by causing a contentious quarrel. Enobarbus, again returning Lepidus's word, gives no ground: "Every time / Serves for the matter that is then born in't" (2.2.9–10). Every affront should be met when it is offered. And when Lepidus then suggests that "small to greater matters must give way" (2.2.11), Enobarbus, yet again using Lepidus's word against him, once more contradicts him: "Not if the small come first" (2.2.11). Honor comes before peace. Lepidus, although initially still critical ("Your speech is passion" [2.2.12]), finally retreats. No longer asking him to moderate Antony's speech, he entreats Enobarbus simply to speak moderately himself: "But pray you stir no embers up" (2.2.12–13). If Enobarbus will not quench Antony's anger, he should at least not kindle it.

2.

Before the triumvirs meet, we hear the ends of Antony's conversation with Ventidius and Caesar's with Maecenas. Although both triumvirs work through lieutenants, there is a difference. "If we compose well here, to Parthia," Antony tells Ventidius (2.2.15). Ventidius will command Antony's army in Parthia, but Antony makes the decision whether to go. "I do not know, Maecenas. / Ask Agrippa," Caesar says (2.2.17). Where Antony answers for himself, Agrippa answers for Caesar. Caesar yields to Agrippa's judgment; Antony follows his own.[5]

While neither Antony nor Caesar, jockeying for advantage, initially acknowledges the other, Lepidus, again urging that the smaller ("leaner" [2.2.20]) matters should make way for the greatest ("most great" 2.2.19]) and that what is amiss should be "gently heard" (2.2.21), exhorts the "[n]oble friends," the "noble partners" (2.2.18, 23),[6] to speak of their sourest points in the sweetest terms and not to add ill temper to what they are discussing. To debate their "trivial" differences "loud," he says, is to "commit / Murder in healing wounds" (2.2.22–23). Antony appears to approve. "'Tis spoken well. / Were we before our armies, and to fight, / I should do thus" (2.2.26–28), he says, making a courteous gesture. Antony will do just what he would if they were before their armies when their armies were set to fight. Victory over their common enemy, not over his political rival, is his paramount concern.

Caesar, acknowledging Antony, welcomes him to Rome and invites him to sit ("Sit" [2.2.31]). But Antony, seeing or fearing that Caesar perceives his hospitable gesture as a sign of his superiority, tells him to sit first ("Sit, sir" [2.2.32]). Honor goes with giving,[7] and the more competitive the rivalry, the more unremitting the comparisons. But even though he is always guarding his status among the triumvirs, Caesar accepts the invitation ("Nay then" [2.2.33]). Although he does not want to appear subordinate, he needs the support of Antony's arms and aid.

As Lepidus fears, the discussion begins tensely. Responding to Caesar's earlier charges, Antony, in his first words, accuses Caesar of taking things ill which are not so or which do not concern him. Caesar, deftly combining reproach and flattery,[8] turns the accusation back against Antony, arguing that Caesar would make himself look ridiculous if he quarreled over nothing or over what did not concern him, "and with you / Chiefly i'th' world" (2.2.37–38). Antony, forced to defend himself, specifies his complaint: "My being in Egypt, Caesar, / What was't to you?" (2.2.40–41).[9] Caesar, who says nothing about what he had complained to Lepidus (1.4.23–25), answers by raising a new complaint: "No more than my residing here at Rome / Might be to you in Egypt. Yet if you there / Did practice on my state, your being in Egypt / Might be my question" (2.2.42–45). Antony, riled by the suggestion that he plotted against Caesar, indignantly challenges, "How intend you, 'practiced'?" (2.2.45). Antony's deliberately provoked question allows Caesar to attack him in the guise of answering.

Caesar cites the wars that Fulvia and Lucius Antonius made against him, which he says were carried out for Antony's sake ("[T]heir contestation / Was theme for you; you were the word of war" [2.2.48–49]). Antony, rejecting the charge, denies that his brother claimed to be fighting in his behalf and suggests that Caesar knows better ("I did enquire it, / And have my learning from some true reports / That drew their swords with you" [2.2.51–53]). Lucius, a man of republican sentiments, had been a consul, the highest elected office in republican Rome and one that continued in name after the Republic's downfall. The war between Lucius and Caesar stemmed from a conflict between the consuls' powers and the triumvirs' legally authorized but strictly unconstitutional powers. As with virtually every step in the erosion of Rome's republican order, the institution of the triumvirate proceeded in the guise of legitimate, traditional authority.[10] Arguing that his brother's war was thus a rebellion against the authority of all the triumvirs, Antony claims to have as much reason as Caesar to be displeased ("against my stomach"

[2.2.55]) with his brother. Moreover, Antony adds, repeating his tacit charge of disingenuousness, his earlier letters to Caesar informed him completely ("did satisfy you" [2.2.57]) on the matter. If he wants to piece ("patch" [2.2.57]) together a quarrel and make it seem substantial, Antony concludes, Caesar needs more than this. His accusation is flimsy as well as artificial.

Despite Antony's attempt to be dismissive, Caesar turns Antony's answer around and uses the fact that Antony defends himself and criticizes Caesar's accusation as a fresh offense. "You praise yourself / By laying defects of judgement to me, but / You patched up your excuses," he replies (2.2.59–60), insultingly repeating Antony's word, "patch," against Antony himself: In blaming Caesar, Antony praises himself, while fabricating excuses. Forcefully denying the charge ("Not so, not so!" [2.2.61]), Antony says that Caesar certainly must know that he could not look favorably on his brother's wars. Since Antony was Caesar's partner in the cause against which Lucius fought, self-interest alone should acquit him.

Turning to Fulvia, Antony, both praising and criticizing her, says he wishes Caesar had so spirited a wife ("I would you had her spirit in such another" [2.2.67]) so that he would know how difficult she was to control. "The third o'th' world is yours, which with a snaffle / You may pace easy, but not such a wife" (2.2.68–69). Fulvia was harder to handle than a third of the world. Enobarbus seconds Antony: "Would we had all such wives, that the men might go to wars with the women!" (2.2.70–71). "[W]ith" could mean "on the same side" or "on the opposite side." "[To] go to wars with the women" could mean to fight alongside or to fight against them. Enobarbus's equivocal quip, obscuring the distinction between love and war, suggests that the parties seek victory over each other in both.[11] Antony, continuing, uses Fulvia's unruliness to acquit himself. Fulvia being so unmanageable ("uncurbable" [2.2.72]), he says, he concedes that her disturbances, produced by her impatience at his absence in Egypt ("Made out of her impatience— which not wanted / Shrewdness of policy too" [2.2.73–74]), caused Caesar much trouble. But what caused Caesar trouble, exonerates Antony: "For that, you must / But say I could not help it" (2.2.75–76). Caesar is obliged to grant ("must / But say . . .") that Antony was unable to prevent Fulvia's trouble and is therefore free of blame. As Lepidus argued earlier, Antony should not be blamed for what he could not have avoided (1.4.13–15). Inability absolves.

Caesar, perhaps gratified by his admission of weakness, raises a new grievance concerning Antony's own actions. He wrote to Antony "[w]hen rioting in Alexandria" (2.2.77), but Antony ignored his letters and tauntingly flouted his messenger, whom he would not hear. Antony, while blaming the

Messenger for approaching him before having been properly admitted, explains, "Three kings I had newly feasted, and did want / Of what I was i'th' morning" (2.2.81–82). Antony's explanation, although confirming that he was "rioting" and was not himself the next morning, may suppress something else. We shall later learn that, as a defensive step before the Parthian campaign, Antony reorganized client kingdoms in the East, placing on the thrones reliable kings whose political sentiments serve his and Rome's interests (3.6.68–77). His feasting three Eastern kings may have been political preparation for the campaign, though, for reasons we shall soon see, he may not want Caesar to know of his plans. Whatever the case, Antony explains that the following day he told the Messenger what his condition had been, "which was as much / As to have asked him pardon" (2.2.83–84). Antony went as far as his dignity would allow. If he and Caesar are to quarrel, he declares, it should not be over an insignificant person. Caesar's own dignity, he suggests, would be debased by such a quarrel.

Caesar accused Antony of praising himself by blaming him (2.2.59–61). Now, he does what he accused Antony of doing. "You have broken / The article of your oath, which you shall never / Have tongue to charge me with" (2.2.86–88). The seriousness of Caesar's accusation is evident from Lepidus's caution: "Soft, Caesar!" (2.2.89).[12] But precisely because the violation of his oath would concern his honor, Antony wants to hear the particular charge so he can vindicate himself: "No, Lepidus, let him speak. / The honour is sacred which he talks on now, / Supposing that I lacked it" (2.2.90–92). To give one's oath is to give one's word of honor. It is to pledge one's honor as the guarantor of one's promise. To violate one's oath is thus to violate one's honor.

Caesar states Antony's violation: "To lend me arms and aid when I required them, / The which you both denied" (2.2.94–95). Antony quibbles in his defense: "Neglected, rather; / And then when poisoned hours had bound me up / From mine own knowledge" (2.2.96–97). Implicitly distinguishing between failure through neglect and failure through intent, Antony, taking for granted that only intentional failure would constitute the violation of an oath, pleads his innocence by claiming his drunken neglect. He neglected his oath to Caesar because he was too drunk to know what he was doing (or not doing). Ignorance argues innocence; drunken negligence therefore excuses, for one can be guilty only of what one knows or intends. Recognizing the weakness of his self-vindication,[13] Antony offers a vague apology. "As nearly as I may / I'll play the penitent to you," he says, "but mine honesty / Shall not make poor my greatness, nor my power / Work without it" (2.2.97–100). Antony tries to reconcile the demands of greatness and honesty, dignity and honor. His honesty will prompt him to apologize, he says, but only to the extent that it does not compromise his greatness, yet his greatness will not cause him to ignore his duty to act with honesty. While repentant to Caesar, he will act with dignity and honor. Antony, although often careless of his dignity, particularly in front of subordinates, is always attentive to it in front of Caesar. Where Caesar is always concerned about his dignity, Antony seems most concerned about it before his great rival. Thus, concluding, Antony elaborates his innocence regarding Fulvia and offers a qualified apology for her actions:

> Truth is that Fulvia,
> To have me out of Egypt, made wars here,
> For which myself, the ignorant motive, do
> So far ask pardon as befits mine honour
> To stoop in such a case.

(2.2.100–104)

After Lepidus, always praising what promises peace among the triumvirs, commends Antony's apology ("'Tis noble spoken" [2.2.104]), Maecenas, no doubt well prepared by Caesar, opens negotiations between Caesar and Antony by hesitatingly offering advice.[14] "If it might please you to enforce no further / The griefs between ye," he suggests, in his distinctive mincing diction,[15] "to forget them quite / Were to remember that the present need / Speaks to atone you" (2.2.105–8). The present need for agreement should cause Antony and Caesar to forget their differences. Lepidus, of course, approves: "Worthily spoken, Maecenas" (2.2.108). But Enobarbus, neither deferential nor tactful, shrewdly if cynically comments, "Or, if you borrow one another's love for the instant, you may, when you hear no more words of Pompey, return it again. You shall have time to wrangle in when you have nothing else to do" (2.2.109–12). The reconciliation between Caesar and Antony can be only temporary. It can last only as long as Pompey threatens. When Antony, trying to maintain diplomatic decorum, rebukes him for impertinence ("Thou art a soldier only. Speak no more" [2.2.113]), Enobarbus misunderstands him—or, pretending to misunderstand him, understands him correctly—to refer to the truth of what he says rather than to his inferior rank: "That truth should be silent, I had almost forgot" (2.2.114–15). Diplomatic exchanges are apt to leave unstated or half-stated at least some of the truth, even when otherwise brutally blunt. "[I]f you . . . / . . . tak[e] / Antony's course, you shall . . . / . . . put your children / To that destruction which I'll guard them from / If thereon you rely," Caesar will tell Cleopatra, silent about both his plans to parade her in triumph in Rome and his intention to kill at least her eldest child, Caesarion, no matter what she does (5.2.127–32). There, Caesar disguises his threat as a promise; here, his agent disguises his opening of negotiations as deferential, conditional advice.[16]

After Antony reiterates his rebuke ("You wrong this presence; therefore speak no more" [2.2.116]), Enobarbus impatiently, though mildly, remonstrates: "Go to, then! Your considerate stone" (2.2.117). Punning on "considerate," he states that he will be considerate of Antony's wishes and therefore be silent as a stone, but that he will not stop thinking. He will be considerate and yet continue to consider.

Notwithstanding his rebuke, Antony may welcome Enobarbus's original impertinent comment. Antony, we shall soon see, has good reason to want a marriage with Octavia. Just as Caesar has put up Maecenas to lay the foundation for the subject, Antony may have instructed Enobarbus to do the same. Enobarbus's apparent impertinence may actually be perfectly pertinent service.

Thus Caesar takes advantage of Enobarbus's words. Saying that he dislikes not the matter but the manner of his speech, he agrees with Enobarbus, "for't cannot be / We shall remain in friendship, our conditions / So differing in their acts" (2.2.119–21). Differing so in their temperaments or characters ("conditions"), Antony and Caesar differ greatly in their conduct ("acts"), and where the conduct is so different, men can remain friends only when some external constraint requires it. Caesar, pointedly limiting himself to their personal differences, says nothing about their rival political interests. Then, as if at a loss, he wishfully declares, "Yet, if I knew / What hoop should hold us staunch, from edge to edge / O'th' world I would pursue it" (2.2.121–23). Caesar's metaphor is that of a hoop holding a barrel together to make it watertight. Just as the metal hoops bind together the barrel's wooden staves, Caesar wishes for something to hold the triumvirs, and hence the entire world, together as one.

Agrippa, on cue, proposes a marriage between Antony and Caesar's half-sister. He proceeds cautiously. Agrippa says that Caesar has a half-sister, "[a]dmired Octavia" (2.2.126), and that Antony is now a widower. Caesar, as though speaking for Antony and even Cleopatra, quickly admonishes him: "Say not so, Agrippa. If Cleopatra heard you, your reproof / Were well deserved of rashness" (2.2.127–29). Caesar covers his carefully contrived course by accusing his spokesman of rashness, allowing Antony to end the discussion with no embarrassment to Caesar. Antony, however, corrects him ("I am not married, Caesar" [2.2.130]) and asks to hear more. Delivering a well-rehearsed speech ("'tis a studied, not a present thought" [2.2.145]), Agrippa, using overblown rhetoric throughout, first states in three ways—literally ("To hold you in perpetual amity" [2.2.132]), synecdochically ("To make you brothers" [2.2.133]) and metaphorically ("to knit your hearts / With an un-slipping knot" [2.2.133–34])—the political purpose of the proposed marriage. Next, he describes Octavia's personal merits: her beauty ("whose beauty claims / No worse a husband than the best of men" [2.2.135–36]) and her virtue and graces ("Whose virtue and whose general graces speak / That which none else can utter" [2.2.137–38]). While her beauty is worthy of the best of men, no words can do justice to her virtue and graces. Agrippa then returns to his proposal's policy, stating it again in three ways—literally ("By this marriage / All little jealousies which now seem great, / And all great fears which now import their dangers / Would then be nothing" [2.2.138–41]), synecdochically ("Truths would be tales, / Where now half-tales be truths" [2.2.141–42]), and incrementally ("Her love to both / Would each to other, and all loves to both / Draw after her" [2.2.142–44]).[17] Great suspicions and fears would become nothing; where rumors are now taken as truths, even truths would be dismissed as mere rumors; Octavia's loves for her husband and her brother would inspire their loves for each other, and the public's ad-miration for her would turn into its love for both men, as well. Octavia would not only reconcile the two triumvirs, but end the public's hostility to them. Agrippa closes his speech by asking for pardon for a contemplated ("studied") rather than a sudden ("present") thought, "[b]y duty ruminated" (2.2.145, 146). His curious apology seems meant to indicate to Antony that the pro-posal comes from Caesar.

Antony wants more than an implicit assurance. "Will Caesar speak?" he asks (2.2.147). Caesar, however, does not want to speak until he knows "how Antony is touched / With what is spoke already" (2.2.148–49). Neither man wants to accept what the other might withhold or reject. Thus Antony asks specifically, "What power is in Agrippa, / If I would say, 'Agrippa, be it so,' / To make this good?" (2.2.149–51). And Caesar assures him, "The power of Caesar, and / His power unto Octavia" (2.2.151–52). Both his public power as Caesar and his private power as a brother would make good the proposal. Antony without hesitation accepts. "May I never, / To this good purpose that so fairly shows, / Dream of impediment!" he says, stressing how hopeful the proposal looks (2.2.152–54). Asking for Caesar's hand to ratify the agree-ment, Antony declares, with similarly overblown language, that "from this hour / The heart of brothers govern in our loves / And sway our great designs" (2.2.155–57). Caesar accepts his hand. "There's my hand," he returns, offer-ing a traditional Roman pledge of trust or faith.

A sister I bequeath you, whom no brother
Did ever love so dearly. Let her live
To join our kingdoms and our hearts; and never
Fly off our loves again!

                    (2.2.157–61)

Although Antony, offering his hand ("Let me have thy hand" [2.2.154]),
changes to the familiar pronoun "thy," Caesar, accepting his hand, retains
the distant "you" to the end.[18]

Families have always been essential to Rome. From the beginning a city of
sovereign fathers,[19] Rome has rested on the prominence and perpetuation of
particular families. Yet, despite the traditional sanctity of Roman marriages,[20]
political marriages and divorces, at least among families possessing or seeking
political power, have become the rule rather than the rare exception.[21] We
see almost nothing but imitations or semblances of traditional Roman families in Antony and Cleopatra. With the exception of Pompey's family, which
will in fact end with his death, the only traditional Roman family is the one
Antony regrets he never had (3.13.111–13).[22] The sanctity of marriage has
become largely an empty shadow.

Caesar will, of course, exploit Antony's (predictable) betrayal of Octavia
to rally Roman opinion against him. Antony's betrayal of a virtuous Roman
wife for a dissolute Egyptian queen will add to the Romans' disgust of him
and give Caesar a casus belli (see 3.6.1–24). The decision to marry Octavia
may nevertheless show the same political astuteness which Antony demonstrates in Julius Caesar and which had made him the dominating member of
the triumvirate. Following Caesar's assassination, Antony left the Senate
"more praised, and better esteemed, than ever man was," for he was thought
to have put an end to Rome's long civil war and to have resolved an excep-
tionally difficult and confused situation in a very prudent and statesmanlike
manner (Plutarch, Antony, 14.2; North, 6:14). But his extraordinary glory
quickly faded, as Rome became outraged by his "rul[ing] absolutely" in everything (Plutarch, Antony, 15.3; North, 6:15). And while Antony, meanwhile,
had nothing but contempt for him because of his young age, Octavius
shrewdly won the support of the Senate and the goodwill of the people, and
succeeded in mobilizing many of Julius Caesar's veterans from the colonies to
which they had retired. At Modena, Antony was crushed by Caesar's parti-
sans and forced to retreat (see 1.4.57ff.). And although he was subsequently
able to rally his allies and make himself formidable, once back in Rome he
again became odious to the Romans with his public crimes, including the

proscriptions, and his private debaucheries (Plutarch, *Antony*, 9; 21.1–3). At Phillippi, however, Antony "did all" in defeating Brutus and Cassius and "had the chiefest glory of all [for] this victory" (Plutarch, *Antony*, 22.1, 4; North, 6:21; see 3.11.35–40). Yet, still again, his glory and power soon dwindled as Antony, turning to the East, committed new outrages while succumbing to new temptations. Defeat of the Parthians, however, promises Antony unrivaled power and glory. Victory would bring the entire East under Roman control, revenge Roman honor for Crassus's disgraceful defeat at Carrhae twenty years earlier, prove Antony in the eyes of the Romans, especially the legionaries, and, earning him a massive triumph in Rome, eclipse the unpopular Caesar, leaving Antony the sole ruler of the world. But a Parthian campaign presupposes peace in the West—peace between Pompey and the triumvirs, on the one hand, and Antony and Caesar, on the other. And, for that, Antony needs the proposed marriage: "If we compose well here, to Parthia" (2.2.15). Once he has his Roman triumph, he need not care about offending Caesar or playing into his hands.

The triumvirs direct their attention to Pompey, whose threat is the immediate reason for the marriage. Antony expresses surprise at his fighting Pompey, to whom he owes gratitude for an unusual and large favor ("strange courtesies and great" [2.2.163]). As we learn later, Pompey gave Antony's mother refuge when Caesar drove her and Fulvia out of Italy (2.6.44–46).[23] Antony, mindful of his honor, does not want to be thought to have forgotten his debt, but he also does not want his debt to impede his action: "I must thank him only, / Lest my remembrance suffer ill report; / At heel of that, defy him" (2.2.164–66). Antony will thank Pompey in order to protect his honor, but then attack him right afterward. Gratitude requires acknowledgment, not forbearance.

Lepidus warns, "Time calls upon's" (2.2.166). The triumvirs must attack Pompey at once, he says, or else Pompey, who has the advantage, will attack them. Caesar says that Pompey is located at Mount Misena, and, though by land his strength is "[g]reat and increasing," by sea he is "an absolute master," to which Antony adds, or qualifies, that that is at least the common report ("So is the fame" [2.2.172, 173]). Whether or not his touch of skepticism is meant to defend himself against Caesar's charge that he failed to deliver assistance when needed (2.2.94–95), Antony declares wishfully, "Would we had spoke together!" (2.2.174). Despite apparently discounting Caesar's assessment of Pompey's forces, he wishes that Pompey's threat had been confronted sooner. But although urging haste ("Haste we for [the battle]" [2.2.174]), Antony seeks a delay. "Yet, ere we put ourselves in arms, dispatch we / The business we have talked of" (2.2.175–76). The battle may be urgent, but the marital has precedence over the martial. Caesar has no objection. "With most gladness" (2.2.176) he will take Antony to see Octavia. And even Lepidus, who warned that time was pressing and that the triumvirs must act right away, would not miss the occasion for anything. "[N]ot sickness should detain me," he declares, with a mixture of obligingness and valetudinarianism, as though sickness might be the grandest thing that could oppose his going (2.2.180).[24]

3.

The three Romans left behind, now that their leaders are gone, speak with greater familiarity and freedom. Maecenas and Agrippa are Caesar's "two chief friends," as Plutarch says (Plutarch, *Antony*, 35.2; North, 6:35) and Enobarbus strongly suggests ("Half the heart of Caesar, worthy Maecenas" [2.2.182–83]). Both men are Caesar's intimate and trusted friends from childhood and owe their remarkable powers and positions entirely to their friendships with him.[25] Maecenas was with Caesar at Philippi (Pliny, 7.148), was his envoy to Antony when Caesar needed arms and aid against Pompey, and will rule Rome and Italy for him in his absence (Appian, *Civil Wars*, 5.92, 99). Agrippa, who will remain Caesar's closest and most trusted friend to the end of Agrippa's life (Seneca, *On Benefits*, 6.32.2; Dio, 54.29), will crush Pompey's fleet at Mylae and Naulochus (Appian, *Civil Wars*, 5.105, 119–21; Dio, 49.9–10), defeat Antony at Actium (Plutarch, *Antony*, 66.3; Velleius Paterculus, 2.85.2), organize the army, navy and administration of the Empire (Velleius Paterculus, 2.90.1; Augustus, *Res Gestae*, 8), marry Caesar's daughter (Plutarch, *Antony*, 87.2–3; Suetonius, *Augustus*, 42.1; 63.1; Velleius Paterculus, 2.93.2), and become his co-regent of the Empire (Dio, 54.12.4–5; Tacitus, *Annals*, 3.56.3, *History*, 1.15; Velleius Paterculus, 2.90.1) and his presumptive successor (Tacitus, *Annals*, 6.51.2). Maecenas and Agrippa, while men of extraordinary ability, personify the personalism of post-republican Rome. They are tied to Caesar not through Rome, but through private friendship. In this crucial respect, they mirror the marriage that Agrippa has proposed.

Maecenas, welcoming Enobarbus "from Egypt," immediately asks about his and Antony's pleasures "in Egypt" (2.2.181, 186). His interest in Egyptian pleasures is no surprise. Maecenas is a man who prominently displays his own taste for profligate pleasures, particularly those of soft luxury, indolence, food and sex.[26] Enobarbus, answering, tells that he and Antony slept through the day and, punning on "light" (2.2.188), says that they made the night bright, merry, light-headed and debauched with drinking.[27] Maecenas responds by asking Enobarbus to confirm what he has heard about Alexandrian feasts: "Eight wild boars roasted whole at breakfast, and but twelve persons there. Is this true?" (2.2.189–90). Maecenas exaggerates Plutarch's already-extravagant description. Where Plutarch speaks of "supper" (Plutarch, *Antony*, 28.3–4; North, 6:27–28), Maecenas speaks of breakfast. Enobarbus, nevertheless, goes still further. Eager to impress, he magnifies Egyptian indulgence by belittling the sumptuous breakfast. "This was but as a fly by an eagle. We had much more monstrous matter of feast, which worthily deserved noting" (2.2.191–93).[28] Alexandrian feasts exceed even Maecenas's most immoderate imaginings.[29]

Enobarbus's mention of yet greater Egyptian feasts leads the pleasure-loving Maecenas, without pause, to the topic of Cleopatra, whom he describes with an appreciative superlative ("She's a most triumphant lady, if report be square to her" [2.2.194–95]). The topics of the sumptuous feasts and the splendid Cleopatra—or perhaps, more generally, gluttony and lechery—seem so close in Maecenas's mind that he can pass from the one to the other without even mentioning her name. Enobarbus, at once gratifying and astounding his listeners, begins to describe Antony's first meeting with Cleopatra, when "she pursed up his heart upon the river Cydnus" (2.2.196–97). And Agrippa, who showed no interest in the topic of food, immediately and enthusiastically speaks of the reported rare splendor of her spectacle. "There she appeared indeed! Or my reporter devised well for her" (2.2.198–99). Enobarbus is delighted to tell ("I will tell you" [2.2.200]). Although his speech is usually pithy and blunt, often aphoristic,[30] his account of Cleopatra on the Cydnus contains nothing but magnificent, lyrical hyperbole. In style and substance, it runs counter to Philo's and Caesar's seamy characterizations of Cleopatra as well as Enobarbus's own unseemly disparagement of her.

Enobarbus first describes Cleopatra's barge, stressing its royal colors and sheen: "The barge she sat in, like a burnished throne, / Burned on the water; the poop was beaten gold; / Purple the sails" (2.2.201–3). Turning from sight to smell, Enobarbus then describes the effect of the perfumed purple sails on the winds: "[A]nd so perfumed that / The winds were love-sick with them" (2.2.203–4). The scent of the sails animated the winds, which languished in love for them. Then turning from smell to touch, Enobarbus describes the oars' similar effect on the water: "[T]he oars were silver, / Which to the tune of flutes kept stroke, and made / The water which they beat to follow faster, / As amorous of their strokes" (2.2.204–7). Where the queen's throne was made of gold, the oars, more distant from and more inferior to Cleopatra, were silver. And while the winds fell in love with the perfumed sails, the water fell in love with the oars stroking it to the music of flutes. Just as the winds were lovesick, the water was enamored. Cleopatra's barge, while arousing the senses, animated the winds and water with ardent amorous desire.

Enobarbus next speaks of Cleopatra herself ("her own person"), whom he says "beggared all description" (2.2.207, 208). Where his account of the barge stressed the senses, his depiction of Cleopatra stresses the imagination. "[S]he did lie / In her pavilion, cloth-of-gold, of tissue," he says, "O'er-picturing that Venus where we see / The fancy outwork nature" (2.2.208–11). Cleopatra, dressed like Venus, surpassed a picture of Venus in which the artist's imagination surpassed nature itself. While she herself became a work of art, she was superior to art, which is superior to nature. Where Enobarbus's description of the barge animated the inanimate, his portrayal of Cleopatra renders her an imitation of Venus surpassing the most beautiful idealization of Venus.

Enobarbus then describes "pretty dimpled boys, like smiling cupids," standing on each side of Cleopatra "[w]ith divers-coloured fans, whose wind did seem / To glow the delicate cheeks which they did cool, / And what they undid did" (2.2.212–15). While his depiction of the barge stressed the senses and his depiction of Cleopatra stressed the imagination, Enobarbus's description of the fanned wind stresses the lack of distinction between contraries. The boys' fanning has simultaneous contrary effects, both specifically and generally. What the boys cooled, they heated; what they undid, did.

"O, rare for Antony!" (2.2.215). Agrippa's exclamation seems to emphasize the theatrical character of Cleopatra's spectacle. Putting himself in Antony's place, Agrippa sees the spectacle as a theatrical masterpiece staged for Antony. Just as Cleopatra presented herself as Venus and the boys were in the guise of ("like") smiling cupids, Cleopatra's gentlewomen, Enobarbus continues, "like the Nereides, / So many mermaids, tended her i'th' eyes, / And made their bends adornings" (2.2.216–18). Dressed in the manner of ("like") the lovely divine or semidivine escorts of divinities,[31] the women made a show of their obeisant bowings. They turned their submission to Cleopatra into an adornment of her presentation of herself as Venus. And as her gentlewomen were so many mermaids, "[a]t the helm, / A seeming mermaid steers," Enobarbus recounts, shifting to the vivid present tense (2.2.218–19). And just as the perfumed sails and stroking oars aroused the love of the winds and of the water, the touch of the gentlewomen aroused the erotic desire of the animated sails: "The silken tackle / Swell with the touches of those flower-soft hands / That yarely frame the office" (2.2.219–21). Throughout his description, Enobarbus pairs stage performance and indeterminacy. While everyone is in costume and performing a part, distinctions disappear—distinctions not only between the imitation and the imitated, but between the human and the divine, on the one hand, and the human and sea creatures, on the other, as well as between the animate and the inanimate, and between the sexes. Everything in Egypt, including its palaces and fleets, Plutarch notes, is stage acting and painted scenery (Plutarch, *Aratus*, 15.2). And where everything is pretense or simulation, anyone can be anything.

Antony was Cleopatra's intended audience, but he was the only one in the city who did not see the spectacle. Personifying both the wharfs and the city (and, soon, the city's air), Enobarbus says that when an invisible perfume from the barge reached "the sense / Of the adjacent wharfs, [t]he city cast / Her people out upon her, and Antony, / Enthroned i'th' market-place, did sit alone, / Whistling to th'air" (2.2.222–26). Antony, having summoned her to appear before him,[32] had expected to greet Cleopatra as king upon his throne ("Enthroned i'th' market-place"). Instead, Cleopatra, sitting on her "burnished throne," stripped him of his subjects. Indeed, Antony, sitting alone, whistled to the air "which, but for vacancy, / Had gone to gaze on Cleopatra, too, / And made a gap in nature" (2.2.226–28). Nature finally constrained Cleopatra's spectacle—or the spectacle of her spectacle's effects. While void is by definition indeterminate, the principle that there can be no void ("gap") in nature prevented the city's air from going to gaze on her. Whereas Cleopatra's magnificent spectacle, subordinating nature to her art, combined stage performance and indeterminacy, nature, as the source of order and determinacy, prevailed in the end. Even in the world of Cleopatra's art, the determinate finally set limits on the indeterminate.[33]

Enobarbus, turning to the events after Cleopatra had landed, no longer speaks of her theatrical spectacle and replaces his lyrical description with his habitual satirical humor.[34] Since providing the first entertainment is a mark of honor, Antony invited Cleopatra to supper, but, for the same reason, she, instead, entreated him to be her guest. And "[o]ur courteous Antony, / Whom ne'er the word of 'No' woman heard speak," having been consummately groomed by the barber, "goes to the feast, / And, for his ordinary, pays his heart / For what his eyes eat only" (2.2.232–36). Antony sat feasting his eyes on Cleopatra. Yet he purchased the supper at the price of his heart. He devoured with his eyes and paid with his heart. Right from the start, Antony has been beguiled and dominated by Cleopatra.

Agrippa, who appreciates extravagant women, praises Cleopatra and her power over men. "Royal wench! / She made great Caesar lay his sword to bed," he says, playing crudely on the phallic and martial senses of the word "sword. "He ploughed her, and she cropped" (2.2.236–38). Cleopatra forced

Caesar to turn his sword into a ploughshare, and she bore the fruit of a child. Agrippa's army gossip is the play's first hint of Caesar and Cleopatra's son, Caesarion. Agrippa alludes to him with an appreciative jest. Later, Octavius will see him not as an object of bawdy humor, but as his rival for the claim to being Caesar's heir. Here, a testament to the strength of Cleopatra's sexual power; there, he will be a threat to Octavius's political strength.

Antony had said that everything becomes Cleopatra, everything becomes fair and admired in her (1.1.50–52). Enobarbus, claiming to report what he has observed firsthand, echoes him. He says that he once saw Cleopatra hop forty paces through the street, "[a]nd, having lost her breath, she spoke and panted, / That she did make defect perfection, / And breathless pour breath forth" (2.2.240–42). Able to breathe—or breathe forth breathless charm— although breathless,[35] she was able to make what is missing present and what is defective perfect. Like her pretty dimpled boys, "what [she] undid did."

Maecenas states that Antony "must leave [Cleopatra] utterly" (2.2.243). He may be speaking as the man responsible for initiating the negotiations that led to Antony's marriage to Octavia (2.2.105–8). Enobarbus, however, once again candid, has no doubt that Antony will never completely leave Cleopatra. "Never. He will not," he declares, and then explains why: "Age cannot wither her, nor custom stale / Her infinite variety" (2.2.245–46). Cleopatra is always new or different, never the same, never boring. She may suffer from ennui (1.5.1ff.; 2.5.1ff.), but never causes it. Her constant changes permit constant pleasure. "Other women cloy / The appetites they feed, but she makes hungry / Where most she satisfies" (2.2.246–48). Cleopatra arouses appetites as she satisfies them, making even the most unworthy things becoming in her, even the most debauched things seem fine: "[F]or vilest things / Become themselves in her, that the holy priests / Bless her when she is riggish" (2.2.248–50). Even licentiousness is decorous in her and receives the holy priests' blessing.

Maecenas, replacing his necessitating "must" with a conditional "if," now seems less certain. "If beauty, wisdom, modesty can settle / The heart of Antony, Octavia is / A blessed lottery to him" (2.2.251–53). No one replies. Instead, Agrippa invites Enobarbus to be his guest, and Enobarbus gladly accepts.

Act Two, Scene Three

1.

Scene 3 comes directly on the heels of Enobarbus's emphatic denial, "Never, [Antony] will not [leave Cleopatra]" (2.2.244). We see Antony, Caesar and

Octavia, but, except for Caesar's "Good night" (2.3.9), we hear only Antony and Octavia. Just as the purpose of their marriage is to link the two men, Octavia literally stands between them (s.d. 2.3.1; see also 3.3.10). Not the city, but a marriage, links the principal triumvirs. Antony tells Octavia that "[t]he world and [his] great office" (2.3.1) will sometimes separate him from her. He speaks as though political matters, not love, will at times pull him away. Octavia, who will later speak of the gods and of her prayers in despair (3.4.12–20), now answers by speaking of them as her comfort: "All which time / Before the gods my knee shall bow my prayers / To them for you" (2.3.2–4). The change from comfort to despair will lie in her being unable to pray for either Antony or Caesar without praying against the other. Using terms of endearment ("My Octavia," "dear lady") and saying good night, Antony acknowledges his wayward past ("I have not kept my square"), but promises to change (". . . but that to come / Shall all be done by th' rule" [2.3.4–7]).

2.

The Soothsayer enters as Caesar and Octavia leave. The Soothsayer, the only Egyptian we see in Rome, is a sign of the replacement of Roman augury by Egyptian soothsaying and, more broadly, of the orientalizing of Rome. The Soothsayer says he wishes he had never come to Rome, nor Antony had gone to Egypt, in the first place (". . . nor you thither" [2.3.11]). This is something he somehow knows, he says, but cannot express ("I see it in my motion; have it not in my tongue" [2.3.13]). It is an inward truth which he cannot articulate. Yet, despite Antony's initial mistake of going to Egypt, the Soothsayer advises him to return there quickly. "But yet hie you to Egypt again," he urges (2.3.14).

Like the Egyptians in 1.2, Antony wants to hear what the future holds for him. "Say to me, / Whose fortunes shall rise higher, Caesar's or mine?" (2.3.14–15). The Soothsayer has no hesitation in answering. "Caesar's. / Therefore, O Antony, stay not by his side. / Thy daemon—that thy spirit which keeps thee—," he explains,

> is
> Noble, courageous, high unmatchable,
> Where Caesar's is not. But near him, thy angel
> Becomes afeard, as being o'erpowered; therefore
> Make space enough between you.
>
> (2.3.18–22)

The Soothsayer distinguishes between Antony and his *daemon*. It is not Antony who is intimidated, but his *daemon*. His *daemon* becomes afraid near Caesar, and so Antony must leave Caesar's company. Offering the example of his ill luck in playing games with Caesar, the Soothsayer says that Antony is certain to lose, despite the odds, no matter what the game: "If thou does play with him at any game, / Thou art sure to lose; and of that natural luck / He beats thee 'gainst the odds" (2.3.24–26). The Soothsayer seems to identify Antony's "*daemon*" with both "[his] spirit which keeps [him]" and "natural luck." On his lips, one's personal guardian is hardly distinguishable from chance or fortune. While the Soothsayer's warning comes directly from Plutarch,[36] Plutarch often obscures the distinction between *daemon* as personal guardian and *daemon* as fortune when the action takes place in the East.[37] As we have seen, the Egyptians, powerless and passive, tend to see fortune as ruling their lives. Thus, in every contest between them, the Soothsayer says, Caesar's greater luck cancels Antony's natural superiority. Antony's nobility counts for nothing. "Thy lustre thickens / When he shines by." Caesar need only appear near Antony to outshine him. "I say again, thy spirit / Is all afraid to govern thee near him; / But, he away, 'tis noble" (2.3.27–29). Caesar's very presence defeats Antony, who away from him is himself, governed by his noble spirit. Contrary to what Philo and Demetrius thought, Antony can be noble in Egypt, but not in Rome. For them, he can be noble so long as he is away from Cleopatra; for the Soothsayer, he can be noble so long as he is away from Caesar.

3.
Antony, telling the Soothsayer to leave, says that Ventidius will go to Parthia. The reconciliation with Caesar permits the campaign. Antony then strongly agrees with the Soothsayer: "Be it art or hap, / He hath spoken true" (2.3.31–32). Caesar's "chance" (2.3.34) always overcomes Antony's "better cunning" (2.3.33), regardless of the sport or the odds. "The very dice obey him" (2.3.32). Caesar wins even when the odds against him are "all to naught," Antony says (2.2.36).[38] Antony, no doubt, greatly exaggerates. Yet, the Soothsayer's identification of Antony's "*daemon*" with both his personal guardian and his fortune may be substantially correct. His "*daemon*" in the sense of his spirit may bring about his "*daemon*" in the sense of his fortune. Antony is frequently—indeed, characteristically—both tardy and impulsive. He is apt to be slow to act when he needs to act, and yet moved by sudden impulse, passion or whim when he does act. He is consequently at a great disadvantage with Caesar, whose great strength lies in his ability to exploit other people's weaknesses and errors. The one man is careless, passionate and able to

act in only one way;[39] the other is coolheaded, calculating and manipulative. The difference in their fortunes may result from the difference in their spirits.

Whether or not the warning of the Soothsayer (who may be in Cleopatra's employ[40]) gives him a needed excuse, Antony says that he will return to Cleopatra. "I will to Egypt; / And though I make this marriage for my peace, / I'th' East my pleasure lies" (2.3.37–39). Antony does not return immediately, however. Nor does he intend to. Matters have not yet been settled with Pompey, and Antony does not yet have his victory over the Parthians. Antony thus ends the scene by giving Ventidius his orders and official appointment: "O come, Ventidius. / You must to Parthia. Your commission's ready. / Follow me and receive't" (2.3.39–41). Once he has celebrated his victory in Rome, he will not need his marriage.

Act Two, Scene Four

Lepidus, Maecenas and Agrippa are discussing preparations for the conference with Pompey. Lepidus, dismissing Caesar's lieutenants who have been assisting him, urges them to hasten their departure for Mount Misena. After Agrippa assures Lepidus that they will leave as soon as the wedding is over, Maecenas says that he and Agrippa will arrive there before Lepidus. Lepidus, although here, as always, attentive to the pressures of time ("Pray you hasten" [2.4.1; also 1.4.77–80; 2.2.8–9, 166–68, 180]), agrees. "My purposes do draw me much about. / You'll win two days upon me" (2.4.8–9). We never learn where Lepidus is going, but we might suspect that his undisclosed "purposes" look ahead to the political situation following the meeting with Pompey. Lepidus's roundabout ("much about") route may take him to Pompey, with the intention of secretly negotiating an alliance (see 3.5.9–10), or to Pompey's allies and sympathizers, with the intention of promoting himself as his successor to lead the anti-Caesarian faction after Pompey is weakened and finally eliminated. Notwithstanding—or precisely in keeping with—his earlier concern for peace among the triumvirs, Lepidus, a mixture of obsequiousness, aggressiveness and duplicity, is perfectly capable of asserting himself when he thinks he sees an opportunity (see 3.5.4–12; 3.6.33–35).

Act Two, Scene Five

1.

Cleopatra, languishing in Antony's continued absence, calls for music, "moody food / Of us that trade in love" (2.5.1–2). She wants "moody" music for her "moody" mood, melancholy music for her melancholy mood. Quickly changing her mind, Cleopatra decides to play billiards to pass the time. Everything, however, reminds her of Antony, yet nothing substitutes for him. When Charmian declines to play and suggests Mardian instead ("Best play with Mardian" [2.5.4]), Cleopatra takes her in a sexual sense: "As well a woman with an eunuch played / As with a woman" (2.5.5–6). And when Mardian, joking ironically again at his own expense (see 1.5.15–17), promises to play with her as well as he can, Cleopatra, suggesting more than she evidently realizes, captures the core of Eastern and post-republican Roman virtue with her risqué reply: "And when good will is showed, though't come too short, / The actor may plead pardon" (2.5.8–9). Good will replaces manly action. When noble action is not possible, morality, becoming internalized, shifts its focus to good intention—to what one would have done if one could have—which pardons the failure to act. Emasculation, whether literal or figurative, leads to a morality of intention and pardon rather than one of action and praise. Inability elevates intention, and intention excuses inaction.[41]

Once again quickly changing her mind, Cleopatra decides to go fishing. Her imagined catch is Antony. With music playing in the background, she will snare the fishes, "and, as I draw them up, / I'll think them every one an Antony, / And say 'Ah, ha! You're caught'" (2.5.13–15). Cleopatra's art of love is an art of angling, a wily art which employs hooks dressed as lures and looks at love from the point of view of gain. Cleopatra's imagined catch reminds Charmian of Antony's imagined catch. As Plutarch tells the story and Charmian briefly summarizes, emphasizing Cleopatra's part, Antony went fishing in the Nile but was embarrassed at not catching anything while Cleopatra and others were watching. So he hired a diver to attach a live fish to his hook underwater. Cleopatra soon discovered the trick. And, with them wagering on the catch, she had her own diver "hang a salt fish on his hook, which he / With fervency drew up," expecting it to be his own diver's (2.5.17–18; Plutarch, *Antony*, 29.3–4). Cleopatra, deflecting Antony's trick back against Antony himself, turned his pretended catch and presumed victory over her into her playful joke on him. Pretending to be fooled, she fooled the angling Antony.

Caesar criticized Antony for fishing, drinking and wasting the night in Alexandria, and for being no more manly than Cleopatra, who was no more womanly than he (1.4.3–7). Now, while Cleopatra's wish to go fishing merrily reminds Charmian of Cleopatra's fishing prank, that prank, in turn, reminds Cleopatra of that day and night and the following morning when she out-laughed and outdrank Antony, dressed him in her clothes and wore his sword:

> That time? O times!
> I laughed him out of patience, and that night

> I laughed him into patience, and next morn,
> Ere the ninth hour, I drunk him to his bed,
> Then put my tires and mantles on him, whilst
> I wore his sword Philippan.

(2.5.18–23)

Cleopatra's reminiscence recalls the story of Hercules, whom Antony claims as his ancestor (4.12.44),[42] and Omphale, Queen of Lydia, who commanded Hercules, at once her lover and slave, to lay aside his lion skin, and dress and work as a woman, while she dressed herself in his lion skin and carried his warrior club.[43] Having gotten Antony drunk, Cleopatra, like Omphale, switched their clothing and took his victorious sword for herself. She emasculated the Roman emperor, who was her lover and slave, and wielded the sword which he used to defeat Brutus and Cassius, and destroy the republican forces, at Philippi (see 3.11.35–38).

2.

An Egyptian messenger returning from Rome enters, and Cleopatra, as though his news could substitute for Antony in a way that Mardian and Charmian cannot, greets him with the order to "[r]am thou thy fruitful tidings in mine ears, / That long time have been barren" (2.5.24–25). But before the man can say anything more than address her, Cleopatra, seeing his sour look, immediately anticipates the worst, perhaps hoping to have the pleasure of being disappointed:[44]

> Antonio's dead! If thou say so, villain,
> Thou kill'st thy mistress; but well and free,
> If thou so yield him, there is gold, and here
> My bluest veins to kiss, a hand that kings
> Have lipped, and trembled, kissing.

(2.5.26–30)

Depending on his news, the Messenger will kill or may kiss and receive gold from his queen.

When told that Antony is well, Cleopatra offers more gold, but then promptly checks herself. Noting we say that of the dead, she threatens the Messenger if he has come to tell her that Antony is dead: "Bring it to that, / The gold I give thee will I melt and pour / Down thy ill-uttering throat" (2.5.33–35).[45] She will repay the man for what comes out of his throat by what she pours back down his throat. News of Antony's death will mean the

Messenger's death. When the Messenger pleads to be heard, Cleopatra says she will listen, but immediately sees bad news in his face. "But there's no goodness in thy face if Antony / Be free and healthful. So tart a favour / To trumpet such good tidings!" (2.5.37–39). Good news should wear a cheerful face. But even as the man's face is too sour if his news is good, it is not nearly grim enough if it is bad: "If not well, / Thou shouldst come like a Fury crowned with snakes, / Not like a formal man" (2.5.39–41). When the man again asks to speak, Cleopatra, having threatened him if his news is bad, now threatens or warns, "I have a mind to strike thee ere thou speak'st" (2.5.42). However, she no sooner threatens to beat him before he speaks than she promises again to shower him with wealth if he tells good news: "Yet if thou say Antony lives, is well, / Or friends with Caesar, or not captive to him, / I'll set thee in a shower of gold and hail / Rich pearls upon thee" (2.5.43–46). Repeating his initial report, the Messenger states, "Madam, he's well" (2.5.46). This time, instead of saying we say that of the dead, Cleopatra, repeating his word, commends the man: "Well said" (2.5.46). When he adds, "And friends with Caesar" (2.5.47), she praises him for his worthiness: "Thou'rt an honest man" (2.5.47). His good news makes him a good man. Intending to increase the good news (and delay the bad), the man goes further: "Caesar and he are greater friends than ever" (2.5.48). Since golden news should receive a golden reward, Cleopatra increases her promise: "Make thee a fortune from me" (2.5.49).

Having run out of good news, the Messenger must finally say what he has come to say: "But yet, madam—" (2.5.49). Cleopatra seizes upon his excepting phrase. "I do not like 'But yet,'" she begins. "It does allay / The good precedence" (2.5.50–51). The phrase detracts from the Messenger's original words. "Fie upon 'But yet'!" Cleopatra continues, "'But yet' is as a gaoler to bring forth / Some monstrous malefactor" (2.5.51–53). Just as the phrase devalued what preceded it, it portends what is to follow it. However, as though suddenly finding strength, Cleopatra asks to hear everything. Describing the news as the mixed material found in a peddler's pack, she implores, "Prithee, friend, / Pour out the pack of matter to mine ear, / The good and bad together" (2.5.53–55).[46] Then, she summarizes what she understands the Messenger to have said: "He's friends with Caesar, / In state of health, thou sayst, and, thou sayst, free" (2.5.55–56). Cleopatra twice before asked or said that Antony is "free," by which she meant not Caesar's captive (2.5.27, 38). Both times the Messenger avoided replying. Now, he must. Shifting implicitly from the military to the matrimonial sense of the word, he answers, "Free, madam? No. I made no such report. / He's bound unto Octavia" (2.5.57–58).

Cleopatra still does not understand him. She takes "bound" to mean "obliged" and asks, "For what good turn" has Octavia placed Antony in her debt? (2.5.58). At a loss for how to break the news, the Messenger blurts it out as a coarse joke: "For the best turn i'th' bed" (2.5.59).[47] The crude joke allows the Messenger to answer truthfully without explicitly saying what he fears to say. Playing on words and employing a synecdoche, he remains at a remove or two from stating the matter.

The Messenger's fears are well founded. After he finally discloses that Antony is "married to Octavia" (2.5.60), Cleopatra begins to berate and beat him (2.5.61, 62, 64 and s.d.). Addressing her courteously (if ironically) as "Gracious madam," he pleads in self-defense, "I that do bring the news made not the match" (2.5.67). But the furious Cleopatra makes no distinction between the Messenger and his message (cp. 1.2.101ff.). Angry at the latter, she will punish the former. She will punish whom she can. But wanting to hear welcome news, Cleopatra quickly encourages the man to deceive her. Ready to kill him for his bad news ("Rogue, thou hast lived too long! *Draw a knife*" [2.5.73 and s.d.]), she offers to reward him lavishly for disavowing it: "Say 'tis not so, a province I will give thee" (2.5.68). If she will kick him brutally for his bad news ("I'll spurn thine eyes / Like balls before me"), she will "boot" him richly for his good news (2.5.63–64, 71).

When the man, pleading his innocence again ("I have made no fault" [2.5.74]), flees for his life, Charmian urges Cleopatra to keep control of herself, citing his innocence: "Good madam, keep yourself within yourself. / The man is innocent" (2.5.75–76). Innocence should be his protection. But Cleopatra rejects any concern for justice: "Some innocents 'scape not the thunderbolt" (2.5.77). Whether justly or unjustly, the gods punish offenses to their honor: "Even the gods are subject unto wrath" (Ovid, *Metamorphoses*, 8.284; Golding, 8.370). A matter of greatness, not of justice, Cleopatra's threatened punishment is indiscriminate. Cleopatra would, accordingly, destroy all of Egypt and transform every animal from its natural kind to serpents: "Melt Egypt into Nile, and kindly creatures / Turn all to serpents!" (2.5.78–79).[48] The consequence would mirror its cause. As Cleopatra does not stay within herself, Egypt and all the animals alike would lose their shape or "kind." Egypt would melt into the river, and its living creatures would disappear into slithering serpents.

Cleopatra, as swiftly as ever, changes her mind. Calling for the Messenger, she assures Charmian, "Though I am mad, I will not bite him" (2.5.80). As it was not justice, but royal greatness, that prompted her threatened punishment, it is not justice, but royal pride, that prompts her promised restraint. "These hands do lack nobility that they strike / A meaner than myself," she explains, "since I myself / Have given myself the cause" (2.5.82–84). Because she is to blame for what has aroused her anger, as she stresses with her emphatic and reflexive "myself's," it would be ignoble of her, she says, to strike someone beneath herself in stature. Cleopatra does not say what she had done to cause her anger. She leaves unclear whether it was her letting Antony return to Rome or her loving him in the first place.

When the frightened Messenger reluctantly returns, Cleopatra gives him a lesson in discretion. "Though it be honest, it is never good / To bring bad news," she admonishes him. "Give to a gracious message / An host of tongues, but let ill tidings tell / Themselves when they be felt" (2.5.85–88). Cleopatra would permit only good news to be spoken and would await bad news to announce itself by its effects. While effects force themselves upon one and cannot be avoided, speech is voluntary and therefore can be avoided or postponed, and only what is pleasant should be voluntary. But when the Messenger defends himself again by claiming that he has done his duty in telling the truth, Cleopatra expressly asks him whether Antony is married ("Is he married?" [2.5.89])—the answer to which had caused her to draw a knife and threaten to kill him (2.5.73 and s.d.). Instead of attacking him, however, she assures him of his safety. "I cannot hate thee worser than I do / If thou again say 'Yes'" (2.5.90–91). The man can safely tell her that Antony is married, for Cleopatra could not possibly hate him any more than she already does for telling her that he is married. Cleopatra's promise of safety thus rings hollow, for she has shown that she already hates him enough to kill him. When the Messenger repeats that Antony is married, Cleopatra first curses him with destruction by the gods ("The gods confound thee!") and then asks whether he still maintains his answer ("Dost thou hold there still?" [2.5.92]). She seems to expect that her frightening curse will change his report. And when the Messenger, evidently certain that no one would want to be deceived, asks incredulously, "Should I lie, madam?" (2.5.93), Cleopatra answers affirmatively, "Oh, I would thou didst," saying that she would wish it even if "half my Egypt were submerged and made / A cistern for scaled snakes!" (2.5.93–95).[49] Just a moment ago, Cleopatra, indifferent to justice, would indiscriminately destroy Egypt and its natural creatures in her furious punishment (2.5.78–79). Now, indifferent to truth, she would have half of Egypt sink under a pool of snake-infested water in order to have the report denied. Her desperate wish closely matches her threatened punishment.

Dismissing the Messenger, Cleopatra declares, "Hadst thou Narcissus in thy face, to me / Thou wouldst appear most ugly" (2.5.96–97). While Narcissus loved no one until he saw a reflection of his own face in water and fell in love with it, all those who saw him fell in love with him for his extraordinary beauty. To Cleopatra, however, even such irresistible beauty would appear most ugly. The greatest beauty would seem to be the greatest ugliness. Cleopatra twice again asks, "He is married?" (2.5.97, 98). In keeping with the ancient tale, she repeats or echoes herself and the Messenger (2.5.60, 72, 89, 91, 97, 98). The nymph Echo, spurned by Narcissus, wasted away until there was nothing left of her but her echoing voice. Both she and Narcissus finally died of unreturned love (Ovid, *Metamorphoses*, 3.339–510).

The Messenger, asked twice again whether Antony is married, tries to avoid repeating his mistake: "Take no offense that I would not offend you" (2.5.99). The Messenger, afraid that his speech and silence alike would offend her—his speech for what it contains, his silence for his refusal to answer—tacitly appeals to Cleopatra's lesson in discretion. Only good news should be spoken. Since his answer would offend her, Cleopatra should take no offense at his attempt not to answer. "To punish me for what you make me do," he protests, "Seems much unequal" (2.5.100–101). It is unjust for her to force him to speak and then punish him for saying what she has forced him to say. Yet, despite the injustice and because of the compulsion, the Messenger answers, "He's married to Octavia" (2.5.101), repeating his fullest and clearest report, the one that initially caused Cleopatra to strike him (2.5.60–61 and s.d.). Notwithstanding her initial insistence that only welcome news should be uttered, Cleopatra finally insists that unwelcome news should also be told. Her repeated question ("He is married?" [2.1.97, 98]) concedes, in spite of herself, that truth telling cannot simply be avoided but contains its own compulsion.

Implicitly acknowledging her injustice, Cleopatra, at last distinguishing between the Messenger and his news, wishes that he were as guilty as Antony, that Antony's fault should carry over to him, so that she could justly punish him: "Oh, that his fault should make a knave of thee / That art not what thou'rt sure of!" (2.5.102–3). If the Messenger was caught between offending by speaking and by not speaking, Cleopatra is caught between punishing unjustly and not punishing. As he wished that he did not have to speak, she wishes that he were guilty enough to punish. Just as she distinguishes for the first time between the Messenger and his news, she blames Antony for the first time in the scene. Thus, dismissing the Messenger (and resuming her peddler metaphor [cp. 2.5.54–55]), Cleopatra says how costly his news has been to her ("The merchandise which thou hast brought from Rome / Are all too dear for me" [2.5.104–5]), but then curses the man for the merchandise by wishing that he will be unable to sell it and be financially ruined by it ("Lie they upon thy hand / And be undone by 'em" [2.5.105–6]).

Where earlier she wanted to kill the man, she now wants only to bankrupt him. Instead of losing his life, he would lose only his investment.

3.

The scene ends, as it began, with Cleopatra and her women. Regret has replaced melancholic loneliness and merry memory. When Charmian urges patience, Cleopatra ruefully states, "In praising Antony, I have dispraised Caesar" (2.5.107). And when Charmian confirms that she has many times, Cleopatra concludes, "I am paid for't now" (2.5.108). Cleopatra, who does indeed "trade in love" (2.5.2), seems to be thinking of her damaged political interests. Politically, she is back where she was following Pharsalia. Neither triumvir will now support or protect her. It seems telling that Cleopatra found it necessary to dispraise Caesar when praising Antony. Her praise of her lover could not be separated from her disparaging his political rival. Cleopatra often describes Antony in superlatives—"the greatest soldier in the world" (1.3.39), a "Herculean Roman" (1.3.85), "The demi-Atlas of this earth, the arm / And burgonet of men" (1.5.24–25), her "man of men" (1.5.75)—but she cannot praise him without comparing him to another. His excellence may be superlative, but is nevertheless necessarily comparative. Characteristically Roman, it can be known only by invidious comparisons.[50]

Asking to be led away and fainting or claiming to, Cleopatra tells Alexas to go to the Messenger and bid him to report Octavia's physical appearance, age and temperament, and to do so right away: "Bring me word quickly" (2.5.114). She has evidently not given up hope of winning back Antony. Cleopatra's hope, though, swiftly turns to ambivalence: "Let him for ever go! Let him not, Charmian" (2.5.115). As Cleopatra is of two minds, Antony is of two faces, having, she says, a nature which appears contrary as one's perspective changes. "Though he be painted one way like a Gorgon," she says, "The other way's a Mars" (2.5.116–17). Cleopatra alludes to a painting on a furrowed surface which when looked at from one way shows one thing and from another way shows something quite contrary.[51] Seen from one side, Antony appears like Gorgon, whose face, wreathed in snakes, turns whoever sees it to stone.[52] But seen from the opposite side, he appears like Mars. The most manly god from one side, Antony is a hideous monster from another. Cleopatra's ambivalence, however, is brief. Realizing that she had forgotten, Cleopatra quickly tells Iras to have Alexas report also on Octavia's height. Then, asking for pity and silence, she concludes by asking again to be led to her chamber.

Act Two, Scene Six

1.

The meeting between the triumvirs and Pompey and his allies takes place. In keeping with his pompous personal pretensions, Pompey enters with "*drum and trumpet*" (s.d. 2.6.1). After Pompey, who begins the exchange, says that the two sides have exchanged hostages and will talk before they fight, Caesar states that the triumvirs have sent their proposals in writing and want to know whether they will satisfy Pompey: "[L]et us know, / If 'twill tie up thy discontented sword / And carry back to Sicily much tall youth / That else must perish here" (2.6.5–8). Caesar speaks of the troops, but not of the battle, that Pompey would lose. He combines discretion with intimidation, careful not to overstate his warning. Pompey, after all, commands the sea, threatens the coast of Italy and is loved by the people, even though he is causing them famine by blockading the ports (1.2.190–99; 1.3.45–55; 1.4.36–39, 76–80).

Pompey addresses Caesar, Antony and Lepidus, at once deferentially and bitterly, as "[t]he senators alone of this great world" (2.6.9). While Rome has expanded to rule the world, the Roman Senate has contracted to—or been replaced by—"three" men who, ruling the world, are now "[c]hief factors for the gods" (2.6.8, 10). This is the play's sole mention of the Roman Senate. Apart from a single mention of the "consuls" who defeated Antony but were killed by him at Modena (1.4.59) and of "the triumvirate" when Caesar says that he has deposed Lepidus from it (3.6.29), it is the only mention of any Roman office. The triumvirs, having divided the Roman Empire among themselves "as if it had been their own inheritance" (Plutarch, *Antony*, 19.1; North, 6:19), rule it as their own property.

Pompey, instead of responding to their terms or making his own demands, defends his rebellion against the triumvirs. He offers two justifications. The first is revenge for his father. Pompey the Great, having a son and friends, Sextus says, should not lack revengers, considering that ("since" [2.6.12]) Julius Caesar's ghost saw Octavius and Antony work for his revenge against Brutus at Philippi. Pompey's parallel focuses entirely on those getting revenge rather than on the cause for which the revenge is due. As Caesar's ghost saw his adopted son (Octavius) and friend (Antony) fighting to avenge him, Pompey the Great, who has a son and friends, should get revenge from them. Pompey, considering nothing but the private relations of the people involved, overlooks the difference between military defeat and political murder. While Caesar was assassinated by Brutus in the Senate, Pompey was defeated by Caesar at Pharsalia. And although defeated by him, he was killed not by Caesar or his forces, but by Caesar's (and Cleopatra's) enemies, who murdered Pompey in Egypt, where he had fled for safety (Plutarch, *Pompey*, 67ff., 72ff.).

Pompey's second justification is the republican cause. "What was't / That moved pale Cassius to conspire?" Pompey asks.

> And what
> Made the all-honoured, honest Roman, Brutus,
> With the armed rest, courtiers of beauteous freedom,
> To drench the Capitol, but that they would
> Have one man but a man?

> (2.6.14–19)

Pompey, the only character in the play who claims to champion the republican cause, describes Caesar's assassins, particularly Brutus, in the most admiring terms. While Brutus, standing above the others, was an honorable ("honest") Roman honored by all, all the assassins, he says, were lovers of political freedom who drowned the Capitol with Caesar's blood because they refused to be ruled by only one man, lest he thereby become more than a man (see JC, 1.2.114–17, 152–57). Pompey's two justifications seem at odds. According to the first, Pompey wishes to imitate the actions of Caesar's faction against Brutus and Cassius. According to the second, he wishes to imitate the actions of Brutus and Cassius against Caesar. Always indecisive and inconsistent, Pompey would emulate both sides in Rome's civil war.

Pompey is unable to separate support for the republican cause from revenge for his father. Although he was "moderate in all things except his thirst for power" (Sallust, *Histories*, 2.18), Pompey the Great won glory for having defended the republican cause. His covetous ambition for sole power was always moderated, not by the power which he sought, but by the wish that it be granted to him by the votes of the people or the goodwill of the Senate.[53] Like Sulla and unlike Caesar, Pompey retained some respect for the republican regime.[54] Thus, in defending the republican cause, Sextus defends his father's cause. "And that is it," he concludes, "Hath made me rig my navy . . . / . . . with which I meant / To scourge th'ingratitude that despiteful Rome / Cast on my noble father" (2.6.19–23). The last of the family of Pompey, Sextus cares only to vindicate his father and family. Just as heredity is the basis for his political power and preeminence (1.2.191–201; 1.3.50–51), the defense of his family's property and honor is his highest—indeed, his only—political cause. The personal always prevails over the political with Pompey, as he proves right away.

After Caesar coolly tries to calm Pompey ("Take your time" [2.6.23]), Antony, while denying that the triumvirs will be frightened by his naval strength, warns him, "At land thou know'st / How much we do o'ercount thee" (2.6.25–26). Antony means that Pompey is weaker than the triumvirs on land. Pompey, however, deliberately twists his verb "o'ercount": "At land indeed / Thou dost o'ercount me of my father's house" (2.6.26–27). Pompey's quibbling taunt alludes to Antony's expropriation of Pompey the Great's splendid house in Rome.[55] Where Antony meant "out-" or "over-number," Pompey, turning a military matter into his private grievance, means "cheat" or "overreach." Pompey thus continues with a combination of personal taunt and threat: "But since the cuckoo builds not for himself, / Remain in't as thou mayst" (2.6.28–29). Like a cuckoo, which seizes the nests of other birds, Antony has stolen another's house, unable to build one for himself. But Antony may remain in it as long as he can ("as thou mayst"),[56] Pompey jeers, which is to say, perhaps not long at all.

Lepidus, wanting to avoid personal offense ("For this is from the present—" [2.6.30]), tries to bring Pompey back to the triumvirs' terms ("[H]ow you take / The offers we have sent you" [2.6.30–31]). Both Antony and Caesar second his effort. Antony tells Pompey to consider how the proposal would serve his interests ("Which do not be entreated to, but weigh / What it is worth embraced" [2.6.32–33]), while Caesar, mixing a veiled threat with a promise ("And what may follow / To try a larger fortune" [2.6.34–35]), warns of his possible loss if he holds out and suggests his possible further gain if he accepts. The risk goes with refusing; the advantage, with accepting. The triumvirs' terms are that, in exchange for his retaining Sicily and Sardinia, Pompey must rid all the sea of pirates and send wheat to Rome (2.6.34–39).[57] Pompey, who makes no counterdemands whatever, says that he came prepared to accept the terms, "but Mark Antony / Put me to some impatience" (2.6.41–42). As he explains, Pompey provided Antony's mother refuge when his brother made war upon Caesar (see 2.2.162–64). Pompey is mindful that his reminder may cost him praise ("Though I lose / The praise of it by telling" [2.6.42–43]). To tell of his hospitality is to praise himself, and self-praise amounts to offensive boasting. Self-praise, Pompey fears, may cost him praise. Still, he cannot resist telling Antony of his hospitality. Pompey, like his famously vain father,[58] praises or flatters himself at every chance. More important, although he is mindful of the danger of losing praise, he fails to give a moment's thought to the danger of losing his military advantage, even in pursuance of his father's cause. In this, too, he resembles his father, who, according to Julius Caesar, "knew not how to use a victory" (Suetonius, Divus Caesar, 36; Holland, 1:42).

Pompey's failure is fully in character. When Antony offers his thanks ("[I] am well studied for a liberal thanks / Which I do owe you" [2.6.47–48]), Pompey accepts them by offering his hand. With his handshake, Pompey, easily placated by his enemies, accepts not only Antony's thanks, but the triumvirs' terms for peace (see 2.6.57). When Pompey, contrary to what he had finally concluded earlier (2.1.32–50), says that he did not expect to see him here, Antony replies that, thanks to Pompey, he came sooner than he had intended: "The beds i'th' East are soft; and thanks to you / That called me timelier than the purpose hither, / For I have gained by't" (2.6.50–52). Antony's reply, while avoiding mentioning Cleopatra,[59] acknowledges the seriousness of Pompey's threat. Pompey, seeking to become "the main soldier" in the world (1.2.198), is the power to be negotiated with. Yet, although his power is at its zenith and he has forced his enemies to make peace, Pompey accepts their terms with nothing more than personal protests concerning the loss of his father's house and the lack of thanks for helping Antony's mother. Although fortune has often handed him excellent opportunities, Appian writes, Pompey is "slow to invade, content to defend." Despite his opportunities, "he . . . never take[s] the advantage of his enemies; neglecting many occasions, he . . . lie[s] still" (Appian, *Civil Wars*, 5.91, 143).[60] Concerned above all with regaining the position and wealth that are due him as his father's son, he would "rather defend his own than invade others, till so he was overcome also" (Appian, *Civil Wars*, 5.25; W. B., 318).[61] Lacking resolution, he has no strength of purpose to match his strength of naval power, and his irresolution will cost him everything. He will be the first to fall.

Caesar, perhaps wanting to let Pompey flatter himself and to avert his giving thought to Antony's acknowledgment, comments on Pompey's appearance. "Since I saw you last, / There is a change upon you" (2.6.52–53). The comment, indefinite in content, gives Pompey a chance to praise himself. "Well, I know not / What counts harsh Fortune casts upon my face," he replies. "But in my bosom shall she never come / To make my heart her vassal" (2.6.53–56). In effect claiming Stoic virtue, Pompey boasts that his heart stands above the consequences of Fortune. Harsh Fortune may mark his face, but it can never master his heart.

When the soothing Lepidus concludes that the meeting went well ("Well met here" [2.6.56]), Pompey says, "I hope so," adding, "Thus we are agreed" (2.6.57). Besides confirming that his handshake signified his acceptance of the triumvirs' terms, Pompey indicates that he believes all of the parties want the agreement to work and none wants simply to buy time or to improve his relative situation. Trusting the triumvirs, he thinks next to put the agreement in writing and have it sealed: "I crave our composition may be written

/ And sealed between us" (2.6.58–59). Notwithstanding the lessons he might have learned from his own and his father's wars, Pompey seems to take for granted that a written agreement carrying each cosigner's official seal will not—or cannot—be broken. One's sealed word is one's inviolable bond. Caesar, of course, has no objection: "That's the next to do" (2.6.59). Caesar will break the agreement just as soon as he can (3.4.3–4; 3.5.4).

Pompey, imagining that he has been triumphant and now commands the meeting, announces that the parties will feast each other before they leave and draw lots for who shall begin. Antony offers to host the first feast, but Pompey refuses him. "No, Antony, take the lot," he says. "But, first or last, your fine Egyptian cookery / Shall have the fame. I have heard that Julius Caesar / Grew fat with feasting there" (2.6.62–65). Whether thoughtless stumbling or deliberate nettling, Pompey's prurient praise of Egypt's cookery, although outwardly gracious, offends the two principal triumvirs—Antony, by suggesting that his lover is well-known as a whore, and Caesar, by reminding him of his rival to the claim of being Julius Caesar's son and legitimate heir ("Caesarion, whom they call my father's son . . ." [3.6.6]). When Antony, cutting him off, replies curtly, "You have heard much" (2.6.65), Pompey pleads his innocence: "I have fair meanings, sir" (2.6.66). And, when Antony, whether with sarcasm or feigned indifference, pretends to compliment him on his choice of words ("And fair words to them" [2.6.66]), Pompey first suggests that he meant only that Caesar literally grew fat with Egyptian feasting ("Then so much have I heard" [2.6.67]),[62] but then immediately introduces another story which only underscores the first. "And I have heard Apollodorus carried—." he continues (2.6.68), beginning the story of Cleopatra's seduction of Caesar. After following Pompey the Great to Egypt, Caesar, having arrived in Alexandria, wanted to resolve the dispute between Cleopatra and her brother, who had exiled her. So he summoned her. But Cleopatra knew that she could not cross the enemy's lines safely. Needing a stratagem to enter Alexandria, she boarded a small boat and landed near Caesar's castle at dusk.

> Then having no other means to come into the court without being known, she laid herself down upon a mattress or flockbed, which Apollodorus, her friend, tied and bound up together like a bundle with a great leather thong, and so took her up on his back and brought her thus hampered in this fardel unto Caesar.
>
> (Plutarch, *Caesar*, 49.1; North, 5:50–51)

Caesar, astonished at the sight of the Egyptian queen rolling out of the mattress and springing to her feet, was immediately taken by her cleverness, daring and charm. "This was the first occasion . . . that made Caesar to love her" (Plutarch, *Caesar*, 49.2; North, 5.51). Enobarbus tries to stop Pompey, at once cutting short and confirming the story: "No more of that. He did so" (2.6.69). But Pompey, seeking to draw more out of him, pretends not to know what Caesar did: "What, I pray you?" (2.6.69). Enobarbus, forced to answer, tries to be discreet: "A certain queen to Caesar in a mattress" (2.6.70). That Antony and Caesar have been offended seems clear. Neither says another word except to take leave (2.6.81).

Pompey, recognizing Enobarbus, asks how he fares ("How far'st thou . . . ?" [2.6.71]), and Enobarbus, playing on the word "fare" while making no attempt to conceal his newfound Egyptian taste, answers that he not only has fared well but is likely to do so in the near future, "for I perceive / Four feasts are toward" (2.6.72–73). Pompey, requesting to shake his hand, praises Enobarbus: "I never hated thee. I have seen thee fight / When I have envied thy behaviour" (2.6.74–75). And Enobarbus, turning the compliment around, offers an oblique compliment in the guise of a direct discourtesy: "Sir, / I never loved you much, but I have praised ye / When you have well deserved ten times as much / As I have said you did" (2.76–78). Enobarbus combines his partisan reluctance to praise Pompey with his confession that Pompey deserves high praise. His proclaimed stinginess bespeaks Pompey's worthiness. Pompey thus welcomes Enobarbus's bluntness. "Enjoy thy plainness," he tells Enobarbus; "It nothing ill becomes thee" (2.6.78–79). Bluntness sharpens the praise while blunting the discourtesy. It flatters while pretending to cause pain.

Pompey, who originally proposed drawing lots for who is to have the first feast, and who refused to let Antony go first, now peremptorily claims the honor for himself: "Aboard my galley I invite you all" (2.6.80). No one objects or declines.

3.

Enobarbus and Menas, staying behind when the others leave, discuss their leaders' actions as well as their own status as thieves. Menas, first, declares, "Thy father, Pompey, would ne'er have made this treaty" (2.6.82–83). In spite of his strength, Pompey settles for Sicily and Sardinia, which are already his, promises to rid the sea of pirates, who are his allies, and undertakes to send wheat to Rome, whose starvation is his most effective tactic. The wheat will not only provide Caesar with much-needed food, but also bring upon Pompey, and spare Caesar, the disfavor of those from whom he will have to collect it (see 1.4.37–40). Pompey, in a word, gives away his advantages, strengthens his enemies, particularly Caesar, and gets nothing in return— and he expects that a sealed written agreement will protect him against any future attacks from the triumvirs.[63] Pompey originally said that his powers are "crescent" and his auguring hope told him they will come to "th' full" (2.1.10, 11). He seems not to appreciate that although a crescent moon waxes until it becomes full, the full moon then wanes until it is no longer seen.

Menas reminds Enobarbus that they have previously met. And when the two men agree that it was at sea, Enobarbus says that Menas has done well by sea, and Menas replies that Enobarbus has done well by land. The moral equivalence between them quickly becomes apparent when Enobarbus says that he cannot deny that he has done well by land, and Menas, echoing him, says the same is true of him by water. Each then expressly if playfully accuses the other of being "a great thief": "you . . . by sea" and "you by land" (2.6.93, 94). The difference between a Roman officer and a pirate disappears in the absence of a public good. Armies, we have seen, now fight for Rome, not in the sense of defending or extending it, but in the sense of winning or acquiring it. They fight not against Rome's foreign enemies, but against their leaders' domestic enemies. And because they fight not for the public good but for each man's own private good, all fighters, however glorious, are on the same moral level as pirates.[64]

Although Enobarbus, with mock indignation, momentarily denies his thievery ("There I deny my land service" [2.6.95]), he soon readily admits it. Shaking Menas's hand, he describes what their eyes might see if they had the authority to make arrests: "[H]ere they might take two thieves kissing" (2.6.97–98). Like their thieving hands clasping, the men themselves are two thieves consorting. Menas generalizes Enobarbus's jest. "All men's faces are true, whatsome'er their hands are" (2.6.99–100). Men always look honest no matter how guilty their actions. Enobarbus, shifting the sense of Menas's word "true," applies it to the faces of women: "But there is never a fair woman has a true face" (2.6.101–2). A beautiful woman's face is always untrue because the woman uses cosmetics. Menas then turns the word's meaning back to his original sense: "No slander. They steal hearts" (2.6.103). Beautiful women are thieves because their deceptive looks steal men's loves. Both men and women are thieves. Men's faces look innocent, and women's faces look beautiful. But neither is the way his or her face appears. The men steal with their guilty hands, the women with their made-up faces.

Enobarbus returns the conversation to Menas's original comment. "We came hither to fight with you," he states (2.6.104). Menas clearly thinks that Pompey had an excellent chance of winning that battle: "For my part, I am sorry it has turned to a drinking. Pompey doth this day laugh away his fortune" (2.6.105–7). Pompey has foolishly abandoned his power and prospects. Enobarbus, confirming Menas's thought, responds, "If he do, sure he cannot weep't back again" (2.6.108–9). Regret cannot reverse folly.

In 2.1, Pompey, completely changing his initial opinion, had finally concluded that Antony was on his way to join Caesar and Lepidus against him, while Menas, holding fast to his original opinion, remained unconvinced (2.1.32ff.). Earlier in the present scene, Pompey, tacitly reversing himself again, reverted to Menas's opinion (2.6.49). Now, Menas, speaking for Pompey as well as for himself, repeats his original opinion: "We looked not for Mark Antony here" (2.6.109–10). Aside from demonstrating his general vacillation, Pompey's reversion to Menas's (incorrect) view and stating it as though he had never thought otherwise ("I did not think, sir, to have met you here" [2.6.49]) seem to illustrate the stinging reproach that Pompey is a slave among his own slaves, a freedman among his own freedmen. Far from his guiding their thinking, they guide his. Just as he envies men of dignity, he is subservient to the meanest (Velleius Paterculus, 2.73.1).[65]

Menas asks whether Antony is married to Cleopatra. The question is not mere personal gossip. Antony's marriage to Cleopatra would give Caesar an immediate political advantage. While making Antony an Eastern monarch, it would give Cleopatra the claim of being the Empress of Rome. Romans would consequently come to fear—or to fear more than ever—that, instead of Rome's ruling Egypt, Rome itself would become ruled from Alexandria by absolute Eastern monarchs. Conquered Egypt would conquer Rome (see 3.6.1–22).

Told that Antony is married to Octavia, Menas, incredulous, asks, "Then is Caesar and he for ever knit together" (2.6.117). When Enobarbus doubts that they are ("If I were bound to divine of this unity, I would not prophesy so" [2.6.118–19]), Menas says he thinks that political expediency played more of a role than the love of the parties. Enobarbus agrees that the purpose was political, but doubts that the marriage will keep Antony and Caesar together. "[Y]ou shall find the band that seemed to tie their friendship together will be the very strangler of their amity" (2.6.122–24). What appears meant to bring them together will set them apart. The marriage will be the cause of their new enmity. As though to explain, Enobarbus states simply, "Octavia is of a holy, cold and still conversation" (2.6.124–25). And when Menas asks, "Who would not have his wife so?" (2.6.126), Enobarbus excludes Antony: "Not he that himself is not so; which is Mark Antony" (2.6.127–28). Enobarbus describes what to expect:

> He will to his Egyptian dish again. Then shall the sighs of Octavia blow the fire up in Caesar, and, as I said before, that which is the strength of their amity shall prove the immediate author of their variance.

> (2.6.128–32)

Enobarbus predicts Antony's misbehavior and its effect on Caesar and on their friendship, but seems not at all troubled by its untoward effect. "Antony will use his affection where it is. He married but his occasion here" (2.6.132–33). Without telling why, Enobarbus suggests that Antony believes that the marriage must meet only his immediate need ("his occasion"). Once that need has been met, he will not have to be concerned about falling out with Caesar.

Menas, ending the scene, invites Enobarbus to drink with him. And Enobarbus, who never refuses a drink, again boasting of his Egyptian drinking ("We have used our throats in Egypt" [2.6.136–37]), is quite happy to join him.

Act Two, Scene Seven

1.

Pompey invited the triumvirs aboard his boat for a feast. Now, before the final course of dessert with wine ("*a banquet*" [s.d. 2.7.1]) is served, two of his servants, describing the company, especially Lepidus, with sharp disrespect, discuss the men's drinking. While everything in the scene reflects the replacement of Roman political institutions by the persons of the rulers, "all three / . . . senators alone of this great world" (2.6.8–9) are reduced to their purely personal foibles, tastes, traits, interests and abilities.

Punning on "plant" as the sole of a man's foot as well as a young tree,[66] the First Servant remarks, "Some o' their plants are ill-rooted already; the least wind i'th' world will blow them down" (2.7.1–3). The most trifling wind in the world will topple the pillars of the world. Lepidus, in particular, is already flush ("high-coloured" [2.7.4]). As the others irritate ("pinch" [2.7.6]) one another, Lepidus "cries out 'No more,' reconciles them to his entreaty, and himself to th' drink" (2.7.7–8). He urges the others to stop their bickering, for which they toast his every effort, forcing him to accept still another round of drinks. Drinking to keep the peace, he cannot keep on his feet or maintain his judgment: "But it raises the greater war between him and his discretion" (2.7.9–10). His attempt at discretion costs him his discretion. While Lepidus, ironically, tries to live up to his name (literally, "pleasantly agreeable"), his peacemaking puts him at war with himself.

The two servants deride Lepidus's general character, finding him nothing more than a "name in great men's fellowship" (2.7.11–12). Lepidus is a mere name, without any ability or power. One servant says that he would rather have a reed that would do him no service than a long-handled, double-edged spear ("partisan" [2.7.13]) that he could not heave. Neither would do him any good, but the spear would not only make him appear ridiculous; in such company, its showy pretentiousness would invite attack. The other servant goes further. "To be called into a huge sphere and not to be seen to move in't," he says, "are the holes where the eyes should be, which pitifully disaster the cheeks" (2.7.14–16). Having a triumvir's high position but no function or authority is like a planet's having no fixed sphere of its own, which, in turn, is like an eye socket having no eye, which, further, as the Servant adds with a pun and another astronomical term ("pitifully disaster"), can strike only with calamity by giving the pitiful appearance of pits instead of eyes. As suits his disparagement of Lepidus, the Servant's metaphor rapidly shrinks from the astronomical to the facial and from the facial to the farcical, from the cosmic to the personal and from the personal to the pitiable.[67] Events will prove the servants correct. We might wonder, though, what they would say of their own master. Would they consider Pompey to measure up to his circumstances?

2.

The guests enter to the ceremonial sound of a sennet. Caesar has place of precedence, followed by Antony and then Pompey and Lepidus (s.d. 2.7.16). Antony, presumably answering Caesar's questions about the economic effects of the Nile, is describing the way the Egyptians measure the rise of the river and judge from it how much harvest to expect. According to Antony, the greater the Nile's flood, the greater its fertility: "The higher Nilus swells, / The more it promises" (2.7.18–21). Antony is characteristically mistaken. While the quantity of Egypt's food depends on the quantity of the Nile's floods, the Nile, in a rare instance of Egyptian moderation, produces dearth when it floods too much as well as too little. "As it ebbs," Antony continues, "the seedsman / Upon the slime and ooze scatters his grain, / And shortly comes to harvest" (2.7.21–23). But just as a small overflow impedes planting by limiting the ground covered by the mud, a large overflow retards planting by retiring too slowly and even endangering all the country with destruction. "If the water reaches only to the fifteenth cubit of [a specific] pillar," John Leo Africanus writes,

> [the Egyptians] hope for a fruitful year following; but if it stays between the twelfth cubit and the fifteenth, then the increase of the year will prove but mean. . . . But if it arises to the eighteenth cubit, there is likely to follow great scarcity in regard to too much moisture; and if the eighteenth cubit be surmounted, all Egypt is in danger to be swallowed by the inundation of Nilus.[68]

While a moderate amount of water produces plenty of food, plenty of water produces a scarcity of food, as Charmian, in spite of herself, seemed to get right (1.2.51–52). For Antony, however, as for Cleopatra (1.5.56–64), more is never too much. Excess always produces plenty.

Although no ancient writer records that a pyramid was used to measure the Nile's flow, Antony reports that the Egyptians measure it "[b]y certain scales i'th' pyramid" (2.7.18).[69] As he presents it, the tomb of the dead contains the scales of "dearth / Or foison" (2.7.19–20). What houses the dead contains the measure of what nurtures life. As though taking his cue from Antony, Lepidus, at once curious, sycophantic and drunk, tells him, "You've strange serpents there" (2.7.24). When Antony concurs, the pretentious, pedantic Lepidus offers an abiogenetic account of their origin: "Your serpent of Egypt is bred, now, of your mud by the operation of your sun; so is your crocodile" (2.7.26–27). Life in Egypt is produced by nonlife, the animate by the inanimate. The mud and the sun—or perhaps the union of the moist and the dry—produce not only living, but sacred creatures.[70] As the importance or prominence of the pyramids might suggest ("I have heard the Ptolemies' pyramises are very goodly things. Without contradiction I have heard that" [2.7.34–36]), although sensuality pervades Egypt, death is primary, there.[71] Indeed, the connection between sensuality and mortality may be close. Life in Egypt, as we have seen, depends radically on fortune. Living at the arbitrary pleasure of an absolute monarch ("Thou shalt be whipped with wire and stewed in brine, / Smarting in lingering pickle!" [2.5.65–66]), Egyptians have good reason to regard life as often short and always precarious (see 1.5.79–81; 2.5.77–79, 93–95) and therefore to make the pleasure of the moment everything.[72] Egyptian subjection and sybaritism may be reciprocally cause and effect.

Just as Maecenas and Agrippa could not hear enough of Egyptian pleasures and spectacles (2.2.186ff.), Lepidus cannot hear enough of Egyptian marvels. After Pompey twice more toasts the already intoxicated Lepidus (2.7.29, 40; note 2.7.30–33), Lepidus, having spoken of the crocodile's origin, asks about its nature: "What manner o' thing is your crocodile?" (2.7.41). Antony answers with a mocking, manifold tautology, which identifies the crocodile simply by its own characteristics (". . . shaped . . . like itself, . . . as broad as it hath breadth . . . . just so high as it is, . . . moves with it own organs . . . lives by that which nourisheth it, . . . [o]f it own colour too" [2.7.42–46, 48]). Lepidus, besides confusing crocodiles and serpents, takes the manifest as the marvelous: "'Tis a strange serpent" (2.7.49). In one respect, however, he is correct. The crocodile Antony describes is indeed strange. "[A]nd the elements once out of it," he says, "it transmigrates" (2.7.45–46). According to Herodotus, the Egyptians believe that animals are depositories of the soul and life. When an animal dies, the soul, which they hold to be immortal, enters the body of another creature just as it is being born. Hence, the "transmigrat[ion]" of the souls of animals and, with it, the worship of animals, including the crocodile (Herodotus, 2.65–76, 123). Egyptian metempsychosis implies Egyptian zoolatry. The low and the high—beasts, souls and gods—are hard to distinguish. The worship of animals implicit in Antony's answer may further explain Egyptian submissiveness. Egyptians revere the subhuman. They look down at (not up to) what they worship.[73] With nothing radically separating them from other animals and nothing therefore stamping them with a specific excellence, they come to despise rather than to respect themselves as humans. They have nothing above them to which they may aspire and by which they may judge themselves.[74] Caesar asks with amused incredulity whether Antony's description will satisfy Lepidus. "With the health that Pompey gives him, else he is a very epicure," Antony answers (2.7.52–53). Only a confirmed atheist ("a very epicure") could drink as much as Lepidus and not believe whatever he is told.[75]

3.

Repeatedly rebuffed (2.7.37, 40, 54–55, 57), Menas persists and finally manages to convince Pompey, on the basis of his past service ("for the sake of merit" [2.7.56]), to hear him in private, although Pompey would rather drink ("Go hang, sir, hang! . . . Away! / . . . Where's this cup I called for?" [2.7.54–55]). Menas begins by offering his deference and loyalty: "I have ever held my cap off to thy fortunes" (2.7.58). Pompey, although irritated by the distraction, agrees that Menas has served him with "much faith" (2.7.59). Pompey's best naval commanders are freedmen inherited from his father.[76] Their ability, if not their loyalty, can be trusted. Menas then boldly asks, "Wilt thou be lord of all the world?" (2.7.62). Pompey, however, forces him to repeat his extraordinary question, as Menas impatiently and perhaps disdainfully notes: "Wilt thou be lord of the whole world? / That's twice" (2.7.63–64). Pompey, unable to understand, asks Menas to explain ("How should that be?" [2.7.64]). He cannot imagine Menas's meaning. Menas, wishing not to be explicit, answers that Pompey need only accept his offer ("But entertain it"), "And, though thou think me poor, I am the man / Will give thee all the world" (2.7.64–66). A former slave with nothing but daring will give the entire world to the son of Pompey the Great. He will do what even Pompey the Great himself could not do. Menas, whom Pompey thinks has drunk too much, assures him that he is perfectly sober: "No, Pompey, I have kept me from the cup. / Thou art, if thou dar'st be, the earthly Jove, / Whate'er the ocean pales or sky inclips / Is thine, if thou wilt ha't"

(2.7.67–70). Menas speaks of Pompey's boldness or daring, but Pompey need only give his approval. He can become ruler of the entire world—"the earthly Jove"—by doing nothing more than giving his lieutenant his consent.

Pompey, still not understanding, forces Menas to be explicit. "These three world-sharers, these competitors, / Are in thy vessel," Menas tells him; "Let me cut the cable, / And when we are put off, fall to their throats. / All then is thine" (2.7.71–74). Rule of the world hangs on a cable.[77] Pompey, however, refuses. "Ah, this thou shouldst have done / And not have spoke on't," he faults Menas (2.7.74–75). Menas's silence would have shielded Pompey. "In me 'tis villainy; / In thee't had been good service" (2.7.75–76). What would be good service from a man such as Menas would be treachery from a man such as himself. Thus, continuing, Pompey explains, "Thou must know / 'Tis not my profit that does lead mine honour; / Mine honour, it" (2.7.76–78). Speaking with the combined stress of an antithesis, negative, chiasmus, emphatic "does" and necessitating "must," Pompey tries to be entirely unequivocal. Yet, his declaration is ambiguous. Pompey says that his profit does not lead his honor; on the contrary, his honor leads his profit. But he means only that his profit does not overtly direct his honor; instead, his honor covertly silences his profit. His honor permits him to profit from a dishonorable act so long as he does not have to expressly approve or permit it before it is done—so long as he can keep his hands clean and Menas keeps his tongue silent. The distinction between Pompey's honor and dishonor lies in the distinction between Menas's silence and speech and Pompey's own ignorance and knowledge. Thus, telling Menas to "[r]epent that e'er thy tongue / Hath so betrayed thine act," Pompey concludes, "Being done unknown, / I should have found it afterwards well done, / But must condemn it now" (2.7.78–81). Menas should repent his speech, not his proposed deed, which his speech "betrayed" by mentioning it. Like his father, Pompey refuses to act to take something to which he has no legitimate claim, but would gladly accept it if handed to him. Although claiming to champion the republican cause, he would gladly become "the earthly Jove," "lord of all the world," possessor of "[w]hate'er the ocean pales or sky inclips," if only given the power. Despite his claiming to defend his honor, Pompey's refusal may merely mask his typical reluctance to act.

Appian describes Menas as "a traitor by nature" (Appian, *Civil Wars*, 5.96; W. B., 349), yet Pompey seems to take his loyalty for granted. He seems not to consider that Menas's loyalty may depend not upon his goodwill toward Pompey, as Menas seemed initially to suggest (2.7.56–59), but upon Pompey's ability and willingness to satisfy his desire to command an army and a province.[78] When Pompey, telling Menas to "[d]esist and drink" (2.7.81), returns to the others, Menas, in an aside, vows to leave him. "For this," he says, "I'll never follow thy palled fortunes more. / Who seeks and will not take, when once 'tis offered, / Shall never find it more" (2.7.82–85). Pompey has refused an opportunity that Fortune offers no more than once in a lifetime. Menas's decision to abandon him is the first of many desertions in the play.

4.

Pompey once more toasts Lepidus, but Lepidus is dead drunk and must be carried ashore. Enobarbus, pointing to the servant carrying him off, jokes, "There's a strong fellow, Menas. / . . . 'A bears / The third part of the world, man" (2.7.89–91). The joke points up the reduction of politics to the personal. What is true of the ruler is true of the entire part of the world which he rules.[79] As the rulers embody the world, Lepidus's third of the world will soon be carried off and change hands. "Would it were all [drunk]," Menas wishes, "That it might go on wheels!" (2.7.92–94). One might suppose that if all the triumvirs were drunk, Menas could carry out his plan quite easily.[80] Unwilling to follow Pompey's fortunes any longer, he might be able to follow his own and make the whole world his. He could do for himself what he would have done for Pompey. But Menas, who is now drinking (see 2.7.87ff.), shows no interest in taking action or seizing power, but wants only to enjoy the party. Menas may be disloyal by both nature and circumstances, but he does not have unbounded ambition. He may want to add to what he already has, but, in spite of his treachery, he seems content with lieutenancy. Even though he offers to give the world to Pompey, he continues to be dependent on a superior. Treachery and dependence go together with the former slave.[81]

Just as Pompey takes Menas's loyalty for granted when refusing him, Menas takes Pompey's loyalty for granted when proposing his plan. It seems never to cross his mind that Pompey would have a compelling reason to kill him after he carried out his murderous deed. Besides having a treacherous assassin to fear, he would need someone to blame and punish.

When Pompey, evidently competing with Antony for the distinction of hosting such a party, protests that "[t]his is not yet an Alexandrian feast" (2.7.96), Antony tries to make it one ("It ripens towards it. Strike the vessels, ho! / Here's to Caesar" [2.7.97–98]). The play's only example of Alexandrian revelry takes place entirely in a Roman context.[82] Caesar, however, does not want to drink. "I could well forbear't," he replies, and then complains, "It's monstrous labour when I wash my brain / And it grows fouler"

(2.7.98–100). His body is simply not up to the effects of heavy drinking. As noted earlier, Caesar's fear prompts his moderation. "His virtues, and even his vices, [are] artificial" (Gibbon, 3, 1:63).

When Antony, voicing what could be his motto, coaxes Caesar to "[b]e a child o'th' time," Caesar counters with what could be his: "'Possess it,' I'll make answer" (2.7.101). Where Antony would go along with others, Caesar would master the situation. The one would submit; the other would dominate or control. "But," Caesar continues, consenting to another drink, "I had rather fast from all, four days, / Than drink so much in one" (2.7.102–3). Contrary to his wish, Caesar accommodates himself to the others. He goes along with them, if only because he thinks he must.

The Romans link dancing and drinking. No one dances, they believe, unless he is drunk (or crazy).[83] Enobarbus, accordingly, asks to dance the "Egyptian Bacchanals" and "celebrate" the revelers' drink (2.7.104, 105). Pompey, who sought an Alexandrian feast, urges the suggestion, and Antony agrees. "Come, let's all take hands," he says, "Till that the conquering wine hath steeped our sense / In soft and delicate Lethe" (2.7.106–8). Traditional Roman wakefulness has given way to the stupor and languor of the East.[84] Egyptian softness, sensuality and oblivion replace Roman hardness, austerity and alertness. Rather than conquering one's bodily desires as well as one's enemies, one surrenders to the conquering wine (see 2.1.26–27). Thus Enobarbus, adulterating the language of war, calls for loud music to assault ("Make battery to") the celebrants' ears, and instructs the revelers to join hands and "beat" out the rhythm of the last chorus as loudly and as rapidly as their strong sides can "volley" (2.7.109, 111, 112). In addition to containing vernacular language that includes dialect ("fats"), archaic ("eyne") and newly minted English ("Plumpy"), along with a proverbial expression ("Cup us till the world go round" [2.7.113–18]), the celebratory song, sung by a boy, incongruously resembles a Christian hymn addressed to the holy spirit. It begins with an appeal to a deity, proceeds in lines of four stresses, and seeks a divine gift to make men other than themselves.[85]

When the riotous song is concluded, Caesar tries to bring the party to an end. Telling everyone good night, he reproaches the celebrants for their lack of seriousness: "Our graver business / Frowns at this levity" (2.7.120–21). He criticizes in the name of their weightier business the frivolity that he has unwillingly endured. Pompey, although getting ready to leave, has not yet had enough and challenges Antony to a drinking match on land ("I'll try you on the shore" [2.7.127]), and Antony accepts ("And shall, sir" [2.7.128]). A drinking contest replaces a military contest, which Pompey was likely to have won. As though there has never been any contention between them, Pompey leaves with Antony to continue drinking. "O, Antony, you have my father's house. / But what? We are friends" (2.7.129–30). Nor are they alone. Although he no doubt had intended to cut his throat along with those of the triumvirs, Menas invites Enobarbus for more drinking in his cabin ("Hoo! Noble captain, come" [2.7.136]), and Enobarbus, as always, accepts.

Notes

1. Livy, *Periochae*, 99; Plutarch, *Pompey*, 28.2; Velleius Paterculus, 2.73.3; Appian, *Civil Wars*, 2.1; Dio, 36.20–37.

2. Livy, *Periochae*, 123; Dio, 48.17.2–6, 19.4. On Menas and Menecrates as freedmen, see Appian, *Civil Wars*, 5.76, 96; Dio, 48.30.4; Velleius Paterculus, 2.73.3. On freedmen serving in Pompey's forces, see Appian, *Civil Wars*, 5.72. Caesar will claim that his war against Pompey was a war against pirates and slaves; see Augustus, *Res Gestae*, 25.1; Horace, *Epodes*, 4.19; 9.7–10; also Strabo, 5.4.4; Lucan, *Civil War*, 6.421; Florus, 2.18.1.

3. See, e.g., Plato, *Laws*, 687c–88b, 801b; Seneca, *Letters*, 60–1–2; Juvenal, *Satires*, 10.346–52.

4. See Homer, *The Iliad*, 5.859–61.

5. See, e.g., Dio, 50.31.1–2.

6. Lepidus addresses or describes Antony, Antony and Caesar, or Antony's speech as "noble" five times in the scene (2.2.14, 18, 23, 104, 180). Except for pronouns, prepositions, articles, negatives and copulative verbs, the obsequious "noble" is his most frequent word in the play.

7. See 2.2.229–32; 3.13.69–73. On the hostility behind ritual competition in generosity, see, e.g., Livy, *History*, 2.41.5–7.

8. Bevington, 115.

9. See Suetonius, *Augustus*, 69.2.

10. On the establishment and legal authority of the triumvirate, see Livy, *Perioche*, 120; Velleius Paterculus, 2.65; Plutarch, *Antony*, 19–20; Appian, *Civil Wars*, 4.2–12; Dio, 46.54–56; on Lucius Antonius, see Appian, *Civil Wars*, 5.19ff.; Suetonius, *Augustus*, 14.1.

11. See, e.g., 1.2.65–80; 2.1.11–13; 3.7.5ff.; 3.10.7ff.; 3.11.51ff.; 3.12.20ff.; 3.13.2ff.; 4.4.6–11; 4.8.1–2.

12. Lepidus's "Soft," "[u]sed as an exclamation with imperative force" (*OED*, s.v. Soft, *adv* 8), is the closest Lepidus ever comes to a command or an injunction.

13. On such a defense as a last resort, see Aristotle, *Rhetoric to Alexander*, 1429a15–19; see also Aristotle, *Nicomachean Ethics*, 1111a24; Anonymous, 2.24.

14. Bevington, 119.

15. On Maecenas's diction, see Seneca, *Letters*, 114.4–8; Suetonius, *Augustus*, 86; Tacitus, *Dialogue*, 26.1. Note also 4.1.7–11; 5.1.34–35.

16. See Cicero, *De inventione*, 2.156–69; Anonymous, 3.3; Quintilian, 3.8.22ff.

17. See, e.g., Quintilian, 8.4.3–9, 6.4–22. Each of the latter three formulations is also a chiasmus.

18. Furness, 106. Throughout the play, Caesar addresses Antony with the familiar pronoun only when apostrophizing him, never to his face (1.4.56–72; 5.1.35–48).

19. Livy, *History*, 1.8; Plutarch, *Romulus*, 13.1–4.

20. See, e.g., Dionysius of Halicarnassus, *Roman Antiquities*, 2.25; Plutarch, *Roman Questions*, 1, 86, 87. The first divorce in Rome did not occur until some five centuries after the city's founding; see Dionysius of Halicarnassus, 2.25.7; Aulus Gellus, *Attic Nights*, 4.3, 17.21.44; Valerius Maximus, 2.1.4. Plutarch says it was not for two hundred and thirty years; see Plutarch, *Comparison of Theseus and Romulus*, 6.3–4.

21. Among the many instances, Julius Caesar, although related to Marius, took as his second wife, Pompeia, the daughter of a consul of the Sullan party (Quintus Pompeius) and a granddaughter of Sulla (Suetonius, *Divus Julius*, 6.2). Sulla married into the prominent Metellus family (Caecilia Mettela), while Pompey, whose support Sulla sought, was persuaded by him to divorce his wife and marry Sulla's stepdaughter and Metella's daughter by a previous marriage, Aemilia, although she was married and pregnant at the time. When Aemelia died, Pompey married another member of the Metellus family, Mucia, who bore him Sextus and Gnaeus (Plutarch, *Pompey*, 9.1–2; 42.7, *Sulla*, 33.3; Cicero, *Letters to Atticus*, 1.12.3). Some time later, Caesar, needing to strengthen his political ties to his fellow triumvir, Pompey, married his daughter, Julia, to him, although she was already engaged to Caepio and was going to be married to him within a few days. To appease Caepio, Pompey promised him his own daughter, although she, too, was already engaged (Suetonius, *Divus Julius*, 21.1; Plutarch, *Caesar*, 14.4, *Pompey*, 47.2, *Cato the Younger*, 31.4). When Crassus's death in Parthia increased the chance of a split with Pompey, Caesar, whose daughter, Julia, had died, proposed a new marriage alliance with Pompey: Pompey should marry Octavia, his grandniece (whom Antony is about to marry and to whom he had previously married Caius Marcellus [2.6.112; Suetonius, *Divus Julius*, 27.1]), who was then presently married, and he, Caesar, would divorce Calpurnia and marry another of Pompey's daughters, who was already promised to someone else (Suetonius, *Divus Julius*, 27.1). As Caesar had been Pompey's father-in-law, Pompey would now become his. Each would be his father-in-law's father-in-law. Pompey rejected the proposal, although he later married Cornelia, daughter of Metellus Scipio, Caesar's third wife (Plutarch, *Pompey*, 55.1, *Caesar*, 6.3).

In addition to marrying his sister to Antony, Octavius Caesar, for his part, first married the aunt of Sextus Pompey's wife in the hope of countering Antony's power and prestige, and then, in an effort to reconcile with Antony, married Fulvia's stepdaughter, who was hardly of marriageable age (Suetonius, *Augustus*, 62.2; Plutarch, *Antony*, 20.1; Appian, *Civil Wars*, 5.53). After falling out with Fulvia, Octavius divorced her stepdaughter and married the sister of Lepidus's father-in-law, whom he also divorced, and, seeking to attract to his cause a certain group of senators, he immediately took Livia from her husband, although she was pregnant at the time (Suetonius, *Augustus*, 62.1; Dio, 48.44.1–2). See also Livy, *History*, 38.57.

22. Shakespeare, while mentioning that Antony has children by Cleopatra (3.6.7–8, 13–16), suppresses that he has several children by Octavia (as well as by Fulvia); see Plutarch, *Antony*, 33.3–4; 35.1–2, 5; 57.3; 87.1. Cleopatra exaggerates when she calls Julius Caesar, Octavius's adoptive father, "[y]our Caesar's father" (3.13.87), as does Octavius himself while implicitly denying Caesar's son by Cleopatra ("Caesarion, whom they call my father's son" [3.6.6]). Similarly, although repeatedly called his sister (2.2.158, 177; 2.6.111; 3.2.25, 39; 3.6.44, 66, 99, 100), Octavia is "a sister by [Caesar's] mother's side" (2.2.125).

23. Plutarch, *Antony*, 32.1; Dio, 48.15.2.

24. Robert D. Hume, "Individuation and Development of Character through Language in *Antony and Cleopatra*," *Shakespeare Quarterly*, 24 (1973), 283.

25. Suetonius, *Augustus*, 66.3; Velleius Paterculus, 2.88.2, 90.1, 127.1; Tacitus, *Annals*, 1.3.1; Dio, 48.20.2.

26. See, e.g., Seneca, *Letters*, 114.4–8; 120.19; Horace, *Satires*, 2.8.16, 22; Tacitus, *Annals*, 1.54; Velleius Paterculus, 2.88.2. Maecenas also becomes a lavish patron of the arts. Horace dedicates his first ode, the place of honor, to him (Horace, *Odes*, 1.1.1), and Virgil dedicates the *Georgics* to him (Virgil, *Georgics*, 1.2). See, further, Suetonius, *The Lives of Illustrious Men*, Horace; Virgil, 20, 27.

27. On "light" as debauched, see Partridge, s.v. Light; note 1.2.183; 1.4.25; also 2.7.121.

28. "For verily the foreign excess and strange superfluities [in Rome] took beginning from the Asian army, who brought all with them into the city. . . . Then began the board to be furnished and set out with more exquisite and dainty viands, and of great expense. The cooks, who in old time were reputed the most contemptible of slaves, as well for calling as estimation, as for use they were put to, came to be in great request, and that which before was a mechanical kind of service grew now to be accounted a science of deep skill and understanding." Livy, *History*, 39.6.7–9; Holland, 823. See also Pliny, 33.53.

29. As an indication of his immoderate taste in food, "Maecenas was the first that at feasts made a dainty dish of young ass foles, and preferred their flesh in his time before the venison of wild asses." Pliny, 8.170; 223.

30. For his frequent use of aphorisms, see, e.g., 1.2.140–42, 144–47, 168–72, 175–77; 2.2.9–10, 11, 70–71, 114–15; 2.6.101, 127; 3.5.13–15; 3.7.7–9; 3.13.31–34, 43–47, 99–100, 200–202, 204–5.

31. Hesiod, *Theogony*, 240–64; Pindar, *Olympian Odes*, 2.29.

32. Plutarch, *Antony*, 25.1.

33. On the impossibility of a void in nature implying the primacy of a determined natural world, see Aristotle, *Physics*, 213a11ff.

34. Kittredge, 1372.

35. For the gloss and the ambiguity of "breathless pour breath forth," see N. F. Blake, *Shakespeare's Language: An Introduction* (New York: St. Martin's Press, 1983), 59.

36. Plutarch, *Antony*, 33.2–3, *The Fortune of the Romans*, 7 (319f–20a).

37. Frederick E. Brenk, *In Mist Appareled* (Lugduni Batavorum: Brill, 1977), 151ff. See, e.g., Plutarch, *Artaxerxes*, 15.5, *Timoleon*, 16.6–12, *Phocion*, 30.5–6, *Alexander*, 30; 50.1, *Sulla*, 24.2, *Crassus*, 22.4–6, *Lucullus*, 27.5, *Sertorius*, 25.2, *Pompey*, 74–76, *Brutus*, 36.3–4, *Caesar*, 69.7–8. See also *JC*, 4.3.274–85; 5.5.16–20.

38. Suetonius, *Augustus*, 70.2–71.4.

39. Plutarch, *Antony*, 24.6.

40. Plutarch leaves uncertain whether the Soothsayer warned Antony "to please Cleopatra or else for that he found it so by his art" (Plutarch, *Antony*, 33.2; North 6:33).

41. See, further, Blits, *Ancient Republic*, 39–61, *Deadly Thought: "Hamlet" and the Human Soul* (Lanham: Lexington Books, 2001), 5–6, 38–39, 163–64, 247.

42. Plutarch, *Antony*, 4.1–2; Appian, *Civil Wars*, 3.16, 19. See also 1.3.85; 4.3.21.

43. Plutarch, *Comparison of Demetrius and Antony*, 3.3, *Old Men in Public Affairs*, 4 (785e–f); Ovid, *Heroides*, 9.53–118, *Fasti*, 2.317–26.

44. Anna B. Jameson, *Shakespeare's Heroines: Characteristics of Women* (London: George Bell and Sons, 1879), 262.

45. On the Parthians' similar treatment of Crassus, see Florus, 1.46.10; Dio, 40.27.3.

46. Cleopatra uses "friend" as a term of address only for subordinates or servants whose assistance she needs; see also 4.8.26; 4.15.4, 32.

47. Kittredge, 1374.

48. "[I]t is impossible to tell whether we have an imperative with a vocative, or a subjunctive used optatively or conditionally." Abbott, §364.

49. On "So" (2.5.94) as "even if," see Abbott, §133.

50. Blits, *Ancient Republic*, 3ff.

51. "[T]hey are like those double or turning pictures; stand before which, you see a fair maid on the one side, an ape on the other, an owl; look upon them at the first sight, all is well; but further examine, you shall find them wise on the one side and fools on the other; in some few things praiseworthy, in the rest incomparably faulty." Robert Burton, *The Anatomy of Melancholy*, Democritus to the Reader, ed. Thomas C. Faulkner, 3 vols. (Oxford: Clarendon Press, 1989), 1:105.

52. Apollodorus, *Library*, 2.4.2.

53. See, e.g., Velleius Paterculus, 2.29.1; Dio, 41.54.1.

54. Suetonius, *Divus Julius*, 76–79.

55. Cicero, *Philippics*, 2.64ff.; Plutarch, *Antony*, 10.2, 32.3; Dio, 45.9.4; 48.38.2. On the recovery of his family's property as Pompey's principal motive, see Sextus Aurelius Victor, *On Distinguished Men*, 79.2; also Dio, 45.10.6.

56. On "mayst" maintaining the original meaning of "can," see Abbott, §307; note, e.g., 1.5.13; 3.9.3; 3.11.60; 3.13.85; 5.2.76, 133.

57. Plutarch, *Antony*, 32.2–3; Appian, *Civil Wars*, 5.72; Dio, 48.36.

58. Plutarch, *Pompey*, 23.3–4; 42.6; 57.3–5; 67.4, *Caesar*, 29.5.

59. Antony never mentions her name in Italy. Nor does anyone mention it to him, except Caesar when ostensibly correcting Agrippa's marriage proposal (2.2.128–29).

60. Appian, *An Ancient History and Exquisite Chronicle of the Roman Wars, Both Civil and Foreign*, trans. W. B. (London: Raulfe Newberrie and Henrie [B]ynniman, 1578), 347, 369.

61. See also Appian, *Civil Wars*, 5.110, 140. On a similar trait in his father, see Plutarch, *Pompey*, 55.5, 67.4, *Caesar*, 39.5.

62. Bevington, 140–41.

63. MacCallum, 375–76.

64. Cicero, *Republic*, 3.24; Augustine, 4.4.

65. Also Appian, *Civil Wars*, 5.78.

66. "[F]rom the Latin [*planta*]." Samuel Johnson, *The Plays of William Shakespeare*, ed. Samuel Johnson and George Steevens, 10 vols. (London: 1778; rpt. London: Routledge/Thommes, 1995), 8:193.

67. Janet Adelman, *The Common Liar: An Essay on "Antony and Cleopatra"* (New Haven: Yale University Press, 1973), 118.

68. John Leo Africanus, *A Geographical History of Africa*, trans. John Pory (London: Impensis Georg. Bishop, 1600; rpt. Amsterdam: Da Capo Press, 1969), 312. See also Pliny, 5.58; John Mandeville, *Mandeville's Travels*, 6 (c. 1357; rpt. Oxford: Claredon Press, 1967), 31; George Abbot, *A Brief Description of the Whole World* (London, 1599; rpt. New York: De Capo Press, 1970), C3.

69. Pliny says that "certain pits" were used (Pliny, 5.9; Holland, 98). Plutarch, reporting local myths, tells that the female crocodile lays her eggs at the point to which the Nile is destined to reach (Plutarch, *Isis and Osirus*, 75 [381b], *Whether Land or Sea Animals are Cleverer*, 34 [982c]). And Leo Africanus describes "the isle of measure, in which isle (according to the inundation of Nilus) they have a kind of device invented by the ancient Egyptians whereby they most certainly foresee the plenty or scarcity of the year following" (Leo Africanus, 312). See also Aelian, *On The Characteristics of Animals*, 5.52.

70. Diodorus, 1.10. On Egypt itself being composed of water and earth, see Herodotus, 2.4.3–18.

71. See, e.g., Herodotus, 2.78; Plutarch, *Dinner of the Seven Wise Men*, 2 (148a–b). On the pyramids as marvels, see Diodorus, 1.63.3–9; on their having been built as royal tombs, see Herodotus, 2.124–35; Diodorus, 1.64.4.

72. See Horace, *Odes*, 1.11; Ovid, *Art of Love*, 3.59ff. On the small value of human life in Egypt, see Herodotus, 2.158.

73. See Herodotus, 2.46, 65–76; Diodorus, 1.83–85; on crocodiles as sacred in Egypt, see Herodotus, 2.69; Diodorus, 1.83.1, 89.1–3; Philo, *The Decalogue*, 78; Plutarch, *Table Talk*, 4.5 (670a), *Whether Land or Sea Animals are Cleverer*, 23 (976b).

74. Following his victory over Antony and Cleopatra, Caesar declined to view Apis, incarnate as a live bull, saying that he was accustomed to worshipping gods, not cattle (Dio, 51.16.5). Note, e.g., Herodotus, 2.46; Diodorus, 1.88.1. See, further, Seth Benardete, *Herodotean Inquiries* (The Hague: Martinus Nijhoff, 1969), 45–46.

75. Bevington, 146.

76. See Act 2, n. 2, above.

77. Of the forty-four mentions of the word "world" in the play, eight occur in this scene, including three ending lines for emphasis in the present exchange (2.7.2, 62, 63, 66, 71, 91, 117, 118). In addition, in the present exchange "all" and "whole" thrice explicitly and once implicitly modify "world" (2.7.62, 63, 66, 74). Note also 2.7.69–70.

78. Appian, *Civil Wars*, 5.71.

79. Hence, the apparently superfluous pronoun in Menas's reply, "The third part then he is drunk" (2.7.92).

80. Benjamin G. Kinnear, *Cruces Shakespearean: Difficult Passages in the Works of Shakespeare* (London: George Bell, 1883), 456.

81. Caesar will raise Menas to the equestrian rank (Dio, 48.45.7) and entertain him at his own table (Suetonius, *Augustus*, 74), but Menas will subsequently abandon him, too (Appian, *Civil Wars*, 5.100–102; see also Dio, 49.1.2–5; Orosius, 6.18.25).

82. David Lindley, *Shakespeare and Music* (London: Arden, 2006), 187.

83. Cicero, *Pro Murena*, 13.

84. On traditional Roman wakefulness, see Blits, *Ancient Republic*, 5–6.

85. See Richmond Noble, *Shakespeare's Use of Song with the Texts of the Principal Songs* (London: Oxford University Press, 1923), 127–28; F. W. Sternfeld, *Music in Shakespeare Tragedy* (London: Routledge and Kegan Paul, 1963), 81–87; Peter J. Seng, "Shakespearean Hymn-Parody?" *Renaissance News*, 18 (1965), 4–6, *Vocal Songs in the Plays of Shakespeare* (Cambridge: Harvard University Press, 1967), 211–13.

~

Act Three

Act Three, Scene One

Antony sent Ventidius to fight the Parthians, who, taking advantage of the unstable political conditions in both the West and the East, and particularly of Antony's idleness in Egypt, had extended their empire from the Euphrates all the way to Ionia (1.2.105–9; 2.3.30–31, 39–41). Act 3 opens in Syria, where Ventidius has won a resounding victory over the Parthians, killing the king's son, Pacorus. "*Enter Ventidius as it were in triumph, the dead body of Pacorus borne before him*" (s.d. 3.1.1). Ventidius's victory is the defeat of the last foreign enemy seriously able to threaten Rome. With the victory, the East is essentially secured, as the West now is, following Pompey's agreement. Rome, however, has always been in danger from itself when it has had no foreign enemies to contend with. "[E]ven now are we in greatest danger, being at this pass that we have left ourselves none to fear . . ." (quoted from Nasica, Plutarch, *How to Profit by One's Enemies*, 3 [88a]; Holland, 239). The elimination of Rome's last serious foreign enemy removes the last serious threat that could force the Romans to unite for the common good.[1] While Ventidius alone in the play fights Rome's enemy instead of fellow Romans,[2] his victory, ironically, ensures that he will be the last to do so.

Ventidius's triumph is also Rome's long-sought revenge. Crassus led an army into Parthia, but was utterly defeated and treacherously killed by Orodes, Pacorus's father, during a conference after Orodes's victory. The Parthians killed twenty thousand Romans and took another ten thousand prisoners.[3] They then ridiculed a Roman triumph, dressing Roman prisoners as women and "singing . . . songs of mockery and derision of Crassus's womanish cowardice" (Plutarch, *Crassus*, 32.1–2; North, 4:88). After decapitating Crassus, besides pouring molten gold into his gaping mouth to mock him for his greed, they used his head as a stage prop in a farcical performance of Euripides's *Bacchae*.[4] "This noble exploit," Plutarch says of Ventidius's victory, "as famous as ever any was, was a full revenge to the Romans of the shame and loss they had received before by the death of Marcus Crassus" (Plutarch, *Antony*, 34.2; North, 6:34).[5]

Thus Ventidius begins, "Now, darting Parthia, art thou struck, and now / Pleased Fortune does of Marcus Crassus' death / Make me revenger" (3.1.1–3). Ventidius puns on the "darting" Parthians' famous weapon and tactic—their arrows and their flight. After shooting their arrows at the enemy, the Parthians flee to avoid close combat, but then turn in their saddles and shoot their arrows behind them as they go.[6] The Parthians have now been punished ("struck"). They who have often struck others with their arrows, are now struck themselves.[7] And Pacorus's death revenges Crassus's death, just as the Roman victory revenges the Roman defeat. "Thy Pacorus, Orodes, / Pays this for Marcus Crassus" (3.1.4–5). The son of Crassus's killer pays for Crassus's death.

Ventidius, exulting in his victory, addresses Parthia and Orodes as though they were before him. Illustrating spiritedness's tendency to animate the inanimate in order to punish it, he apostrophizes both while personifying Parthia, so that he can punish them—or imagine he is punishing them—to their faces. While displaying the body of the king's son as his trophy for his army to admire, he tells Parthia and Orodes explicitly and directly what they have suffered and lost.

Ventidius also personifies Fortune: "Pleased Fortune does . . . / Make me revenger." Ventidius at once raises and lowers himself. By personifying Fortune, he elevates his actions and his victory: He serves not simply Antony, but Fortune, who is pleased with his vengeful victory. But, on the other hand, he attributes his victory not to his virtue but to Fortune's favor. It is she, not he, who gave him victory and vengeance. His victory is not really his own.[8]

Silius, one of his officers, urges Ventidius to pursue the fleeing Parthians without delay: "Spur through Media, / Mesopotamia, and the shelters whither / The routed fly" (3.1.7–9). If successful, such a pursuit would drive the Parthians back, deep within their original territory. Silius thinks that Antony would welcome Ventidius's further victory. "So thy grand captain Antony / Shall set thee on triumphant chariots and / Put garlands on thy head," he says, describing a Roman triumph (3.1.9–11). The cautious Ventidius corrects him. Declaring that he has "done enough" (3.1.12), he explains the danger of doing more. "A lower place, note well, / May make too great an act. For learn this, Silius," he stresses, "Better to leave undone than, by our deed, / Acquire too high a fame when him we serve's away" (3.1.12–15). During the Republic, fame was the reward of and the spur to noble action. To advance, a Roman needed to please Rome, not his superior, whose position his success, in fact, threatened.[9] Ventidius, however, serves Antony, not Rome. To advance, or even to maintain his position, he must please his superior, his "grand captain," as Silius calls him. And so, as Ventidius emphasizes while speaking like a teacher, it is better to compromise one's own campaign—"to leave undone"—than to win too much fame when he whom one serves is not present. Thus, continuing, Ventidius says that Caesar and Antony have won more through lieutenancy than through their own command (". . . ever won / More in their officer than person" [3.1.16–17]). But even though Antony wishes the enemy be defeated, whatever further glory his lieutenant might gain is—or Antony thinks it is—taken from him.[10] Ventidius offers the cautionary example of "Sossius, / One of my place in Syria, [Antony's] lieutenant, [who] / For quick accumulation of renown, / Which he achiev'd by th' minute, lost his favour" (3.1.18–20).[11] The more battles Sossius won, the less favor he enjoyed. "Who does i'th' wars more than his captain can, / Becomes his captain's captain; and ambition, / The soldier's virtue, rather makes choice of loss / Than gain which darkens him" (3.1.21–24). A soldier's ambition, which should spur him to achieve more, now prompts him instead to limit his achievements.[12] What guides his ambition is not the gain of his own glory but the loss of his captain's. And so Ventidius concludes, "I could do more to do Antonius good, / But 'twould offend him, and in his offence / Should my performance perish" (3.1.25–27). A further victory might prove as much Ventidius's defeat as the Parthians'.

Silius answers like a thoroughly post-republican Roman. "Thou hast, Ventidius, that / Without the which a soldier and his sword / Grants scarce distinction" (3.1.28–30). Without such calculation, Silius says, there is hardly a difference between a solider and his sword: the soldier is simply his mindless weapon. A soldier's virtue is no longer knowing how to win in battle, but now includes, as Ventidius said, knowing when not to win—knowing how to bring success and glory to his captain without incurring his jealousy and anger.

Evidently pleased by Silius's compliment, Ventidius tells what he will write to Antony. He will "humbly signify what in his name" the army has done. "How, with his banners and his well-paid ranks, / The ne'er-yet-beaten horse of Parthia / We have jaded out o'th' field" (3.1.31, 33–35). What is done in his name, under his banners, and by the troops he has paid, is

Antony's victory, despite his absence. Although he is "the only man that ever triumphed [over] the Parthians until this present day" (Plutarch, *Antony*, 34.5; North, 6:35),[13] Ventidius dissembles his own great achievement. He sacrifices his glory to his discretion.

Act Three, Scene Two

1.

Agrippa and Enobarbus are together again, back in Rome, where the triumvirs, having finished their business with Pompey, are concluding their own affairs. According to Enobarbus, Octavia is weeping because she must leave Rome, Caesar is sad, "and Lepidus / Since Pompey's feast, as Menas says, is troubled / With the green-sickness" (3.2.4–6). Throughout their exchange, Agrippa and Enobarbus mockingly mimic Lepidus's obsequious praise of Caesar and Antony. Enobarbus, beginning the parody, describes a symptom of Lepidus's hangover as the symptom of a young girl's lovesickness ("green-sickness"): The infatuated Lepidus is besotted with Caesar and Antony.[14] Then Agrippa and Enobarbus, each ostensibly championing the worthiness of the other's captain, vie with each other in expressing Lepidus's effusive admiration and love for the two captains, each of whom is equally unequalled:

> *Eno.:* Oh, how he loves Caesar!
> *Agr.:* Nay, but how dearly he adores Mark Antony!
> *Eno.:* Caesar? Why he's the Jupiter of men.
> *Agr.:* What's Antony? The god of Jupiter.
> *Eno.:* Spake you of Caesar? Hoo! The nonpareil!
> *Agr.:* O Antony! O thou Arabian bird!
> *Eno.:* Would you praise Caesar, say 'Caesar.' Go no further.
>
> (3.2.7–13)

Enobarbus and Agrippa try to top not only each other, but the previous round of praise. The putative praise ascends, increasingly exaggerating in order to further diminish Lepidus. Its climax is unintentionally ironic, however, for, as the praise rises from men to gods, and from gods to the incomparable or singular, it culminates in Enobarbus's giving Caesar's name as the highest possible praise. To have the name "Caesar" is to be unsurpassable ("Go no further").[15] Enobarbus's joke on Lepidus is an unwitting warning to Antony.

Enobarbus continues by lampooning Lepidus's indescribable love for Antony and his even greater love for Caesar: "But he loves Caesar best. Yet he loves Antony. / Hoo! Hearts, tongues, figures, scribes, bards, poets, cannot / Think, speak, cast, write, sing, number—hoo! — / His love to Antony" (3.2.15–18). Enobarbus piles up ridiculously excessive rhetoric, made to seem even more excessive by his respective construction and asyndeton,[16] to mock Lepidus's ridiculously excessive love. Scribes with their hearts cannot think or write, bards with their tongues cannot speak or sing, poets with their figures cannot cast into verse or number Lepidus's love for Antony. But if Lepidus loves Antony beyond description, he nevertheless more than worships Caesar: "But as for Caesar, / Kneel down, kneel down, and wonder" (3.2.18–19). Lepidus's love for Antony may be ineffable, but his love for Caesar elevates Caesar to the divine. Having ridiculed the fawning Lepidus for his flattery of his fellow triumvirs, Enobarbus, sardonically summing up, scorns his professed love as an imitation of the obscene behavior of beetles. "They are his shards and he their beetle," he dryly states (3.2.20). According to Plutarch, the Egyptians hold that there are no female beetles,

> but all the males do blow or cast their seed into a certain globus or round matter [of dung] in form of balls, which they drive from them and roll to and fro contrariwise, like as the sun, when he moves himself from the West to the East, seems to turn about the Heaven clean contrary.
>
> (Plutarch, *Isis and Osiris*, 74 [381a]; Holland, 1071)

If to a servant he resembles a planet without a fixed sphere and an eye socket without an eye (2.7.14–16), to Enobarbus, Lepidus, scurrying back and forth with fulsome praise between Caesar in the West and Antony in the East, resembles a beetle generating by rolling a ball of dung backward and forward, just as the sun seems to travel west by day and east by night.[17] Lepidus, a triumvir of the world, resembles nothing so much as a ludicrous, loathsome, low insect attempting to emulate the motions of the sun in the sky.

2.

The jocular derision of Lepidus is followed by the tearful farewell of Octavia. Politely told that he need not accompany them any further ("No further, sir" [3.2.23]), Caesar tries gently to admonish the newlyweds, prefacing his comments by telling Antony, "You take from me a great part of myself," and then urging or warning him, "Use me well in't" (3.2.24–25). Caesar speaks of love twice in the scene, but of the love between Antony and himself (3.2.29, 32), not of his love for Octavia. However much he may love Octavia, her marriage to Antony is meant to link the brothers-in-law. Thus, urging Octavia to be the sort of wife he is sure she will be, Caesar adopts the language of a business transaction, saying that he has provided a surety for the quality of his goods: He will pledge ("pass on") his utmost credit ("my farthest bond") that she will stand the test ("approof" [3.2.26–27]). As his language is commercial, so his thought is chiefly of himself. Then, addressing Antony and turning to metaphors of architecture and war, Caesar makes explicit both the purpose and the peril of the marriage. An exemplar of virtue ("piece of virtue"), Octavia is the uniting part ("piece") "which is set / Betwixt us, as the cement of our love / To keep it builded" and must not "be the ram to batter / The fortress of it" (3.2.28–31).[18] What holds them together must not be allowed to set them apart (see 2.6.122–24). "For better might we / Have loved without this mean," Caesar concludes, referring to his sister as a means as well as an intermediary ("mean"), "if on both parts / This be not cherished" (3.2.31–33).

Although Caesar spoke of the need for both Antony and himself ("both parts") cherishing Octavia, Antony takes umbrage: "Make me not offended / In your distrust" (3.2.33–34). And when Caesar replies that he will say no more, Antony, answering the distrust, offers his absolute assurance: "You shall not find, / Though you be therein curious, the least cause / For what you seem to fear" (3.2.34–36). No matter how determined Caesar is to find fault, he will find not the slightest in Antony's behavior. Antony speaks as though he does not intend to return to Egypt, as though he "married [more than] his occasion here" (2.6.133). Despite taking offense, however, Antony concludes graciously, "So the gods keep you, / And make the hearts of Romans serve your ends" (3.2.36–37). Yet, notwithstanding his graciousness, throughout the scene Antony, unlike when accepting the marriage proposal (2.2.154), addresses Caesar, as Caesar addresses him, only with the distant pronoun "you" (3.2.24, 34, 35, 36 [twice], 38, 62, 63 [twice], 64).

When Caesar, bidding Octavia farewell, wishes that all of nature's powers and life's circumstances combine to treat her kindly and keep her always happy ("The elements be kind to thee, and make / Thy spirits all of comfort!" [3.2.40–41]), Octavia cries and cannot speak. Antony takes her tears as an expression of her love: "The April's in her eyes; it is love's spring / And these the showers to bring it on" (3.2.43–44). And when Octavia, unable or unwilling to speak aloud, whispers in her brother's ear, Antony remarks, "Her tongue will not obey her heart, nor can / Her heart inform her tongue" (3.2.47–48). Antony then describes why Octavia's tongue cannot express what is in her heart: "—the swan's-down feather / That stands upon the swell at full tide, / And neither way inclines" (3.2.48–50). Divided equally between her loves for each of them, Octavia's heart is balanced between sorrow at parting from her brother and desire to accompany her husband, and so, like a feather on still water just before the full tide turns, she is not inclined either way. It is not surprising that Antony speaks of "the swell at full tide" rather than the ebb at low tide, although the delicate balancing would be true of both. He speaks of the fullness of her love for both men. Nevertheless, the inadvertent implication seems clear: The tide, now at its height, will soon begin to decline, and the water will flow one way.

Enobarbus and Agrippa, seeing Caesar on the point of crying ("He has a cloud in's face" [3.2.51]), banter about men weeping. According to Enobarbus, who quibbles on the word "cloud," just as a horse is less valuable for having a dark spot ("cloud" [3.2.51]) on its face, "So is [Caesar], being a man" (3.2.53). Weeping is a sign of unmanliness. Agrippa, playfully deflecting the denigration away from Caesar and onto Antony, reminds Enobarbus of Antony's own weeping: "Why, Enobarbus, / When Antony found Julius Caesar dead, / He cried almost to roaring, and he wept / When at Philippi he found Brutus slain" (3.2.53–56). Agrippa, with maudlin mirth, fabricates or exaggerates his report. Antony did not cry when he found either Caesar or Brutus slain (JC, 3.1.148ff.; 5.5.68–75), though his eyes "[began] to water" when he saw Octavius's servant weep at the sight of Caesar's corpse, and he did feign tears at Caesar's funeral (JC, 3.1.285; 3.2.117). Enobarbus, pretending to take Agrippa's remarks at face value, sarcastically replies, "That year, indeed, he was troubled with a rheum. / What willingly he did confound he wailed, / Believe't, till I weep too" (3.2.57–59). Antony wept, he says, at the destruction he readily sought, as Caesar will at the sight of the sword that kills Antony (5.1.24–27). Such displays of tears, whether simulated or real, enjoy a long ancient tradition, following Alexander's enormous conquests and sudden death at an early age. Eumenes weeps for Craterus (Plutarch, *Eumenes*, 7.8), Antigonus for Pyrrhus (Plutarch, *Pyrrhus*, 34.4), Antiochus for Achaeus (Polybius, 8.20.9–10), Aemilius Paullus for Perseus (Plutarch, *Aemilius Paulus*, 26.5–6; Polybius, 39.20.1–4), Scipio Africanus for the captured royal women of Carthago Nova (Polybius, 10.18.13), Scipio Aemilianus for destroyed Carthage (Polybius, 38.21.1–3, 22; Diodorus, 32.24; Appian, *Punic Wars*, 132) and Julius Caesar for Pompey (Plutarch, *Caesar*, 48.2, *Pompey*, 80.5). The tears are meant to acknowledge the mutability of Fortune and the uncertainty of human affairs." Is there any man living, my friends," Aemilius Paullus asks his men after defeating Perseus,

who having fortune at will, should therefore boast and glory in the prosperity of his doings, for that he has conquered a country, city or realm; and not rather to fear the inconstancy of Fortune? . . . [T]he common frailty of men does plainly teach us to think that there is nothing constant or perdurable in this

world. For when is it that men may think themselves assured, considering that
when they have overcome others, then are they driven to mistrust fortune
most, and to mingle fear and distrust with joy of victory, if they will wisely consider the common course of fatal destiny that alters daily, sometime favoring
one, otherwise throwing down another?

(Plutarch, *Aemilius Paulus*, 27.1–2; North, 2:228)

However great the conquest, the conqueror may become the conquered.[19]

Caesar, responding aloud to at least some of what Octavia has whispered,
promises, "No, sweet Octavia, / You shall hear from me still" (3.2.59–60).
Octavia is concerned that Caesar will forget her when she is gone from
Rome. She seems not to suspect that he may intend to use her and her marriage as a pretext for war with Antony. Caesar strongly reassures Octavia that
he will think of her constantly: "The time shall not / Outgo my thinking on
you" (3.2.60–61). He may mean just what he says, though not in the heartfelt spirit in which he says it.

Lepidus, the butt of scathing jokes early in the scene, has virtually the final word. His words, addressed to Octavia, express his delight with her marriage: "Let all the number of the stars give light / To thy fair way!"
(3.2.65–66). Lepidus's surprisingly lyrical words—his only words in the scene
and his last in the play—ironically echo his first words. There, Antony's
faults resembled the stars (". . . seem as the spots of heaven, / More fiery by
night's blackness" [1.4.12–13]). Here, the stars will guide Octavia's way. Contrary to what Lepidus evidently intends, Antony's faults will, in fact, determine her way.

Act Three, Scene Three

The Messenger, whom Cleopatra had abused and beaten for bringing her
news of Antony's marriage, is still afraid to address her. Alexas, who has himself served as a messenger to Cleopatra (1.5.36ff.), tries tactfully to explain
the man's fear. "Herod of Jewry," he reminds her, "dare not look upon you /
But when you are well pleased" (3.3.3–4). Even the terrifying Herod, notorious for cruelty, is intimidated by Cleopatra except when she is pleased with
him. Her displeasure is daunting. Cleopatra initially confirms Alexas's obser-
vation. "That Herod's head / I'll have," she threatens (3.3.4–5). However,
she immediately catches herself: "But how, when Antony is gone, / Through
whom I might command it?" (3.3.5–6). Politics is never far from love in
Cleopatra's mind. Her power as queen of Egypt has depended on the support
she has enjoyed from powerful Romans (1.5.30–35), and their support has

rested largely on their love for her. A client kingdom of Rome, Egypt depends on Rome—or on one of its leaders—for its power against foreign enemies.[20] Without Antony, Cleopatra is powerless as well as loveless. If Antony subordinates politics to love, Cleopatra uses love to serve her political ends. What a man is to her includes what he can do for her.

The Messenger has evidently learned from his earlier experience. He carefully avoids saying anything that Cleopatra, his "dread queen" (3.3.8), does not want to hear, turning everything that might offend her into what will please her. And Cleopatra, abetted by Charmian, compounds his gratifying account by jealously and spitefully magnifying it. When the Messenger reports that Octavia is not as tall as Cleopatra and is low voiced, and Charmian, seconding Cleopatra's judgment that "[Antony] cannot like her long" (3.3.14), exclaims, "Like her? O Isis! 'Tis impossible" (3.3.15), Cleopatra, suddenly more confident, declares, "I think so, Charmian. Dull of tongue and dwarfish" (3.3.16). Cleopatra's new-found confidence inspires the Messenger's, who now self-assuredly exaggerates. Asked about the majesty of her gait and reminded that he had previously looked on true majesty (namely, on Cleopatra herself [see 3.3.41–43]), the man describes Octavia as motionless and lifeless. "She creeps," he says, "Her motion and her station are as one. / She shows a body rather than a life, / A statue than a breather" (3.3.18–21). Octavia lacks not only dignity and grace, but even breath and life. When Cleopatra voices some skepticism ("Is this certain?" [3.3.21]), the Messenger, now ready to boast of his reliability, boldly proclaims, "Or I have no observance" (3.3.22). And when Charmian confirms his boast ("Three in Egypt / Cannot make better note" [3.3.22–23]), Cleopatra, as though reaching the conclusion by herself, firmly agrees with both his boast and his judgment: "He's very knowing; / I do perceiv't. There's nothing in her yet. / The fellow has good judgement" (3.3.23–25). The Messenger has good judgment because he tells that there is nothing in Octavia. The less there is in her, the more there is in him. The Messenger, however, briefly stumbles. Replying to a question about Octavia's age, he assures Cleopatra, who will soon be thirty-nine, "I do think she's thirty" (3.3.28). This is the Messenger's only answer which Cleopatra passes over in silence.[21]

After the Messenger satisfies her with disparaging descriptions of Octavia's face, hair and forehead, Cleopatra offers him gold, declares her goodwill, and promises him future work, saying, "I find thee / Most fit for business" (3.3.35–36). She richly rewards him for duping her. And after he leaves, with Charmian's strong encouragement, she concludes, with apparent finality, "Why methinks, by him, / This creature's no such thing" (3.3.39–40). Octavia is nothing remarkable, nothing to worry about.

Yet, despite her seeming confidence, Cleopatra is still not assured. She praises the Messenger's judgment ("The man hath seen some majesty, and should know" [3.3.41]), and Charmian offers her full agreement: "Hath he seen majesty? Isis else defend, / And serving you so long!" (3.3.42–43). Cleopatra is the model of majesty. But Cleopatra still wants to know more about her rival. "I have one more thing to ask him yet, good Charmian," she says of the Messenger (3.3.44). No feature or comparison is too trivial for her to be concerned about.

Cleopatra not only wants to know more. She is still sending Antony messages. She has already written him letters which the Messenger is to deliver ("Go, make thee ready; / Our letters are prepared" [3.3.36–37]). And, as soon as she concludes that Octavia is nothing remarkable, she decides to write more. Her question for the Messenger can wait: "'[T]is no matter; thou shalt bring him to me / Where I will write. All may be well enough" (3.3.45–46). The next time we see Cleopatra, Antony will be back.

Act Three, Scene Four

Caesar had urged Antony not to let Octavia find herself torn between the two of them (3.2.27–22). He also had agreed at Misena to let Pompey have Sicily and Sardinia in exchange for his clearing the sea of pirates and sending wheat to Rome (2.6.34–39). Now, however, Antony tells Octavia that Caesar has waged new wars against Pompey, has made his will, read it in public, presumably promising large bequests to the people, and (as seems most to irritate him) has spoken only grudgingly of Antony when he could not avoid saying something. His praise was minimal, reluctant and forced.[22] Antony sees Caesar's actions as his preparation for a final break. Although Caesar appears to have been planning all along to make war on Pompey and then on Lepidus and finally on Antony, Ventidius's victory over the Parthians, which was won "in [Antony's] name" (3.1.31), seems to have forced him to act at this time. He needs both a victory redounding to his own glory and a way of preventing Antony's triumphant return to Rome. His victory over Pompey promises both.

The normally reticent Octavia replies at length,[23] asking Antony either not to believe all the news or, if he must, not to resent all of it. In Coriolanus, Volumnia described her misery at being divided between her son and her country. She could not pray for one, she said, without praying against the other. But forced to choose between them, she chose her country. The public prevailed over the private (Cor., 5.3.94–182). Octavia faces a dilemma that is superficially similar but fundamentally different. The wife of one triumvir and the sister of another, she is torn not between the public and the private, but between two private loves or concerns. Neither here nor any-where else does she mention Rome or speak of her country (or anything like it). Although she is not at all selfish, "my" is by far her most frequent word.[24] Like Volumnia, Octavia cannot pray without praying against her prayers. "A more unhappy lady, / If this division chance, ne'er stood between, / Praying for both parts," she says in dismay.

> The good gods will mock me presently
> When I shall pray 'O, bless my lord and husband!';
> Undo that prayer by crying out as loud
> 'O, bless my brother!' Husband win, win brother,
> Prays and destroys the prayer.
>
> (3.4.12–19)

Each prayer undoes the other. Both the prayer itself and the one who prays ("prayer") are destroyed. "[N]o midway / 'Twixt these extremes at all" (3.4.19–20). In Coriolanus's Rome, the city tied the citizens together. Not only did the Romans share the city; the city made them who they were. They were citizens first and private individuals second. In praying for any Roman, a Roman was praying also for Rome. If Coriolanus became the ex-ception, Volumnia reaffirmed the rule. In Caesar and Antony's Rome, on the other hand, there is nothing higher than private goods: "Husband . . . brother." Octavia rather than the city unites the two men, and so she is left with nothing between her husband and her brother except herself and her prayers. In the absence of a public realm, everything goes to the private and, consequently, to the extreme. The moderating, mediating middle is missing.

Antony, unable or unwilling to answer, leaves it to Octavia to decide which love to choose: "Let your best love draw to that point which seeks / Best to preserve it" (3.4.21–22). Octavia should choose the love which will best preserve her love. Antony says nothing to retain her love. Having made "this marriage for [his] peace" (2.3.38), he has little reason to keep Octavia from leaving him, now that he has his Parthian victory and Caesar seems to be preparing a showdown.

Antony does, however, defend his resenting Caesar's insulting actions. Speaking as if Octavia as well as he would lose, he declares, "If I lose mine ho-nour, / I lose myself; better I were not yours / Than yours so branchless" (3.4.22–24). Antony, like a traditional Roman, finds his identity in his honor. He cannot be himself unless his retains his honor, and Octavia cannot love him unless he is himself. To be himself and to be worthy of her love, he must defend his honor and take offense at Caesar's affronts. Antony thus uses the word "honor" in its characteristically Roman double sense. It is at once his moral worth and his public reputation. Who he is depends on how others regard him.[25]

Antony, nevertheless, yields to Octavia's request to allow her to try to reconcile himself and Caesar. She who has said that there is "no midway / 'Twixt these extremes at all" is "[her]self [to] go between [them]" (3.4.25). The private is to mediate between the private. Antony couples his granting Octavia's request with a warning or threat to Caesar. "The meantime, lady, / I'll raise the preparation of a war / Shall stain your brother" (3.4.25–27). Antony's preparations for war will eclipse Caesar's. "Make your soonest haste," Antony urges, "So your desires are yours" (3.4.27–28). Not only are Octavia's chances small; time is short and works against them.

Unable to pray for one against the other, Octavia now prays ardently for both. "The Jove of power make me, most weak, most weak, / Your reconciler!" (3.4.29–20). Despite or because her only power is that of love, Octavia is "most weak." But as weak as she is, her task could hardly be greater. "Wars 'twixt you twain would be / As if the world should cleave, and that slain men / Should solder up the rift" (3.4.30–32). War between the two triumvirs would be as though the world had split in two, and only the countless consequent corpses could rejoin the contending camps.

Octavia has spoken of her equal loves of Antony and Caesar, but nothing about who is to blame for the present threat of war. The closest she came was to ask Antony not to believe or resent what he has heard. Antony now ties together the issues of love and blame. "When it appears to you where this begins," he says, referring to cause of the present quarrel, "Turn your displeasure that way, for our faults / Can never be so equal that your love / Can equally move with them" (3.4.33–36). Blame must lessen love. And so, since the faults of Antony and of Caesar cannot be so evenly balanced, neither can Octavia's love. Where Octavia wishes to reconcile her loves, Antony denies the possibility. Octavia must choose between, not stand "midway" between, them. Caesar's provocations and Antony's sense of honor, if nothing else, make reconciliation impossible.

Act Three, Scene Five

Antony told Octavia that Caesar has made war against Pompey, contrary to the Misena agreement (3.4.3–4). Eros now reports that Lepidus joined him in the fight and that

Caesar, having made use of him in the wars 'gainst Pompey, presently denied him rivality; would not let him partake in the glory of the action; and, not resting here, accuses him of letters he had formerly wrote to Pompey; upon his own appeal, seizes him.

(3.5.6–11)

Having deceived Pompey with the pretense of peace and Lepidus with that of friendship,[26] Caesar used Lepidus, whose naval forces he needed, to defeat Pompey in Sicily. Then, having used him, he refused to reward him, accusing Lepidus, instead, of secretly dealing with Pompey, stripped him of his triumviral powers and banished him to an isolated promontory in southwest Italy.[27] No longer needed, Lepidus was no longer kept.[28] "So the poor third is up, till death enlarge his confine" (3.5.11–12). The third triumvir of the world is held prisoner, and only death can release him from his confinement.

Enobarbus clearly grasps the political consequence. "Then, world, thou hast a pair of chaps, no more, / And throw between them all the food thou hast, / They'll grind the one the other" (3.5.13–15). Echoing Octavia's grim vision (3.4.30–32), Enobarbus describes a war between Antony and Caesar in which the two sides, grinding against each other like two voracious jaws, do not stop until they have consumed each other.

Antony, Eros says, is walking in his garden and, kicking at what lies before him, "cries, 'Fool Lepidus!' / And threats the throat of that his officer / That murdered Pompey" (3.5.17–19).[29] Lepidus and the officer are guilty of the same folly. Lepidus and Pompey, whatever their weaknesses, helped to provide a balance of power among the Roman rulers. Caesar could not successfully battle Antony if Antony had the support of at least one of them, nor could Antony successfully battle Caesar if Caesar had such support. The delicate balance kept the peace, though not without sporadic lapses—lapses which were largely kept in check by the fear of a combined opposition. If the Romans are in danger from themselves when they have no foreign danger to fear, that domestic danger is—or, now, was—at least limited by the ever-shifting alliances of the weaker parties. As with first triumvirate of Caesar, Pompey and Crassus, when the three parties are reduced to two, the two quickly become one.[30] Accordingly, as the elimination of Pompey and Lepidus removes a final impediment to Caesar's plans against Antony, Antony's navy is rigged "[f]or Italy and Caesar" (3.5.20).

Hearing that Antony wants to see him right away, Enobarbus remarks, "'Twill be naught" (3.5.22). Enobarbus, whose "naught" is ambiguous, speaks more wisely than he realizes. He seems to mean that Antony wants to speak about something that will come to nothing ("naught"). But "naught" could also mean "disastrous" (see 2.3.36; 3.10.1; 4.15.82). In fact, it will mean both. Antony will not proceed to Italy, and his failure will prove disastrous. The former sense of "naught" will produce the latter.

Act Three, Scene Six

1.

Antony seemed to think that victory over the Parthians would allow him to eclipse Caesar in Rome. By celebrating a triumph in Rome for the victory, he would become sole ruler of the world. But whether because he has once again proved himself a slave to Cleopatra, or whether because Caesar has quickly eliminated Pompey and Lepidus and, gaining control of the seas, has impeded his return, Antony has celebrated a triumph in Alexandria rather than in Rome. Instead of winning their honor and support, he has outraged and horrified the Romans.[31]

Caesar describes the extraordinary spectacle of Antony's display of contempt for Rome ("Contemning Rome" [3.6.1]). Flouting Rome's ancient ways, Antony adopted foreign and hostile ways in their place.[32] Although the Romans have always detested the title of king,[33] Antony presented himself as an Oriental monarch proclaiming a dynasty. Seated amid the people on a throne of gold atop a silver platform (". . . on a tribunal silvered, / . . . in chairs of gold"), he and Cleopatra were "publicly enthroned" (3.6.3–5). At their feet sat "Caesarion, whom they call my father's son, / And all the unlawful issue that their lust / Since then hath made between them" (3.6.6–8).[34] As Caesar describes it, Antony's defiant display smacked of Eastern luxury and extravagance, Asian monarchy and subservience, and Egyptian sensuality and dynastic rule.[35] It is no surprise that Caesar refers to Caesarion as "whom they call my father's son." Despite his very young age, Caesarion, as already noted, is Octavius's rival for the important claim of being Julius Caesar's son: Caesarion by bastard birth, Octavius by posthumous adoption. As the Roman people's honoring Sextus Pompey for his father's deeds seems to show (1.3.50–51), imperial rule tends to be hereditary rule. Since Octavius's position as a triumvir rests in no small part on Julius Caesar's name and parentage—"You, boy, . . . owe everything to a name—" (quoted from Antony, Cicero, *Philippics*, 13.24–25)[36]—, Antony is evidently trying to weaken Octavius's claim to being Caesar's political heir by pointing up that Caesarion has no less title than Octavius to being called Caesar's son.[37] Moreover, by presenting himself as Cleopatra's consort, Antony can claim to be the boy's stepfather, thus bolstering his own claim to being Caesar's legitimate successor. For sound reasons, Caesar will waste no time to hunt down and kill Caesarion.[38] "Too many Caesars is not good" (quoted from Areius, Plutarch, *Antony*, 81.2; North, 6:83).

Instead of presenting his spoils to Capitoline Jupiter, Antony gave them to Cleopatra as she sat on the throne dressed "[i]n th' habiliments of the goddess Isis" (3.6.17).[39] He celebrated in Egypt a sacred victory that could be celebrated only in Rome.[40] "This greatly offended the Romans . . . when they saw that for Cleopatra's sake he deprived his country of [its] due honor and glory, only to gratify the Egyptians" (Plutarch, *Antony*, 50.4: North, 6:53). Caesar lists Antony's political gifts to Cleopatra and Antony's sons by her. To her, he gave the rule of Egypt and made her "[a]bsolute Queen" (3.6.11) of lower Syria, Cyprus and Lydia. To their elder son, Alexander, he gave the newly conquered lands of Great Media, Parthia and Armenia. And, to their younger son, Ptolemy, he assigned Syria, Cilicia and Phoenicia. Antony also proclaimed the sons "kings of kings" (3.6.13). In a single stroke, he restored and even augmented the Ptolemaic empire at its height. As Caesar strongly suggests, Antony has not only denied the Romans the spoils that are properly theirs. Having submitted himself to an Egyptian queen presenting herself as a foreign goddess, he has placed himself at war with the Roman gods as well as with Rome itself.[41] Antony's victory over Caesar would be Egypt's victory over Rome. Rather than ruling Egypt, Rome, conquered by its conquest, would be ruled by despotic Egyptian monarchs claiming to be divine. Antony's infatuation for the Egyptian queen thus threatens not only his capture by her, but Rome's. It portends the shift of the capital of the world from Rome to Alexandria, from West to East.[42]

Maecenas and Agrippa, eager to turn public opinion further against Antony, want the Romans to hear Caesar's report. "[Q]ueasy with his insolence already," Agrippa says, the Romans will withdraw "their good thoughts . . . from him" (3.6.21, 22). Caesar, losing no time, has already informed the people: "The people knows it" (3.6.23).[43]

Caesar tells that Antony has made his own accusations. Referring to himself formally by name or title ("Caesar") and the regal first-person plural ("we" [3.6.25, 26, 30]), he says that Antony has accused him of failing to give him his due portion of the spoils conquered from Pompey in Sicily and of failing to restore the ships that Antony had lent him, ones which he used against Pompey.[44] And Antony is angry that Caesar has expelled Lepidus from the triumvirate and retained all his money.[45] Caesar, demonstrating his customary alacrity, has already answered the accusations ("'Tis done already, and the messenger gone" [3.6.32]). While silent about the unrestored ships and the confiscated wealth, he says he told Antony that "Lepidius was grown too cruel, / That he his high authority abused / And did deserve his change"

120 ∽ New Heaven, New Earth

(3.6.33–35). Caesar does not explain his charge. In a way, it does not matter. Whatever excuse Lepidus handed him for removing him from power,[46] Caesar simply shrugs off Antony's protest. Preemptory toward Lepidus, he is imperious toward Antony. "For what I have conquered," Caesar continues, as though offering reasonable terms, "I grant him part; but then in his Armenia / And other of his conquered kingdom, I / Demand the like" (3.6.35–38). The lands which Caesar is demanding include much of those he will soon accuse Antony of having given to foreign kings. Were he to agree to Caesar's proposed exchange, Antony would lose the political, military and financial support which those new allies provide. Maecenas has no trouble seeing Antony's likely response: "He'll never yield to that" (3.6.38). Caesar, by no means disappointed, seems to welcome Antony's refusal: "Nor must not then be yielded to in this" (3.6.39). Antony's refusal will be Caesar's pretext for his own refusal.

2.

Octavia enters with several attendants, and Caesar immediately calls her a "castaway," saying that she has "stolen upon" him (3.6.41, 43). Indignant that she comes without the pomp and ceremony appropriate to "Caesar's sister" and "[t]he wife of Antony" (3.6.44), he describes with uncharacteristic bombast what her train should have been. Octavia should have an army for an usher and the neighs of horses telling of her approach long before she is seen. More than that, the trees along the way should have been filled with men waiting to see her procession pass by. Still more, the dust stirred up by her many troops should have reached the roof of heaven. "We should have met you / By sea and land," Caesar says, "supplying every stage / With an augmented greeting" (3.6.54–56). Caesar thus describes a victorious general's magnificent return to Rome. Octavia's return should have resembled that of a triumphant general, whose glory is measured by the numbers and quality of the people turning out to greet him, and by the place where he is met: The greater the distance from Rome, the greater the honor.[47] "But you are come / A market maid to Rome," Caesar says with the strongest disapproval, "and have prevented / The ostentation of our love which, left unshown, / Is often left unloved" (3.6.51–54). Caesar's objection, uniting the show of love and love itself, suggests that love must be shown in order to arouse love. Left unshown, it is often unknown. Caesar, who is not likely to lose her love, seems to fear that his lost opportunity to welcome Octavia in such an extravagant fashion may cost him an opportunity to arouse popular sympathy for her and to produce popular opposition toward Antony and popular love for himself. His public display of love would serve to contrast the virtuous, abandoned

Octavia and the dissolute, seductive Cleopatra, and, consequently, the two men who love them—one exemplifying Roman virtues, the other, Oriental vices.

Octavia, correcting his implicit blame of Antony, tells Caesar that she was not constrained, but came as she did on her free will (see 3.4.36–38). Then, saying that Antony told her of Caesar's preparations for war, she explains that she begged him for permission to return. Caesar, turning her protest around, is ready with the charge of Antony's infidelity: "Which soon he granted, / Being an abstract 'tween his lust and him" (3.6.61–62). Antony quickly granted Octavia's request because her return to Rome made it easier for him to return to Cleopatra. Octavia doubts the charge ("Do not say so, my lord" [3.6.63]). But Caesar supports it, first, with the boast that he has spies watching Antony who report to him from everywhere (". . . on the wind" [3.6.64]) and, then, with a confirmatory question, "Where is he now?" (3.6.65). Octavia's incorrect answer ("[I]n Athens" [3.6.65]) allows Caesar to strengthen his accusation by mocking the ease by which Cleopatra summoned Antony: "No, / My most wronged sister. Cleopatra hath / Nodded him to her" (3.6.66–67).

Caesar quickly turns to the issue of war. Where Antony blamed him for his war preparations, Caesar blames him for his own: "He hath given his empire / Up to a whore, who are now levying / The kings o'th' earth for war" (3.6.67–69).[48] Caesar lists ten kings and kingdoms, stretching from Thrace to Media, from Paphlagonia to Libya, to whom Antony has given land and power. While accusing Antony of squandering Roman provinces on an Egyptian whore, he overlooks that Antony's actions may have been in response to his own failure to support him and that they serve Antony's political and military rather than his amorous interests. While punishing client kings who had previously sided with the Parthians, the grants replace them with kings who belong to no established dynasty and therefore owe their positions to Antony.[49] What Caesar presents as an effect of Antony's erotic enslavement may well be an example of astute political judgment. Despite what he suggests here, Caesar will adopt a policy very similar to Antony's in the East.[50] His action will vindicate Antony's.

Her worst fear coming true, Octavia deplores the looming war between Antony and Caesar: "Ay me, most wretched, / That have my heart parted betwixt two friends / That does afflict each other!" (3.6.78–80). Octavia, who still calls Antony her "friend," says nothing about his abandoning her. Her heart is broken not by his having betrayed her, but by her having to choose between two warring friends. Octavia's lack of recrimination will only add to the people's love and pity for her and their hostility toward

Antony. Unintentionally, she will damage Antony by not blaming him. "[T]hinking no hurt, she did Antony great hurt. For her honest love and regard to her husband made every man hate him when they saw he did so unkindly use so noble a lady" (Plutarch, *Antony*, 54.2; North, 6:56–57).

Caesar finally welcomes Octavia ("Welcome hither" [3.6.80]). Using royal plural pronouns thrice in three lines (3.6.81–83), he explains that her letters prevented him from attacking Antony, until he realized how misguided ("wrong led" [3.6.82]) she was in trying to keep the peace and how much danger he faced through negligence. His explanation tacitly confesses that Antony bought time with his marriage. It kept Caesar from attacking him. Urging her to cheer her heart, Caesar exhorts Octavia to have stoic patience. "Be you not troubled with the time, which drives / O'er your content these strong necessities," he counsels, "But let determined things to destiny / Hold unbewailed their way" (3.6.84–87). Octavia should not allow herself to be troubled with the present circumstances, whose necessary events trample over her happiness, but should instead let predestined events go unlamented to their destined end. Except for (disingenuously) blaming Antony's end on their "[u]nreconciliable" "stars" (5.1.46–47), Caesar nowhere else alludes to necessity or destiny. Elsewhere, when he says that something has been "[d]etermine[d]," he means chosen by him (5.1.59). Here, he tries to present his choosing to go to war as impersonal destiny. It is Fate, not he or his ambition, that has determined the situation, and one should not lament what cannot be avoided. Thus, welcoming her again and declaring that nothing is dearer to him than she, Caesar claims that his war is the gods' justice for Antony's abuse of her: "You are abused / Beyond the mark of thought, and the high gods, / To do you justice, makes his ministers / Of us and those that love you" (3.6.88–91). This is the only time Caesar mentions "justice" or anything like it.[51] After Agrippa and Maecenas join in welcoming her, and Maecenas repeats how Antony has outraged her, Caesar concludes by urging Octavia to accustom herself to patience: "Sister, welcome. Pray you / Be ever known to patience. My dear'st sister!" (3.6.99–100). Despite what he says about his "lov[ing]" "[his] dear'st sister," this is the last time Caesar ever mentions Octavia.[52] He forgets her once she has fulfilled her function.

Act Three, Scene Seven

1.

The scene shifts to Actium, a headland on the northwest coast of Greece, where Antony is getting ready for battle. A sign of the expansion of the Roman world, all three of the battles to decide Rome's fate—Philippi, Pharsalus and Actium—occur not in Italy, but in Greece, where West and East meet. With Enobarbus openly and impatiently objecting, Cleopatra insists that she will take part in the battle. Asked why it is "fit" that she fight, she answers, switching to the royal plural pronoun, "Is't not denounced against us?" (3.7.4, 5). By "fit," Enobarbus means suited to the conditions. Cleopatra, on the other hand, means deserving. Caesar has declared ("denounced") war not against Antony, but against only her. He intends to emphasize that the war is not a civil war, but a conflict between Egypt and Rome. The war's purported purpose is to prevent Cleopatra from becoming the Egyptian empress of Rome. Moreover, fully expecting him to remain with her and fight for her, Caesar has sought to present Antony as a traitor to Rome—as having of his own accord taken up war against his own country for the sake of an Egyptian queen, even though no fellow countryman had caused him any personal harm whatever.[53]

Cleopatra, insisting on legal propriety, plays into his hands. Since war has been declared against her, "Why should not we / Be there in person?" she asks (3.7.5–6). Enobarbus responds with a ribald jest: "Well, I could reply / If we should serve with horse and mares together, / The horse were merely lost. The mares would bear / A soldier and his horse" (3.7.6–9). Notwithstanding the great natural spiritedness of horses,[54] a horse's sexual desire would immediately and completely overwhelm it (see 1.5.21–23), and so the horse would lose its military function. It is not clear whether Cleopatra hears Enobarbus's joke or simply pretends not to ("What is't you say?" [3.7.9]). Enobarbus, instead of repeating, bowdlerizes what he said: "Your presence needs must puzzle Antony, / Take from his heart, take from his brain, from's time / What should not then be spared" (3.7.10–13). Enobarbus, although he would prefer to be impudent and obscene, speaks sensibly: Cleopatra would be a paralyzing distraction. Antony's concern for her would draw his attention away from the battle. Enobarbus then adds a political consideration. "[Antony] is already / Traduced for levity, and 'tis said in Rome / That Photinus, an eunuch and your maids / Manage this war" (3.7.12–15). According to the talk in Rome, eunuchs and serving maids conduct Antony's military affairs.[55]

Cleopatra will have none of Enobarbus's political objection. She first curses Rome and the censuring Romans ("Sink Rome, and their tongues rot / That speak against us!" [3.7.15–16]). Then she reasserts more strongly that she will take part: "A charge we bear i'th' war, / And, as the president of my kingdom, will / Appear there for a man" (3.7.16–18). Cleopatra, repeating the royal pronoun, offers a new reason for her to fight. She has contributed money and ships. Therefore, she says, as the ruler of her kingdom, she will "[a]ppear there for a man." What she means is not immediately clear. "[F]or a man" could mean "as though" or "in the capacity of" a man, "in support of" or "to help" a man, or "from a desire for" or "in order to win or keep" a man. The first implies that Cleopatra would usurp the prerogative of a man; the second, that she would fight in behalf of a man; the third, that she would fight to impress or please a man. She could well mean all three. Intending her declaration to be final, Cleopatra, silencing Enobarbus's objection, orders, "Speak not against it!" and then announces determinately, "I will not stay behind" (3.7.18–19). It is striking that Cleopatra, who has mentioned Fulvia more than anyone else has,[56] does not cite her as a Roman precedent. Although Fulvia is dead, Cleopatra seems still to consider her a rival. Jealousy trumps aptness, even when it concerns the dead.

2.

The second part of scene 7 is the central part of the central scene of the central act of *Antony and Cleopatra*. It concerns Antony's needless and disastrous decision to battle Caesar at sea. Only Cleopatra agrees with him. All the others vehemently disagree.

Antony is surprised at how rapidly Caesar has crossed from the heel of Italy and captured a town near Actium. "Is it not strange, Canidius," he asks his victorious lieutenant in Armenia and now commander of his land forces at Actium,[57] "That from Tarentum and Brundusium / He could so quickly cut the Ionian sea / And take in Toryne?" (3.7.20–23). Enobarbus and Eros said that Antony was ready to cross the sea and fight Caesar ("Our great navy's rigged" "[f]or Italy and Caesar" (3.5.19–20). And Plutarch reports that, notwithstanding his defeat of Pompey and Lepidus, Caesar had been afraid Antony, then well prepared, would force him to fight the war during the previous summer. But despite the decisive advantage that time and place can be in war, Antony delayed, just as he has at other crucial moments, and his opportunity slipped away.[58] Antony asks Cleopatra whether she has heard about Caesar's swift crossing, and although she has often caused his delay (e.g., 1.2.122–23; 1.4.57, 73–74; 2.1.20–21, 33–39; 2.6.49–52), she rebukes him for his slowness: "Celerity is never more admired / Than by the negligent" (3.7.24–25). Antony's surprise at Caesar's speed reflects not so much on the swift as on the slow. Antony, heartily approving her rebuke, commends Cleopatra for speaking like a manly man: "A good rebuke, / Which might have well becomed the best of men, / To taunt at slackness" (3.7.25–27). Cleopatra's manly rebuke shows that she is fit for command.[59]

Antony, in his next breath, announces, "Canidius, we / Will fight with [Caesar] by sea," and Cleopatra immediately agrees: "By sea—what else?" (3.7.27–28). Cleopatra speaks as if there could be no other way to fight the battle. Antony and his men, however, have often fought successfully on land, but never a major battle at sea. And Caesar's navy has recently defeated Pompey's formidable fleet.[60] Thus Canidius asks Antony why they will fight at sea. Antony's fleet is largely Cleopatra's and, as Plutarch suggests, Antony may want Cleopatra to have the glory of victory (Plutarch, *Antony*, 62.1). The victory would indeed be Egypt's over Rome. But Antony does not say that he wants to please Cleopatra, though he could hardly say so if it were true. Instead, he attributes his decision to Caesar's dare: "For that he dares us to't" (3.7.29). He will fight at sea because Caesar has challenged him to. It is a question of spirited honor or manly virtue, not of erotic enthrallment. A challenge, however, is only as honorable as he who makes it. Enobarbus therefore quickly points out that Caesar has rebuffed Antony's daring him to a single fight. And Canidius adds that Caesar has also ignored Antony's daring him to wage the forthcoming battle at Pharsalia, where Caesar and Pompey the Great fought.[61] "But these offers, / Which serve not for his vantage, he shakes off, / And so should you" (3.7.32–34). Since Caesar acts for his advantage rather than for his honor, Antony should ignore his challenge, for there can be no honor at stake in a challenge coming from someone simply calculating his advantage. Caesar's challenge is nothing more than a trap to force Antony to fight from his weakness.[62]

Enobarbus thus outlines Antony's drawbacks at sea. Antony's ships are not well manned. His mariners are mule drivers and migrant crop gatherers, forced into service,[63] while many of Caesar's sailors have often fought against Pompey. Nor are Antony's ships favorable. While Caesar's are light and easily managed, Antony's are heavy and hard to handle.[64] "No disgrace / Shall fall you for refusing him at sea, / Being prepared for land" (3.7.38–40). And when Antony nevertheless insists, "By sea, by sea" (3.7.40), Enobarbus argues that, by fighting at sea, Antony would throw away his supreme generalship ("absolute soldiership") on land, divide and perhaps demoralize ("[d]istract") his forces, which consist mostly of veteran foot soldiers ("war-marked footmen"), fail to use his own "renowned knowledge" and thus "quite forgo / The way which promises assurance; and / Give up [him]self merely to chance and hazard / From firm security" (3.7.41–48). Antony can win only by fortune at sea. What he sees as a challenge to his virtue or honor would, on the contrary, prevent him from showing or proving his virtue or defending his honor in the fight.

Antony is unmoved: "I'll fight at sea" (3.7.48). And Cleopatra, answering Enobarbus, boasts, "I have sixty sails, Caesar none better" (3.7.49). She and Antony, she insists, are not overmatched at sea. Antony finally sketches a strategy. His forces will burn their "overplus" of ships "[a]nd with the rest full-manned, from th'head of Actium / Beat th'approaching Caesar" (3.7.51–52). And if they fail, "We then can do't at land" (3.7.53). Antony tacitly concedes Enobarbus's first point. He will burn some of his ships so he can fully man the rest. He does not have a surplus of ships, but a shortage of sailors.[65] Antony suggests that he will fight Caesar's approaching forces by staying close to the shore ("from th'head of Actium / Beat th'approaching Caesar"). His crews must maintain a tight formation and deny Caesar sea room to use his superior numerical strength and greater agility. They must guard against letting the enemy outflank or sail through their formation to attack them from behind. Antony, while thus permitting Caesar to take the offensive and strike first, appears to assume that his land troops will remain loyal even if his ships are defeated.

When a messenger confirms that Caesar has captured Troyne and has been seen there, Antony is incredulous. "Can he be there in person? 'Tis impossible; / Strange that his power should be" (3.7.56–57).[66] Antony marvels that Caesar's army, perhaps even only an advance party, has occupied Troyne. It seems impossible to him that Caesar himself could already be there.

Antony gives Canidius instructions for the land forces. Canidius is to hold Antony's nineteen legions and twelve thousand cavalry while Antony fights at sea.[67] The contrast between Antony's small navy and large army emphasizes his bravado in taking the riskier action first.[68]

"Away, my Thetis!" Antony bids Cleopatra (3.7.60). Thetis, the most famous of the Nereides, is a sea nymph or sea goddess—"watry Thetis," "The Lady of the sea" (Ovid, *Metamorphoses*, 11.221, 228; Golding, 11.251, 260). And Cleopatra, whom women dressed as the Nereides served when she captured Antony's heart on the Cydnus (2.2.216–19), has just led Antony to fight at sea. Moreover, just as Thetis guided Jason and the Argonauts through the hazards of the Scylla and Charybdis with the aid of the Nereides (Apollodorus, 1.9.25), Cleopatra offers to help Antony in the hazards of his sea battle with Caesar. But if Antony's name for Cleopatra seems fitting, it also seems foreboding. For Peleus, her ardent suitor, had to capture Thetis while she took on any shape she pleased—"shifted oftentimes her shape" (Ovid, *Metamorphoses*, 11.221; Golding, 11.276). And after they were married, Peleus abandoned Thetis and, at least according one account, was reunited with her only in death (Euripides, *Andromache*, 1255ff.). With unwitting irony, Antony's fond moniker for Cleopatra captures not only their magnificent past, but their momentous present and their mournful future.

A "worthy soldier" (3.7.60) enters and, addressing Antony as "noble Emperor" while at the same time violating all bounds of military discipline, urges him not to "fight by sea. / Trust not to rotten planks" (3.7.61–62). For the Soldier, who is devoted to Antony and has evidently fought for him many times before, the issue is not a matter of tactics, but of trust: "Do you misdoubt / This sword and these my wounds?" (3.7.62–63). The man's wounds are witness to his loyalty and courage.[69] Moreover, fighting on land rather than on water goes together with manly strength and pride. "Let th'Egyptians / And the Phoenicians go a-ducking," the Soldier disparagingly tells Antony (in the presence of the Egyptian queen); "we / Have used to conquer standing on the earth / And fighting foot to foot" (3.7.63–66).[70] Where the seagoing, effeminate Egyptians and Phoenicians dive into the water and cringe or bow from fear ("a-ducking"), the Romans are accustomed to standing on firm ground and standing tall from pride. They fight man-to-man, face-to-face, "foot to foot." For Antony to choose to fight at sea is thus for him to doubt or deny the manliness of his men. Antony, however, disregards the Soldier's protest. "Well, well, away!" he dismissingly replies, and leaves (3.7.66).

3.

The last part of the scene is paired with the first. In the first, Enobarbus disputed Cleopatra's taking part in the battle. In the last, Canidius and the Soldier dispute Antony's fighting at sea. The former concerned Cleopatra's military presence; the latter, her military strategy. The two parts, framing the play's central section, are also equal in length, each containing ten speeches.

The Soldier, swearing by Hercules, the fiercest ancient hero and Antony's claimed ancestor, is certain that he is correct. Canidius strongly agrees: "But his whole action grows / Not in the power on't" (3.7.68–69). Antony's whole course of action, at once reckless and obstinate, perversely disregards his military strengths. "So our leader's led, / And we are women's men" (3.7.69–70). Where a traditional Roman is a man's man,[71] a man led by a woman becomes a woman's man. He becomes unmanly or womanish. The difficulty, Canidius seems to suggest, is not simply that Antony is led by a woman's whim, but that her whim favors an unmanly manner of war, as the Soldier just protested. Tactics and character go together. If the Roman army has traditionally depended on its leaders for its valor,[72] Antony, repudiating manliness even while claiming to affirm it, reverses the effect. The whole is unmanned from the top.

Canidius and the Soldier review Antony's strategy. While giving Canidius complete command of the legions and the cavalry, Antony has divided command of his fleet among four lieutenants.[73] Evidently expecting the important action on the wings, he has broken up the naval command to increase the fleet's quickness and agility on the flanks. Canidius, using the military metaphor of a projectile's forward motion, remarks on the amazing speed of Caesar's forces crossing from Italy: "This speed of Caesar's / Carries beyond belief" (3.7.74–75). The Soldier, however, corrects him. "While [Caesar] was yet in Rome," he explains, "His power went out in such distractions as / Beguiled all spies" (3.7.75–77). Caesar's forces appear to have moved so swiftly because, clustered in small groups, they were able to avoid being seen by Antony's spies. His detachments ("distractions") serving as diversions ("distractions"), his ruse appears as his rapidity. Antony was not so much slow to attack Caesar crossing the sea as he was deceived by him. The upcoming battle is now producing its own fast pace of events. When a messenger arrives to tell him that Antony is calling for him, Canidius remarks, "With news the time's in labour, and throws forth / Each minute some" (3.7.80–81). The time gives birth to news every minute. War sets its own rapid tempo.

Act Three, Scene Eight

We see the opposing sides, briefly, by turns. Caesar tells his lieutenant not to strike by land. "[K]eep whole; provoke not battle / Till we have done at sea" (3.8.3–4). Antony said that he could fight on land if he faltered at sea; Caesar will fight on land after they are done at sea. Where a land battle is Antony's backup plan, it is Caesar's mop-up plan. Caesar allows his officer no discretion: "Do not exceed / The prescript of this scroll" (3.8.4–5). Caesar's orders are written down and not to be departed from.[74] Caesar, expecting Antony's land forces to have no heart to fight after losing at sea, makes clear that he expects the sea battle to decide the outcome: "Our fortune lies / Upon this jump" (3.8.5–6).

Act Three, Scene Nine

While Caesar gives his officer set written orders, Antony directs Enobarbus to act according to what he sees of Caesar's forces. Antony's land troops are to go on a certain hill from which they can observe Caesar's line of battle and the number of his ships, "[a]nd so proceed accordingly" (3.9.4). Where Caesar's battle plan is fixed, Antony's is flexible. The difference is tactical as well as characteristic. While an offensive force knows what it wants, a defensive force is suspended in uncertainty and must adjust its actions to its opponent's. Permitting Caesar to take and maintain the initiative, Antony must await developments, hoping for the best. As Enobarbus had warned, his success depends on good fortune (3.7.46–48).

Act Three, Scene Ten

The battle of Actium, although not a major military engagement, ranks as one of the Western world's most significant sea battles. Notwithstanding the later fighting at Alexandria (4.7–12), it amounts to Caesar's final victory in his rise to sole power, preparing the way for the institution of the Augustan Principate. It also reestablishes or reaffirms Rome's command over the East. Although largely over before it begins, it marks a turning point for the world.[75]

With the sounds of the sea battle in the background, Enobarbus and Scarus frantically describe the disaster of Cleopatra and then Antony fleeing the fight. Crying out that all has been lost ("Naught, naught, all naught!"), Enobarbus cannot bear to observe any more: "I can behold no longer!" (3.10.1). Cleopatra's flagship and her sixty other ships have taken flight. "To see't mine eyes are blasted" (3.10.4). The sight of such an ignominious action deprives Enobarbus of his sight. The blind act is blinding.

Scarus has seen still worse. Invoking all the gods in despair, disgust and disbelief ("Gods and goddesses! / All the whole synod of them!" [3.10.4–5]), he declares, "The greater cantle of the world is lost / With very ignorance" (3.10.6–7). Through sheer folly, a huge segment of the earth's sphere has been lost. "We have kissed away / Kingdoms and provinces," Scarus thunders with bitter wordplay (3.10.9–10). Then, asked how the fight appears, he fulminates with a series of similes and metaphors, for likenesses lend themselves to hyperbole.[76] Comparing their side to the last stages of the plague, he begins, "On our side, like the tokened pestilence / Where death is sure" (3.10.9–10). Then, with a cluster of outraged, overlapping, obscene puns and metaphors, he curses Cleopatra with a loathsome death: "Yon ribaudred nag of Egypt — / Whom leprosy o'ertake! —" (3.10.10–11). Cleopatra, the ribald-rid nag or whore[77] of Egypt, should be "o'ertake[n]," like an old tired nag, by leprosy. The whore's disease should "o'ertake" (whore-take) the whore.[78] The battle, Scarus says, was undecided and equally favorable to both sides (". . . vantage like a pair of twins appeared / Both as the same") or, as he restates, correcting himself or perhaps angrily exaggerating, even more favorable to Antony's ("—or, rather, ours the elder—" [3.10.12–13]). But then, a gadfly attacking her or a wind filling her sails ("The breeze upon her"),[79] Cleopatra, "[l]ike a cow in June, / Hoists sails and flies" (3.10.14–15). When Enobarbus replies that he saw this and that his eyes, sickened at the sight, could endure to see no more, Scarus describes what Enobarbus did not allow himself to see. Once Cleopatra made ready to sail, "[t]he noble ruin of her magic, Antony," Scarus recounts, using the vivid present tense and likening

Antony to a lovesick duck, "Claps on his sea-wing and, like a doting mallard, / Leaving the fight in height, flies after her" (3.10.19–21). Antony disgraced himself not only as emperor, but as a man. Indeed, Scarus, dropping figurative speech, says he has never seen anything as shameful as Antony's flight. "I never saw an action of such shame. / Experience, manhood, honour, ne'er before / Did violate so itself" (3.10.22–24). Antony's defeat was his debacle.[80]

Canidius, entering, says that Antony's forces could have won at sea. "Had our general / Been what he knew himself, it had gone well" (3.10.26–27). Antony deserted his men because he had deserted himself. He deserted himself in two respects. He acted out of character and was not his own man. Had he been himself—had he shown his courage and had not followed Cleopatra—his fleet would have done well.

Foreshadowed by Menas's desertion of Pompey, Antony's flight sets in motion the many which follow, as Canidius apparently anticipates: "Oh, he has given example for our flight / Most grossly by his own!" (3.10.28–29). Enobarbus, catching his hint, asks whether Canidius is thinking of deserting ("Ay, are you thereabouts?"), adding that if he is, then their cause is finished ("Why, then, good night indeed" [3.10.29–30]). Instead of immediately answering, Canidius reports that Antony and Cleopatra have fled toward the Peloponnesus. Scarus, who will fight again for Antony at Alexandria, says that he will go to the Peloponnesus and wait to see what happens. Canidius, however, declares he will defect to Caesar and hand over his foot soldiers and cavalry, explaining that six kings have already left Antony and "[s]how me the way of yielding" (3.10.35). Just as Antony deserts his men for a foreign queen, Canidius, following the example of foreign kings, deserts him.

Enobarbus, on the other hand, is ambivalent, divided between his loyalty and his reason. "I'll yet follow / The wounded chance of Antony," he says, "though my reason / Sits in the wind against me" (3.10.35–37). Although describing his ambivalence, Enobarbus in effect denies it. He defends his nobility by dividing himself. He ("I," "me") will be loyal to Antony; his ("my") reason, like a contrary wind, urges him to flee. His loyalty comes from within; his disloyalty is prompted from without. Spiritedness tends to simplify or oversimplify the moral world by reducing wholes to parts and taking parts for wholes, particularly when aroused by shame.[81] Enobarbus, accordingly, identifies himself with his loyal part, while alienating his calculating part as though it were external to him. He protects his sense of loyalty by presenting his ambivalence as a conflict between himself and another. It is not he who would deserve shame; his reason would. What would otherwise shame him is not part of him.[82]

Act Three, Scene Eleven

1.

Antony is filled with shame. "Hark! The land bids me tread no more upon't; / It is ashamed to bear me" (3.11.1–2). The land, Antony says, upon which he refused to fight, is now ashamed for him and refuses to support him. Having ignominiously fled at sea, he is left with no ground to stand on. Antony suggests that he has stayed too late in the world. Calling his followers to approach him ("Friends, come hither" [3.11.2]), he describes himself as "so lated in the world" that he has "lost [his] way for ever" (3.11.3, 4). Overtaken by the lateness of the night, he has utterly lost his way.

Antony tells his followers to take his gold, flee and make peace with Caesar. His followers, however, refuse to forsake him ("Fly? Not we" [3.11.6]). As Antony is generous in defeat and solicitous for their safety, they, in turn, are devoted to him. Their ties to him are not simply mercenary. A man of deep love, he is loved by his men.[83]

Antony, echoing Canidius (3.10.26–27), gives his followers a reason to leave him: "I have fled myself" (3.11.7). He fled from battle, because he fled from himself. Antony separates himself from himself, like Enobarbus, but in the contrary fashion. Enobarbus distinguished between himself and his reason. He was the loyal party; his reason, the disloyal party. Antony reverses the parties. "I" is the shameful Antony; "myself," the noble Antony. Antony preserves his noble self, by alienating it and making it the abandoned, offended party. Where Enobarbus, not yet having acted ignobly, alienated the corrupting part of himself by identifying himself with the uncorrupted part, Antony, having acted ignobly, alienates the uncorrupted part by identifying himself with the corrupted part. Both preserve their noble self by separating it, Enobarbus by identifying himself with it, Antony by distinguishing himself from it. Despite his overbearing shame, Antony seeks to maintain his nobility.

Saying that he has instructed cowards by his cowardly example, Antony hints at suicide. "I have myself resolved upon a course / Which has no need of you" (3.11.9–10). Antony wishes to end his shame by ending his life. "Oh, / I followed that I blush to look upon" (3.11.12–13). While shame, perhaps the most reflexive of all passions, involves the self looking at the self, the self, feeling ashamed, wants neither to be seen nor to look. In contrast to pride, which seeks public view, shame seeks privacy or concealment. Pride wishes to display; shame, to disappear.[84] Death would spare Antony from both seeing and being seen.

Antony is unable to continue to maintain his noble self. In saying "I followed that I blush to look upon," he no longer clearly distinguishes between his noble and ignoble self. As before, he divides himself. But instead of sep-arating himself from himself so as to preserve his noble self, he distinguishes between a present "I" that feels shame and a past "I" that acted shamefully. The distinction is merely temporal. Extending the psychic slippage, Antony goes on to describe himself as divided between two mutually recriminating parties: "My very hairs do mutiny, for the white / Reprove the brown for rash-ness, and they them / For fear and doting" (3.11.13–15). In place of a noble and an ignoble self, a contemptuous and a contemptible self, there are now simply two contemporaneous parts blaming each other. An older ("white") part reproves a younger ("brown") part for rashness, while the younger re-proves the older for fear and infatuation. In the mutuality of the recrimina-tions, even the distinction between Antony's past and present "I" vanishes.

Antony himself soon vanishes in shame. Bidding his followers to go, Antony promises to give them letters to help clear their way to Caesar. The letters will, presumably, commend the men for loyal service by stating that they did not abandon Antony, but rather he urged them to leave. Their loy-alty to their leader may be trusted. Antony, entreating them ("Pray you . . ." [3.11.17]), asks his followers not to look sad or to speak of their reluctance to go, but instead to "take the hint / Which my despair proclaims" (3.11.18–19). They should see from his despair that his situation is desperate and take the opportunity to escape. "Let that be left / Which leaves itself," he urges (3.11.19–20). A moment ago, Antony described his self-recrimina-tion in the present tense ("My very hairs do mutiny, for the white / Reprove the brown . . . , and they them . . ."). Now, he describes his self-abandonment in the present tense (". . . leaves itself"). The shameful act, he suggests, is ha-bitual or characteristic, not past or complete. His previous self-divisions also used personal pronouns ("I . . . myself," "I . . . I . . . ," "My . . ."). Now, he avoids using any personal pronoun, but, instead, replaces them with the im-personal pronouns "that" and "itself" (". . . that . . . / Which leaves itself"), pronouns which, in addition, have no antecedent. Just as Antony finds his existence in his honor, he loses it in his dishonor: "If I lose mine honour, I lose myself" (3.4.22).[85]

Antony also loses his ability to command. Concluding his sad, shame-stricken speech, he shows as well as states his inability to give orders: "Leave me, I pray, a little—pray you, now; / Nay, do so; for indeed I have lost com-mand; / Therefore, I pray you" (3.11.22–24). Antony uses the beseeching "pray" four times in the speech, thrice in the last three lines (3.11.17, 22 [twice], 24), the only times he mentions the word in the play. No longer able to command, he begs his men to do as he asks them to do. Unable to order, he is now forced to entreat.[86]

2.

Eros tries to reconcile Antony and Cleopatra. But Antony, utterly hopeless, neither hears him nor notices Cleopatra's presence. Buried in anguished thoughts, he can do nothing but think of his glorious past. He cannot think of it, however, without exaggerating or distorting it. He says that Caesar never drew his sword at Philippi ("kept / His sword e'en like a dancer"), "while I struck / The lean and wrinkled Cassius, and 'twas I / That the mad Brutus ended" (3.11.35–38). Plutarch says that Caesar, conveniently ill, never fought at Philippi: "As for Octavius Caesar himself, he was not in his camp, because he was sick" (Plutarch, *Brutus*, 41.1; North, 6:223). Shakespeare, true to his source, shows Caesar before and after the battle, but not during it (JC, 5.1.63–66; 5.5.52). Caesar's soldiers fought for him in his absence.[87] But even if he is right about Caesar, Antony did not kill either Cassius or Brutus. Cassius was killed by his Parthian slave, Pindarus, and Brutus by his officer, Strato (JC, 5.3.36ff.; 5.5.44–51; also A&C, 3.2.55–56).[88] Nor is it obvious why Antony calls Brutus "the mad Brutus." Brutus may deserve strong criticism for having pursued an imprudent, self-indulgent and ultimately fatal ethic of intention. Showing good moral intentions was more important to him than achieving good political results.[89] But Antony had praised him as "the noblest Roman of them all" precisely for his intentions: "He only, in a general honest thought / And common good to all, made one of them" (JC, 5.5.68, 71–72). Antony in his misery may confuse Brutus with his namesake and putative ancestor, Junius Brutus. In magnifying his own past achievements, he may go so far as to imagine that he killed not only the last defenders of the Republic but its earliest champion.[90] Whatever the case, Antony repeats his indictment of Caesar: "He alone / Dealt on lieutenantry, and no practice had / In the brave squares of war" (3.11.38–40). Antony overlooks his own practice of fighting and winning glory through his subordinates (2.3.31, 39–41; 3.1.16–17; 4.6.1). "Yet now—no matter," he despondently concludes (3.11.38–40). The contrast which Antony emphasizes or exaggerates between himself and Caesar, while in some sense satisfying his deeply mortified pride, serves to make his present misery even worse. Although gratifying his bitter indignation, it underscores that he has been defeated by a man for whom he has complete contempt.

Antony does not respond when Eros announces Cleopatra's presence, and so Iras urges Cleopatra to approach him. "Go to him, madam; speak to him. / He is unqualitied with very shame" (3.11.43–44). Thorough shame has deprived Antony of all the qualities that make him what or who he is. It has stripped him of his nature or character, as Antony himself suggested. Eros, addressing Antony as "[m]ost noble sir" (3.11.46), tries again, this time warning

Antony that only his comforting can save Cleopatra from death. But Antony still hears nothing, except perhaps Eros's term of address: "I have offended reputation, / A most unnoble swerving" (3.11.49–50). As before, Antony, speaking in Rome's time-honored manner, closely identifies virtue and reputation. Life in republican Rome was public in every respect. Because they held that the only thing in life worth seeking is what is worthy of public praise and renown, the Romans believed that a person's actions should be governed by the estimation of others.[91] As honors were conferred by Rome for deeds performed in behalf of the public good, public honor was thought to confirm noble virtue. The good citizen was the citizen thought to be good. "[T]o scorn fame is to scorn virtue" (quoted, Tacitus, Annals, 4.38). The Romans, finding their virtues in the eyes of fellow citizens, even had the same word for virtue and reputation (honestas), for each was held to imply the other.[92] Paradoxically, Antony never sounds more like a traditional Roman than when he is "unqualitied with very shame." Shame at what he has become makes him sound like what he is not.

Antony finally becomes aware of Cleopatra's presence and immediately blames her for leading him astray: "O, whither hast thou led me, Egypt?" (3.11.51). The shame he feels is not for having been led by love or by a woman, but for having been led astray. Antony claims that his looking back on the ruins of his past prevents Cleopatra from seeing the shame in his face. "See / How I convey my shame out of thine eyes / By looking back what I have left behind / 'Stroyed in dishonour" (3.11.51–54). Shame, heightened by the sense of an onlooker's gaze, dwells largely in the face. As noted earlier, when ashamed, we tend to cover or to avert our face, for the face is a synecdoche for the self. We try, literally, to save face.[93] Yet, by turning his face away from Cleopatra so she cannot see his shame, Antony only stresses what his effort aims to avoid. Hence, his self-contradictory imperative: "See / How I convey my shame out of thine eyes . . ." Antony directs Cleopatra to see what he putatively prevents her from seeing and how he prevents her. His "convey[ance]," though meant to keep her from seeing his shame, draws full attention to it.

Cleopatra, blaming her cowardice ("Forgive my fearful sails!"), pleads her innocence: "I little thought / You would have followed" [3.11.55–56]). Antony is sure that she is being disingenuous. "Egypt," he rebukes her, "thou knewst too well / My heart was to thy rudder tied by th' strings / And thou shouldst tow me after" (3.11.56–58). Antony mixes heartstrings and a ship's tow at sea. Both pull another irresistibly in its own direction.[94] "O'er my spirit / Thy full supremacy thou knewst," he continues, dropping metaphors, "and that / Thy beck might from the bidding of the gods / Command me"

(3.11.58–61). Love, by its nature, commands. Cleopatra knew that the power of Antony's love for her would have prevailed over the authority of the gods. She knew that her mere silent gesture ("[t]hy beck") would have overridden the gods' spoken orders ("bidding").

Cleopatra asks for pardon, but Antony, ignoring her request, stresses what his fallen state will mean for him. He must now send humble offers of peace ("humble treaties") to "the young man," as he contemptuously disparages Caesar,[95] and shuffle and prevaricate ("dodge / And palter") in the desperate ways of those who are humiliated or weak ("in the shifts of lowness"), who, he says, again comparing himself to what he was, "[w]ith half the bulk o'th' world played as I pleased, / Making and marring fortunes" (3.11.62–65). He who had the power to do whatever he wanted with half of the world—he who could play or sport with kingdoms, as he declares using a telling gambler's phrase—must now act like a piteous, powerless pauper. Accusing her again, Antony tells Cleopatra, "You did know / How much you were my conqueror, and that / My sword, made weak by my affection, would / Obey it on all cause" (3.11.67–68). Cleopatra knew that his love for her would enfeeble him as a soldier and cause him to do anything, regardless of what was at stake. Yet, despite expressly accusing her of knowingly causing him to desert and dishonor himself, Antony does not suggest a reason for her action. Neither denying nor granting her claim of cowardice, he says that she knew what she did, but not why she did it.

When Cleopatra, again asking for pardon, sheds tears, Antony instantly melts. "Fall not a tear, I say; one of them rates / All that is won and lost" (3.11.69–70). Asking for a kiss, he says that just one "kiss" of hers ("[e]ven this") "repays me" (3.11.70–71). Antony may magnify the worth of a single tear or kiss of Cleopatra's in order to minimize what he has lost. Insofar as he is "repa[id]," he has lost nothing. Although we might think that his melting to Cleopatra's tears and kiss only heightens his folly, he might think—or wish to think—that it redeems his conduct.

Antony, however, quickly, though tacitly, takes back what he just affirmed. He not only still cares about Caesar's terms for peace ("We sent our schoolmaster. Is a come back?" [3.11.72]). He finds himself forced to acknowledge the greatness of his loss: "Fortune knows / We scorn her most when most she offers blows" (3.11.74–75). Despite his stated equivalency of Cleopatra's kiss to his loss, that loss is Fortune's greatest blow. Antony, nevertheless, tries to minimize his loss by rising above it. He tries to find a moral victory in his military defeat. As he underscores with his dolefully defiant closing couplet and double use of "most," the greater the loss, the greater the victory, for the former provides the opportunity for Antony to display stoic indifference and endurance. Scorn of victory replaces—or Antony wishes it to replace—shame of defeat.

Act Three, Scene Twelve

1.

Antony sends "his schoolmaster" (3.12.2), the teacher of his and Cleopatra's children, as his ambassador to Caesar. For a man who had "superfluous kings for messengers" only recently, his need to send "so poor a pinion of his wing" shows that "he is plucked" (3.12.3–5). Deserted by many friends and scarcely knowing whom to trust,[96] Antony is a once-handsome bird stripped of feathers.

2.

No doubt overwhelmed by his extraordinary circumstances, the Ambassador speaks with an incongruous mixture of showy language and self-depreciation. Ordered by Caesar to approach and speak, he describes his own insignificance with a florid trope. "Such as I am, I come from Antony," he says. "I was of late as petty to his ends / As is the morn-dew on the myrtle leaf / To his grand sea" (3.12.7–10). The man's extravagant disproportion between himself and Antony implies a similar disproportion, intended or otherwise, between Antony formerly and presently. What diminishes the Ambassador, diminishes Antony, too. It measures how far Antony has fallen.

When Caesar, evidently impatient with his attempt at eloquence, curtly tells the man to address the business for which he has come, the Ambassador prefaces Antony's request with his confession of defeat: "Lord of his fortunes he salutes thee" (3.12.11). Caesar is the acknowledged master of Antony's fortunes. The emissary then says that Antony asks to live in Egypt or, if not that, to live—"let him breathe between the heavens and earth," he says with a further flourish (3.12.14)—as a private man in Athens. The Ambassador similarly prefaces Cleopatra's request with her statement of submission to Caesar: "Cleopatra does confess thy greatness, / Submits her to thy might, and of thee craves / The circle of the Ptolemies for her heirs, / Now hazarded to thy grace" (3.12.16–19). Cleopatra, acknowledging her submission to Caesar, asks that the Egyptian crown be kept for her descendants. Caesar dismisses Antony's requests out of hand ("I have no ears to his request" [3.12.20]). Political prudence as well as personal hatred speaks against them. Caesar cannot grant either, but especially the first, without endangering his settlement of the East and his position as sole ruler of the world. Nor does Antony seem to expect to receive the former or perhaps either (". . . which not granted, / He lessens his requests . . ." [3.12.12–13]). Cleopatra's request is similarly problematic. In addition to Caesarion representing a powerful challenge to Caesar's claim to be Julius Caesar's legitimate heir, a Ptolemic dynasty in Egypt would, like Antony's request, threaten Caesar's rule of the East and hence of the world. Cleopatra's fruitless request is the last time the name of the Ptolemies is mentioned.

Caesar, however, hopes to use her request to turn Cleopatra against Antony. He promises, with a series of conditionals and double negatives, that she will not fail to receive a hearing or to obtain what she wishes ("Of audience nor desire shall fail"), provided that ("so") "she / From Egypt drive her all-disgraced friend / Or take his life there. This if she perform, / She shall not sue unheard" (3.12.21–24). Cleopatra will be satisfied, or at least not unsatisfied, if she satisfies Caesar.[97]

3.

As soon as the emissary leaves to deliver Caesar's message, Caesar directs Thidias to use his eloquence to promise Cleopatra whatever she wants in order to separate her from Antony. In contrast to his ordering Taurus not to exceed his written instructions in the battle (3.8.4–5), he tells Thidias to promise Cleopatra, on Caesar's authority, whatever she requests and to add whatever Thidias thinks to mention. Caesar seems certain that Cleopatra's betrayal can be bought. The only question is the price. "Women are not / In their best fortunes strong," Caesar flatly states, perhaps forgetting his sister, "but want will perjure / The ne'er-touch'd vestal" (3.12.29–31). While women even in the happiest of circumstances are not strong, want will make any woman disloyal. Thidias need only be clever ("Try thy cunning, Thidias" [3.12.31]). Thidias himself has a price. "Make thine own edict for thy pains, which we / Will answer as a law" (3.12.32–33). If he succeeds, as Caesar seems to assume he will, Thidias may set his own price and Caesar will pay it as if the price were set by law.[98] Caesar is still concerned about Antony, however. He tells Thidias to watch him closely, observe how he bears his misfortune (". . . becomes his flaw" [3.12.34]), and try to read his state of mind from his outward motions ("And what thou think'st his very action speaks / In every power that moves" [3.12.35–36]). Antony, characteristically at his best in great adversity (see 1.4.56–72), might yet rally his spirit.

Act Three, Scene Thirteen

1.

Cleopatra and Enobarbus both seem hopeless. She is at a loss to know what to do ("What shall we do, Enobarbus?"), and he can suggest only brooding on what has happened and dying of despair ("Think, and die" [3.13.1]). There is no future for either of them other than death, Enobarbus seems to say, though he leaves unclear whether death will come from their despondent thought itself or from their suicides.

Cleopatra asks whether she ("we" [3.13.2]) or Antony is to blame. Enobarbus has no doubt: "Antony only, that would make his will / Lord of his reason" (3.13.3–4). Although Cleopatra fled "[f]rom that great face of war, whose several ranges / Frighted each other" (3.13.5–6), why, he asks, should Antony follow? Enobarbus vindicates his own original judgment. Women are not fit to fight, and men will be distracted by their presence. Eros will subdue valor (3.7.7ff.). "The itch of his affection," Enobarbus says, referring to Antony's erotic passion, "should not then / Have nicked his captainship, at such a point, / When half to half the world opposed, he being / The mered question" (3.13.7–10). While he (not Cleopatra [cp. 3.7.5–6]) was the entire issue in the war, and the war, furthermore, involved half the world against the other half, Antony allowed himself to be emasculated ("nicked")[99] by his sexual desire. The stakes could not have been higher, and yet he shamed himself as the slave of his lust. "'Twas a shame no less / Than was his loss, to course your flying flags / And leave his navy gazing" (3.13.10–13). No longer guided by the sentiments of a commander or a brave man, or even by his own judgment, Antony, ignoring everything else, shamefully abandoned and betrayed the men who were fighting and dying for his cause, and chased after the woman who was his ruin.[100]

2.

Antony and his ambassador enter. The Ambassador has reported Caesar's answer, which Antony now repeats in summary, still referring to himself with a royal pronoun: "The Queen shall then have courtesy, so she / Will yield us up" (3.13.15–16). Although he bids the Ambassador to tell Cleopatra, Antony tells her himself in lurid terms. "To the boy Caesar send this grizzled head," he says, contrasting Caesar's age and his, "And he will fill thy wishes to the brim / With principalities" (3.13.17–19). Cleopatra is evidently horrified or stupefied ("That head, my lord?" [3.13.19]). But rather than allowing her the chance to decide, Antony replies to Caesar with a renewed challenge. Instead of belittling him again as a "boy," he now uses Caesar's youth as a reason for the world to expect something outstanding from him: "Tell him he wears the rose / Of youth upon him, from which the world should note / Something particular" (3.13.20–22). As a man in the bloom of youth, Caesar should show his nobility by some brave action. He should act as young Roman men traditionally have (see 4.4.26–27). Otherwise, Antony continues, what he wins through his subordinates could belong to a coward or a child. Antony wishes to shame Caesar to duel him. As he challenged him before Actium (3.7.30), he now dares him to lay aside all the splendid trappings of his office ("gay caparisons") and "answer me declined, sword against sword, / Ourselves alone" (3.13.26–28). Caesar is to dismiss all of his external advantages and face Antony in a single combat in which personal prowess alone would count. Virtue, not fortune, would determine the outcome. The contest would be a duel of valor for rule of the world.[101]

After Antony leaves with the Ambassador to write the challenge, Enobarbus considers the effect of fortune's blows on men's souls. "Yes, like enough high-battled Caesar will / Unstate his happiness, and be staged to th' show / Against a sworder!" (3.13.29–31). Caesar, commanding great armies, Enobarbus says with bitter sarcasm, is likely to divest himself of the enormous advantages which fortune has given him and descend from his lofty position and be shown upon a public stage as though fighting against a gladiator. Antony may be certain that Caesar would lose, but even if he won, Enobarbus seems to stress, Caesar would lose the dignity which he is always careful to protect. "I see men's judgements are / A parcel of their fortunes," he reflects, once again aphoristically, "and things outward / Do draw the inward quality after them / To suffer all alike" (3.13.31–34). Antony had vowed stoic constancy (3.11.74–75). Enobarbus, implicitly answering him, denies that men's minds can be independent of their fortunes. On the contrary, outward events shape a man's inner being. Rather than the soul mastering fortune, fortune masters the soul. As a man's fortunes decay, so does his judgment. The inner man declines with the outer man. Antony, moreover, should know better, Enobarbus continues. He has known every degree of fortune, from the highest to the lowest, and so he should know how Caesar will reply: "That he should dream, / Knowing all measures, the full Caesar will / Answer his emptiness!" (3.13.34–36).[102] Caesar will never fight someone as weak as Antony, for he would have nothing to gain. If he won, he would keep what he already has; if he lost, he would lose what he has. "Caesar," Enobarbus concludes, "thou hast subdued / His judgement too" (3.13.36–37). Antony's military defeat has produced his mind's defeat.

A servant enters and announces to Cleopatra, "A messenger from Caesar" (3.13.37). Formerly, servants, expressing the deference and respect due to royalty, have addressed her as "dear queen," "[g]ood majesty," "[m]ost gracious majesty," "dread queen," "most dear queen," "good empress" and "your highness" (1.5.9, 41; 2.5.98, 106; 3.3.2, 7, 8; 3.11.26, 33) as well as "lady," "madam," "gracious madam," "gentle madam," and "good madam." This servant, however, omits any locution of honor. "What, no more ceremony?"

Cleopatra asks in dismay. "See, my women, / Against the blown rose they may stop their nose / That kneeled unto the buds" (3.13.39–41). Where Enobarbus sees a person's change of fortune affecting the person himself, Cleopatra sees it affecting others. He sees a person's withering fortunes withering the person's own judgment; she sees it withering the respect others have for him. He sees the effect as internal; she, as external.

Having seen Antony's loss of judgment and the servant's loss of respect for Cleopatra, Enobarbus considers abandoning Antony. "Mine honesty and I begin to square," he says. "The loyalty well held to fools does make / Our faith mere folly" (3.13.42–44). As when he first mentioned the possibility of abandoning Antony ("I'll yet follow / . . . though my reason . . ." [3.10.35–36]), Enobarbus divides and simplifies himself. But whereas previously he identified himself with his loyalty and distinguished himself from his calculation, now he reverses the parties. "[His] honesty" says one thing, he ("I") says the opposite. He identifies himself with the corrupted party, while alienating his honesty. Closer now to acting dishonorably, he, like Antony (3.11.7ff.), separates his honesty from himself in order to preserve it.

Enobarbus, however, introduces another consideration. "Yet," he continues, "he that can endure / To follow with allegiance a fallen lord / Does conquer him that did his master conquer, / And earns a place i'th' story" (3.13.44–47). Enobarbus does not have to choose between honesty and calculation. The two can go together. Loyalty to a fallen lord may not be folly, for it may bring renown. In an earlier day, when disloyalty was considered dishonorable and unforgivable in Rome, loyalty would have been taken for granted. Disloyalty would have been severely punished; loyalty would not have won fame. But men are now free to switch their loyalties as they wish. And so loyalty to a defeated leader can earn honorable renown, precisely because it demonstrates the fortitude to disregard ordinary self-interest. Refusing to bow to the victor, the loyal follower can conquer his master's conqueror by willingly enduring his master's defeat and "earn a place i'th' story."

Enobarbus speaks of allegiance to his "master." Before Actium, the word "master" appeared only once, referring to Pompey's control of the sea (". . . by sea / He is an absolute master" [2.2.172–73]). Beginning now, in the aftermath of Actium, the word appears eighteen times, always as a title or term of address, all but once designating someone with absolute command of, or authority over, another person or other people.[103]

3.

When Thidias enters, Cleopatra will not hear Caesar's reply in private, as Thidias requests. All those present, she tells him, are her friends. Therefore, he should speak to all. Thidias, however, trying to divide Cleopatra and Antony, forcefully but politely distinguishes between her friends and Antony's: "So haply are they friends to Antony" (3.13.51). Neither she nor Antony may be able to trust the other's friends, Thidias suggests. Her interests and Antony's differ. Answering Thidias, Enobarbus, with typical flippant cynicism, defends his loyalty to Antony by saying that Antony, in his present circumstances, needs as many friends as Caesar has or else needs none. Possessing fewer friends than Caesar would be as useless as possessing no friends at all. Having thus emphasized Antony's desperate prospects while appearing to declare his allegiance to him, Enobarbus voices his conditional friendship for Caesar: "If Caesar please, our master / Will leap to be his friend" (3.13.53–54). And since Antony's friends are the friends of one another, they will become the friends of Caesar ("Whose he is we are, and that is Caesar's" [3.13.55]). Taking their cue from Antony, they can be loyal to Antony and still be Caesar's friends. All depends on whether Caesar wants Antony for a friend.

Thidias, ignoring Enobarbus, attempts to cajole Cleopatra. Addressing her as "thou most renowned," he combines generous language and an empty promise: "Caesar entreats / Not to consider in what case thou stand'st / Further than he is Caesar" (3.13.56–58). Caesar is, literally and figuratively, the beginning and the end of the promise. Cleopatra need not be concerned about her situation, but instead consider only that Caesar is Caesar. Thidias, presumably deliberately, leaves unclear whether she should take for granted Caesar's magnanimity to her or his power over her—his generous forgiveness or her hopeless submission. He prods Cleopatra's fear while ostensibly comforting her hope.

Cleopatra appears to take encouragement from his words. "Go on; right royal," she urges Thidias, evidently referring to both Caesar and his generosity as "royal" (3.13.58). Acquitting her of blame, Thidias continues by denying that Cleopatra ever loved Antony: "[Caesar] knows that you embrace not Antony / As you did love, but as you feared him" (3.13.59–60). Where he just tried to color her fear of Caesar as hope, Thidias now exonerates her love of Antony by calling it fear. Since fear constrains or compels and people are responsible only for what they could have done otherwise, fear of Antony acquits Cleopatra. Her love was nothing but fearful calculation.

It is hard to be sure of the tone or tenor of Cleopatra's monosyllabic response: "Oh!" (3.13.60). The exclamation might express surprise, skepticism, scorn, surrender, satisfaction, coyness, incredulity, horror, encouragement or many other things.[104] Cleopatra may be preparing to accept Caesar's promise or simply drawing Thidias on to learn Caesar's plans. Thidias, interpreting her response as confirming his insinuation, continues to exculpate her. "The scars upon your honour, therefore, [Caesar] / Does pity as constrained blemishes, / Not as deserved" (3.13.61–63). Caesar frees Cleopatra from blame, though not from dishonor. Since, in a Roman's eyes, a woman's honor consists in sexual respectability (for which intention does not count),[105] Cleopatra has scars on her honor, but they are undeserved because they were forced upon her and therefore deserve pity rather than blame.

Cleopatra appears to agree. Calling Caesar "a god" and saying that he knows what is true ("What is most right" [3.13.64]), she echoes Thidias's explanation: "Mine honour was not yielded / But conquered merely" (3.13.65–66). She was not Antony's lover, but his helpless prey. As just before, Cleopatra's tone and tenor are uncertain. Cleopatra may be playing false to Antony or playacting to Thidias. Always on stage but never transparent, Cleopatra, the only title character in a Shakespeare tragedy without a soliloquy, typically remains hidden even when in full public view. Like Isis, she is always veiled.[106] Cleopatra is never more opaque, though, than in her exchange with Thidias. Enobarbus, taking her at face value, concludes that she is betraying Antony. "Sir, sir," he apostrophizes Antony, "thou are so leaky / That we must leave thee to thy sinking, for / Thy dearest quit thee" (3.13.67–69). Even those who most love Antony are abandoning him. With these words, Enobarbus leaves. Perhaps to our surprise, he does not desert Antony, but goes to get him and bring him back to stop what he sees as Cleopatra's perfidy.

Caesar wants Cleopatra to ask him to give her what she wants. He wants "[t]o be desired to give" (3.13.71). He wants to be asked because giving shows superiority and strength, while asking another to give acknowledges inferiority and need. To tell "men that value themselves upon their titles, or positions, and have the world at will, . . . *that ever they stood in need of, or were beholden to any man*, is to strike them to the very heart" (Cicero, *De officiis*, 2.69).[107] As is true particularly among the spirited, giving is a form of taking, for it humbles the recipient.[108] Thidias, accordingly, says that it would much please Caesar "[t]hat of his fortunes you should make a staff / To lean upon" (3.13.72–73). Her leaning would lift him still higher. But, Thidias continues, it would "warm [Caesar's] spirits" to hear that Cleopatra had left Antony and "put [her]self under [Caesar's] shroud, / The universal landlord" (3.13.73–76). Caesar is lord of the world. No one remains to contest him. Thidias offers Cleopatra Caesar's protection ("his shroud"), but he describes Caesar as a "landlord" rather than as a ruler. The designation is commercial rather than political. Conquest has turned into commerce. Caesar not only rules, but owns the world. Everything is private, and everyone is his tenant. Rome's universal sovereignty has become the property of a single proprietor.

Cleopatra, who has spoken only briefly to Thidias (all but one of five speeches shorter than a single line), asks his name and makes him her own representative to Caesar. Caesar's emissary to her becomes her emissary to him. "Say to great Caesar this in deputation," she begins, "I kiss his conqu'ring hand. Tell him I am prompt / To lay my crown at's feet, and there to kneel / Till from his all-obeying breath I hear / The doom of Egypt" (3.13.78–82). Cleopatra surrenders to Caesar. Yet, it seems that she does not desert or surrender Antony. Neither confirming nor contradicting Thidias's insinuations, she does not mention Antony at all. She simply submits to Caesar's conquest, making obeisance to him as her conqueror. Ironically, "[her] honour [is] not yielded, / But conquered merely." Circumstances constrain her to act as she does.

Thidias commends Cleopatra for choosing her "noblest course" (3.13.82). As he presents it, nobility is hard to distinguish from utility. "Wisdom and fortune combating together," he says sententiously, "If that the former dare but what it can, / No chance may shake it" (3.13.82–85). Thidias, affecting Stoic wisdom, twists the central Stoic tenet. Stoicism places happiness in virtue and virtue in what a man himself can control. Although no one can control the vicissitudes of fortune, a man can control his disposition toward their effects. So long as nothing external breaks into his will or affects his judgment, no misfortune can touch his soul or disturb his happiness. As Pompey and Antony suggested earlier (2.6.54–56; 3.11.74–75), a Stoic's happiness lies in his self-sufficiency, which his self-mastery sustains.[109] Stoicism thus teaches that fortune cannot shake the wisdom of Stoic virtue. He who regards virtue as the only good and is therefore indifferent to external goods, cannot lose his happiness. Wisdom renders him immune to the blows of fortune. Thidias speaks of "wisdom," but he means prudent calculation, not Stoic self-mastery. If one limits one's daring to what one knows one can accomplish, then no misfortune can shake one's security. The constancy of Stoic virtue becomes the expediency of calculating acquiesence. Mastery of fortune becomes submission to Caesar.

When Thidias asks to kiss her hand to pay her homage, Cleopatra allows him, recalling how "[y]our Caesar's father" (3.13.87), when he would contemplate conquering new kingdoms, "[b]estowed his lips on that unworthy place / As it rained kisses" (3.13.89–90). As with Antony, everything reminds Cleopatra of the past and, by implication, of the contrast between then and now. The royal hand upon which the triumphant Julius Caesar poured down kisses while musing new conquests is now kissed by his adopted son's messenger accepting her surrender.

4.

Warned of Cleopatra's betrayal, Antony, fresh from challenging Caesar and led back by Enobarbus, walks in on the kiss and Cleopatra's talk of kisses, and is immediately enraged. What he sees and hears seem to confirm what Enobarbus thought he saw. "Favours?" he cries out; "By Jove that thunders! / What art thou, fellow?" (3.13.90–91). Thidias, answering Antony's question as if he meant it as a question, proudly boasts of the greatness of the man he serves: "One that but performs / The bidding of the fullest man and worthiest / To have command obeyed" (3.13.91–93). Enobarbus clearly sees that Thidias will pay for his impudence: "You will be whipped" (3.13.93). The man who counseled Cleopatra to confine her courage to her circumstances— and the man whose cunning speech Caesar trusts (3.12.26–33)—finds that his own boastful pride has led him to ignore his own circumstances and foolishly to speak with bluster. Fortune has shaken his wisdom.

Fortune has also shaken Antony's authority. Demonstrating Thidias's implicit insult, Antony calls for servants and no one comes. "Authority melts from me," he bitterly observes; "Of late when I cried 'Ho!', / Like boys unto a muss, kings would start forth / And cry 'Your will?'" (3.13.95–97; see 3.12.2–6). Antony denies there is reason for his waning authority. When a servant finally enters, he insists, "I am / Antony yet" (3.13.97–98). Antony is Antony regardless of his fortune. And to show it, he orders that Thidias be whipped. But, as Enobarbus recognizes, Antony's attempt to demonstrate his authority and power exhibits nothing so much as his lost authority and impotent rage: "'Tis better playing with a lion's whelp / Than with an old one dying" (3.13.99–100). Antony, accustomed to unlimited command, is reduced to punishing the effrontery of a "jack of Caesar's" (3.13.108).

Antony tries to deny that he has been reduced to punishing a petty poltroon. "Whip him. Were't twenty of the greatest tributaries / That do acknowledge Caesar," he declares, "should I find them / So saucy with the hand of she here— what's her name / Since she was Cleopatra?" (3.13.101–4). Antony does not finish his thought, but becomes distracted and diverted by the thought of Cleopatra. Although he is still Antony ("I am / Antony yet"), Cleopatra is no longer Cleopatra. Unfaithful to him (so he believes), she is now a contemptible, nameless "she." Antony retains his identity despite his betrayal of his men; Cleopatra loses hers because of her (suspected) betrayal of him.

Antony intends his punishment to unman Thidias. Thidias is to be whipped until he cringes and cries aloud for mercy "like a boy" (3.13.105).

Antony, who has nothing but contempt for men who are like boys, tries to restore his own manliness by unmanning an already unmanly man. Feeling diminished, he seeks to diminish the man who has diminished him, so as not to feel diminished.

When Thidias is dragged away to be flogged, Antony turns to Cleopatra and rails at her for being a whore. Saying that she was half blighted before he knew her, he compares her to Octavia. He compares the woman for whom he left his wife to the wife whom he left. Antony has gone without "the getting of a lawful race, / And by a gem of women," he says, only to be abused by one who looks favorably on servants ("feeders" [3.13.112–14]).[110] Cleopatra has always played fast and loose ("a boggler" [3.13.115]), Antony charges. But when we grow hard in our vices, he continues, "the wise gods seel our eyes, / In our own filth drop our clear judgements, make us / Adore our errors, laugh at's while we strut / To our confusion" (3.13.117–20). The gods, laughing at our folly, punish us with our own vices by taking away our judgment and making us love the vices which we flaunt but which will bring our destruction. Unable to act, Antony can do nothing but moralize.[111] All he can do is threaten Cleopatra that the gods will punish her by letting her continue her vicious ways until she destroys herself.

Echoing her own ribald description of herself as well as Pompey's and Enobarbus's crude allusions to her (1.5.32; 2.6.64–65, 128), Antony says that he found Cleopatra

> as a morsel, cold upon
> Dead Caesar's trencher—nay, you were a fragment
> Of Gnaeus Pompey's, besides what hotter hours,
> Unregistered in vulgar fame, you have
> Luxuriously picked out.

> (3.13.121–25)

Antony has never used bawdy language before. His language and his moralizing go together. His bawdy description substantiates his moral indictment that nothing about Cleopatra rises above the level of a licentious body. Thus Antony accuses Cleopatra of not knowing what moderation is. "For I am sure, / Though you can guess what temperance should be, / You know not what it is" (3.13.125–27). Cleopatra is a stranger to temperance. At best, she could only guess what it should be. Anger is always self-righteous. In his futile fury, Antony sanctimoniously accuses Cleopatra, whose immoderation he has always relished (see 2.6.124–28), of being ignorant of the moderation that he himself has never shown or sought.

Cleopatra, who has been unable to stop the tirade, finally gets Antony to answer her. When she asks why he is saying all this, he blames the familiarity she allowed Thidias: "To let a fellow that will take rewards / And say 'God quit you!' be familiar with / My playfellow, your hand, this kingly seal / And plighter of high hearts!" (3.13.128–31). Cleopatra has permitted a lowly servant to be intimate with her royal hand, the hand, Antony says, by which she has attested to her heart's love. Antony considers himself to have been cuckolded by Thidias's kiss. Comparing himself to the roaring beasts on the biblical hill of Basan (Psalm 22:12–13), he imagines himself the champion of the herd: "O that I were / Upon the hill of Basan, to outroar / The horned herd!" (3.13.131–33). As he explains, he has cause enough to be savage ("savage cause" [3.13.133]), and to be anything less ("to proclaim it civilly" [3.13.134]) would be to submit compliantly, even gratefully, to his humiliations. Thinking that roaring and beating are thus called for, and hearing that Thidias has been soundly whipped and cried for pardon, Antony taunts the man to his face, "If that thy father live, let him repent / Thou wast not made his daughter" (3.13.139–40). Where Thidias was to be whipped until he cowered and cried "like a boy," now, having been whipped and having cried for pardon, he is no more manly than a girl. From now on, just the sight of a woman's hand should shake him as though he had a fever ("The white hand of a lady fever thee; / Shake thou to look on't" [3.13.143–44]). Antony punishes Thidias, however, not only for kissing Cleopatra's hand, but "for follow[ing] Caesar in his triumph" (3.13.141). Antony has emasculated Thidias for Caesar's victory as well as for Thidias's kiss, for both have emasculated him.

Turning to his real target, Antony sends Thidias back to Caesar with his angry complaint, not (as in Plutarch) that "[Thidias] showed himself proud and disdainful toward him, and now specially when he was easy to be angered, by reason of his present misery" (Plutarch, *Antony*, 73.2; North, 6:76), but that "[Caesar] seems / Proud and disdainful, harping on what I am, / Not what he knew I was. He makes me angry, / And at this time most easy 'tis to do't," when Antony's entire world has come undone (3.13.146–49). Antony transfers to Caesar what Plutarch's Antony complains of Thidias. He punishes the emissary for the emperor's affront. As subordinates win battles for generals, so, too, they are punished for them. The intended harm is the insult to the emperor, not the stripes inflicted on his underling. Antony thus suggests a way for Caesar to requite his insult.

> If he mislike
> My speech and what is done, tell him he has

Hipparchus, my enfranched bondman, whom
He may at pleasure whip or hang or torture,
As he shall like to quit me.

(3.13.152–56)

Caesar may punish Antony through Hipparchus. Plutarch says that Hipparchus was a favorite of Antony, who became the first of his freedmen to defect to Caesar (Plutarch, *Antony*, 67.7). Shakespeare, however, says nothing about his defecting. Shakespeare's silence, which avoids the possible implication that Caesar would be punishing Antony's defector in Antony's behalf, serves to point up Antony's heartless injustice in punishing a presumably innocent, loyal man.[112] In contrast to his magnanimity elsewhere, Antony's treatments of Thidias and Hipparchus, intended to shame those who shamed him, are his most tyrannical acts.

5.

When Thidias exits, Cleopatra, who has said nothing since asking Antony why he accused her of being a whore, now reproachfully asks whether he is done: "Have you done yet?" (3.13.157). She means, Have you finished ranting? Antony takes "done" in a different sense. "Alack, our terrene moon is now eclipsed / And it portends alone the fall of Antony" (3.13.158–59). Antony himself will soon be at an end, he says. Cleopatra—the earthly moon goddess Isis (3.6.16–19; 5.2.239–40)—has withdrawn from him. Without her love, he is done.

With Cleopatra evidently waiting for him to recover himself ("I must stay his time" [3.13.160]), Antony, accusing her again of betrayal, has another outburst of jealous indignation: "To flatter Caesar would you mingle eyes / With one that ties his points?" (3.13.161–62). But when she asks, "Not know me yet?" (3.13.162)—her "yet" meant reprovingly to answer the question—Antony answers with his own rebuking question: "Cold-hearted toward me?" (3.13.163). Taking it as a genuine question and not as a reproach, Cleopatra answers at length, for the first time in the quarrel.[113] Intending her optative imperative as a heroic oath to underscore her willing loss if she is cold-hearted toward him ("From my cold heart let heaven . . ." [3.13.164]),[114] she vehemently wishes, if she is, that heaven engender poisonous hail from her cold heart and, as the hail melts, use it not only to dissolve her life, but to smite Caesarion and her other children, together with all the Egyptians, who should all then lie exposed to the flies and gnats of the Nile. Heaven, she says, should use her cold heart to cause the deaths of herself ("Dissolve my life"), her children ("the memory of my womb") and her subjects ("my brave

Egyptians all"), and feed them all to flies and gnats "for prey" (3.13.167–72). The low should devour the high and everything that is hers.

Antony, satisfied by Cleopatra's grand self-curse, immediately regains heart and talks of battling Caesar. "Caesar sets down in Alexandria, where / I will oppose his fate" (3.13.173–74). It is unclear whether Antony, who speaks not of defeating Caesar but of opposing his fate, expects to win or to die nobly trying. But whether or not he thinks Caesar's victory is inevitable (cp. 2.3.14ff.), Antony offers a sanguine report of his military strength both on land and at sea. Contrary to what seemed to be the case right after Actium, he says that his land force held nobly and his "severed navy too / Have knit again, and fleet, threat'ning most sea-like" (3.13.175–76).[115] He is silent about his officers and foreign allies (see 3.10.33–35). "Where hast thou been, my heart?" he asks, referring to his courage and perhaps to Cleopatra.[116] "If from the field I shall return once more / To kiss these lips, I will appear in blood. / I and my sword will earn our chronicle" (3.13.178–80). Once more, Antony speaks like a traditional Roman. As the sign of bravery is blood (and the metonymy for prowess, a sword), the reward for victory is fame. Antony says nothing about Cleopatra fighting along with him. "There's hope in't yet," he concludes (3.13.181).

Praised by Cleopatra as "my brave lord" (3.13.182), Antony vows heroic courage. Affirming that he will be thrice himself and fight fiercely (". . . trebled-sinewed, hearted, breathed / And fight maliciously" [3.13.183–84]), he, yet again, compares himself to what he had been. This time, however, he compares his present fierceness to his former easygoingness. When his days were pleasant and happy ("nice and lucky" [3.13.185]), Antony would let enemies ransom their lives for a trifle. As his life was soft, so was he. "But now, I'll set my teeth / And send to darkness all that stop me" (3.13.186–87). He will slaughter whoever hinders him. But Antony no sooner vows his ferocity than he calls for a night of revelry. "Come, / Let's have one other gaudy night," he bids Cleopatra, asking for all his melancholy and sober captains ("sad captains" [3.13.189]) to join the festivities. "Fill our bowls once more. / Let's mock the midnight bell" (3.13.189–90). Antony calls for the celebration to last well into the early morning hours. He speaks of mocking the midnight bell, but his bravado seems to mock his bravery.

Cleopatra, responding to Antony's raised spirits, announces that it is her birthday. She says that she had thought to mark the occasion only sparingly, "but since my lord / Is Antony again, I will be Cleopatra" (3.13.191–92). Her birthday celebration will be sumptuous. Cleopatra's announcement, while signaling their reconciliation, answers Antony's denial that she is still Cleopatra (3.13.103–4). His combined desire for fierce fighting and festive revelries makes him Antony again, and that makes her Cleopatra again. Declaring that there is life ("sap" [3.13.197]) in it yet, Antony vows to "make Death love me, for I will contend / Even with his pestilent scythe" (3.13.198–99). Antony, needing an opponent to measure himself against, will compete with Death himself and win his love by out-killing him even in times of the plague. If he cannot duel with Caesar, he will duel with Death. Slaughter will rescue him from shame. Antony's manly virtue will earn him his opponent's love.[117]

6.

Enobarbus, alone after the others leave, reflects on what he has just witnessed. Earlier, he thought that Antony's judgment declined with his fortunes. Now, he thinks that as his judgment waned, his fearlessness grew. "Now he'll outstare the lightning" (3.13.200). Antony will face any danger, not because he is brave, but because he is maddened with rage: "To be furious / Is to be frighted out of fear, and in that mood / The dove will peck the estridge" (3.13.200–202). Shame has frightened Antony out of fear. It has made him fearless with frenzied fury. "[A]nd I see still / A diminution in our captain's brain / Restores his heart" (3.13.202–4). Antony's diminished judgment revives—in fact, replaces—his courage. Desperate shame has deprived him of reason and given him the pseudo-courage of frantic rage. "When valour preys on reason, / It eats the sword it fights with" (3.13.204–5). Valor is not valor unless governed by reason. By consuming reason, it consumes itself. To be valor, it must be emboldened by more than pain.[118] Enobarbus thus concludes that he will leave Antony: "I will seek / Some way to leave him" (3.13.205–6). No longer torn, Enobarbus no longer divides himself between a noble and an ignoble party. Loyalty held to fools, he tacitly concludes, is mere folly.

Notes

1. Cantor, 133.
2. Harley Granville-Barker, *Prefaces to Shakespeare*, 4 vols. (London: Sidgwick and Jackson, 1930), 2:113.
3. Plutarch, *Crassus*, 31.7.
4. Plutarch, *Crassus*, 33.2–4; see act 2, n. 45, above.
5. Also Plutarch, *Crassus*, 33.5; Valerius Maximus, 6.9.9; Tacitus, *Germania*, 37.4; Appian, *Civil Wars*, 6.65; Florus, 2.18.3–7.
6. Horace, *Odes*, 2.13.17–18; Virgil, *Georgics*, 3.31.
7. Johnson, in Johnson-Steevens, 8:200. On Ventidius's battle, see Dio, 49.19–20.
8. Cicero, *De oratore*, 2.342–43.

9. *Cor.*, 1.1.262–75; see, further, Blits, *Spirit, Soul, and City*, 32–33.

10. Quintus Curtius, *History of Alexander*, 6.1.17–18. Agrippa makes the same argument as Ventidius after defeating Pompey in behalf of Caesar (Dio, 49.4).

11. Plutarch, *Antony*, 34.6; Dio, 49.21.1.

12. Dio, 49.23.2.

13. Also Dio, 49.21.3.

14. On green-sickness as chlorosis, see *OED*, s.v. Green-sickness.

15. See Blits, *Ancient Republic*, 87–89.

16. On the tropes, see Anonymous, 4.30.41; Quintilian, 9.3.53–54.

17. *Antony and Cleopatra*, ed. J. H. Walter (Boston: Plays Inc., 1970), 154.

18. On Caesar's pedestrian mode of speech, see Suetonius, *Augustus*, 86–87. Note also, e.g., 2.2.121–23; 2.7.99–100; 5.1.39–40, 43; 5.2.182–83.

19. For the same reason, a victorious Roman general was accompanied, in his triumph, by a slave repeating to him, "Look behind thee; remember thou art a man" (Tertullian, 33.4). See also Plutarch, *Alexander*, 69.2–3; Arrian, *The Discourses of Epictetus*, 3.24.85.

20. On the political hostility between Cleopatra and Herod, and her reliance upon Antony for needed political support, see, e.g., Josephus, *The Jewish War*, 7.300–3. See also 4.6.13–15.

21. Cleopatra "neither excelled Octavia in beauty, nor yet in young years." Plutarch, *Antony*, 57.3; North, 6:60.

22. Plutarch, *Antony*, 35.1.

23. Her speech is nearly twice as long as any of her other speeches and contains nearly one-third of her total words (75 of 237).

24. All but five of the sixteen times, Octavia's "my" modifies either Antony or Caesar (3.2.42, 45; 3.4.10, 16, 18, 28; 3.6.40, 56, 58, 63, 65).

25. See, further, Blits, *Spirit, Soul, and City*, 36–37; and act 3, nn. 91–92, below.

26. Tacitus, *Annals*, 1.10.

27. Suetonius, *Augustus*, 16; Appian, *Civil Wars*, 5.126.

28. See JC, 4.1.19–27, where Antony suggests to Octavius this treatment of Lepidus.

29. On Pompey's death, see Appian, *Civil Wars*, 5.133–45.

30. Plutarch, *Caesar*, 28.1, *Pompey*, 53.6.

31. Plutarch, *Antony*, 50.4.

32. Suetonius, *Augustus*, 17.1.

33. "[The Roman people at the time of Julius Caesar] suffered all things subjects should do by commandment of their kings, and yet could not abide the name of king, detesting it as the utter destruction of their liberty." Plutarch, *Antony*, 12.3–4; North, 6:13. See JC, 2.1.53–54; Blits, *Ancient Republic*, 32–34.

34. Dio, 49.40.3, 54.3.

35. Plutarch, *Antony*, 54.3–6; Dio, 50.5.

36. "Augustus was sensible that mankind is governed by names." Gibbon, 3, 1:64. On his changing his name from "Octavius, son of Octavius," to "Caesar, son of Caesar," see Appian, *Civil Wars*, 3.11.

37. Plutarch, *Brutus*, 22.1; Suetonius, *Augustus*, 7.1; Appian, *Civil Wars*, 3.94; Dio, 49.41.1–3. On Julius Caesar's authorizing the name, see Suetonius, *Divus Julius*, 52.1.

38. Plutarch, *Antony*, 81.2–82.1; Suetonius, *Augustus*, 17.5; Dio, 51.15.5–6.

39. Plutarch, *Antony*, 54.6; Dio, 49.40.3.

40. On the rare (and insolent) exception to celebrating a triumph only in Rome, see Cicero, *Against Piso*, 38, 92, *De provinciis consularibus*, 7, 15.

41. "All monstrous kinded gods, Anubys dog that barking slave, / Against all Roman gods. . . ." Virgil, *Aeneid*, 8.698; *The Aeneid of Thomas Phaer and Thomas Twyne* (1558; rpt. New York: Garland Publishing, 1987), 8.745–46. Also Dio, 50.27.7; Propertius, *Elegies*, 3.11.41; Virgil, *Aeneid*, 8.696–713. On Roman horror at the East, see, e.g., Seneca, *Benefits*, 5.16.6.

42. Dio, 50.4.1–5.4, 24–28; Florus, 2.21.1–3. "Rome, who had never condescended to fear any nation or people, did in her time fear two human beings; one was Hannibal, and the other was a woman." W. W. Tarn, *The Cambridge Ancient History*, 12 vols. (Cambridge: Cambridge University Press, 1934), 10:111.

43. Plutarch, *Antony*, 55.1.

44. Plutarch, *Antony*, 35.4; Appian, *Civil Wars*, 5.93–95, 139; Dio, 48.54.1–2.

45. Plutarch, *Antony*, 55; Dio, 50.1.3–5.

46. Livy, *Perioche*, 129; Dio, 49.11.3–12.4; Velleius Paterculus, 2.80; Appian, *Civil Wars*, 5.123–26.

47. E.g., Velleius Paterculus, 2.89.1; Plutarch, *Antony*, 11.1, *Cicero*, 33.5, *Pompey*, 13.4; Appian, *Civil Wars*, 5.130; Valerius Maximus, 5.1f; Dio, 51.19.2. Note *Augustus*, 12.1.

48. See Rev. 17:1–2.

49. Dio, 49.32.3; Plutarch, *Antony*, 37.3; Appian, *Civil Wars*, 5.75.

50. See *Augustus*, 27; Velleius Paterculus, 2.94.4; Tacitus, *Annals*, 2.3; Dio, 54.9.4.

51. For his only mention of law, which Caesar, using the subjunctive ("as [if] a law"), implicitly identifies with his will, see 3.12.33. For his only other two mentions of the gods, see 3.6.17; 5.1.27. "[T]he high gods," here, seems to be a collective term, used for emphasis (hence the singular verb "makes").

52. The nearest he will come will be to refer to Antony as "[his] brother," after learning of his death (5.1.42). Note especially 5.2.357–59. By contrast, Cleopatra emphatically mentions Octavia ("your wife Octavia" [4.15.28]).

53. Plutarch, *Antony*, 60.1; Dio, 50.4.3–5, 6.1, 21.1, 26.3–4. See Virgil, *Aeneas*, 8.675ff.

54. Xenophon, *The Art of Horsemanship*, 9.2; Plato, *Phaedrus*, 253d3–e1; Aristotle, *Nicomachean Ethics*, 1106a19–21; Plutarch, *Roman Questions*, 97.

55. Plutarch, *Antony*, 60.1.

56. Eight times (to Antony's six). She, similarly, mentions Octavia by name more than anyone else does—five times (to Antony's and Enobarbus's four, each, and Caesar's three).

57. Plutarch, *Antony*, 34.6, 63.3.

58. Plutarch, *Antony*, 58.1.

59. Bevington, 171.

60. Plutarch, *Antony*, 63.4; Dio, 50.28.4.

61. Plutarch, *Antony*, 62.3.

62. Suetonius, *Augustus*, 25.4.

63. Plutarch, *Antony*, 62.1, 65.5; Dio, 50.15.4.

64. Plutarch, *Antony*, 62.2; Dio, 50.29.1–4.

65. Plutarch, *Antony*, 64.1, 65.5; Dio, 50.15.4.

66. Plutarch, *Antony*, 62.3.

67. Plutarch, *Antony*, 68.2.

68. Bevington, 172.

69. See also, e.g., 3.13.178–80; 4.2.5–7; 4.5.2; 4.7.6–10; 4.8.10–11.

70. Plutarch, *Antony*, 64.

71. Blits, *Ancient Republic*, 3–20.

72. Blits, *Spirit, Soul, and City*, 47.

73. Plutarch, *Antony*, 65.1–2.

74. Suetonius, *Augustus*, 84.2.

75. It is also the last important naval battle of antiquity.

76. Aristotle, *Rhetoric*, 1413a18–35; Cicero, *Topica*, 45; Quintilian, 8.6.67–76.

77. On "nag" meaning whore, see *OED*, s.v. Nag n. 1 2b. See, further, 3.7.8–9; 4.8.14–16.

78. Frankie Rubenstein, *A Dictionary of Shakespeare's Sexual Puns and their Significance* (London: Macmillian, 1984), 146.

79. While the secondary meaning of "breeze" is an ordinary kind of breeze (*OED*, s.v. Breeze n. 2), its primary meaning is a gadfly, especially the sort which annoy cattle and horses (*OED*, s.v. Breeze n. 1).

80. "There Antonius showed plainly that he had not only lost the courage and heart of an Emperor, but also of a valiant man." Plutarch, *Antony*, 66.4; North, 6:69.

81. Hence, the frequency in the play of synecdoche (whole for part; part for whole) and metonymy (a closely associated word). On the tropes, see Anonymous, 4.43; Quintilian, 8.6.19–27. On the general tendency, see, further, Blits, *Spirit, Soul, and City*, 6, 12–13, 41–42, 104, 208.

82. Note Scarus's similar division of "[e]xperience, manhood, honor" (3.10.23–24) and Canidius's similar division of Antony (3.10.26–27). Both preserve Antony's nobility by separating it from what violated or abandoned it.

83. Plutarch, *Antony*, 67.6–7.

84. See, e.g., Cicero, *Pro Sulla*, 74; Livy, *History*, 9.7.11; Dionysius of Halicarnassus, 9.27.5; Suetonius, *Augustus*, 65.2.

85. "*Mine* [rather than *my*] is . . . used before words to which it is so frequently prefixed as to become almost a part of them." Abbott, §327.

86. Antony similarly uses the verb "prithee" only when he is mortally wounded and unable to act (4.14.130).

87. Titinius's and Messala's references during the battle to "Octavius" (*JC*, 5.3.6, 51) are synonymous with "Octavius's wing" (*JC*, 5.2.4). On Caesar's fighting through his subordinates, see Suetonius, *Augustus*, 20. No one in *Antony and Cleopatra* men-

tions Caesar's courage except to deny it (e.g., 3.11.38–40; 4.7.2; 4.15.15); see Suetonius, *Augustus*, 10.4; 13.1; 16.1–2.

88. Plutarch, *Antony*, 22.3–4, *Brutus*, 43.5–6, 52.

89. Blits, *Ancient Republic*, 39–61.

90. *Rape of Lucrece*, 1807ff., *JC*, 2.1.53–54; Livy, *History*, 1.56ff.; Plutarch, *Publicola*, 1ff.

91. Cicero, *Paradoxa Stoicorum*, 12–13.

92. The Romans of course also had separate words for each, *virtu* and *fama*. For *honestas* as virtue, see, e.g., Cicero, *De officiis*, 1.5, 6, 152, *De finibus*, 1.61, 2.37–38, 45; for honestas as reputation, see, e.g., Cicero, *Tusculan Disputations*, 2.31, 66; Gellius, 1.3.23ff.; on the word's ambiguity, see Cicero, *De finibus*, 2.48. See, further, Blits, *Spirit, Soul, and City*, 36–37.

93. See, e.g., Livy, *History*, 9.6.8.

94. Note the parallel uses of "rudder," literally for "[t]h' Antoniad," and metaphorically for Antony (3.10.2–3; 3.11.57).

95. While Cleopatra taunted Antony by belittling Caesar as "scarce-bearded" (1.1.22), Antony, who did so in *Julius Caesar* (*JC*, 4.1.18) but had not earlier in this play, will now repeatedly disparage him for his young age ("the young man" [3.11.62]; "the boy Caesar" [3.13.17], "boy" [4.1.1], "this novice" [4.12.14] and "the young Roman boy" [4.12.48]).

96. Plutarch, *Antony*, 72.1.

97. Plutarch, *Antony*, 73.1.

98. For Caesar's use of "law," see act 3, n. 51, above.

99. *The Works of Shakespeare*, ed. Howard Staunton, 4 vols. (London: Routledge, Warne & Routledge, 1864), 4:427.

100. Plutarch, *Antony*, 66.5.

101. Rome has a long tradition of challenged battles, including those of single combat. "[Romans] have done valiantly and courageously, where without any necessity, they enter voluntarily and fight man-to-man in single combat." Polybius, 6.54.4; *History of Polybius*, trans. Edward Grimeston (London: Simon Waterson, 1634), 301. See, e.g., Livy, *History*, 7.9.6–10.4, 7.26.1–10, 8.7.1–22, 23.46.12–47.8, 25.18.4–15, 45.39.16; Plutarch, *Marcellus*, 2.1, *Marius*, 3.2, *Sertorius*, 13.3–4, *Aemilius Paulus*, 31.2; Caesar, *Spanish War*, 25.3–5. Most famously, Livy, *History*, 1.24–26; Dionysius of Halicarnassus, 3.13.1–22.10. See also *Cor.*, 1.1.232–34; 1.8.1–15. However, the only instances of a duel deciding the outcome of a battle, let alone of a war, are probably mythical.

102. Plutarch, *Antony*, 68.2.

103. 3.13.46, 53; 4.2.28, 30; 4.5.16; 4.6.15; 4.9.25; 4.14.74, 90, 103; 5.1.8; 5.2.15, 42, 52, 64, 115, 189. A soldier once addresses his fellow sentries with the polite "masters" (4.3.27).

104. Walter, 200.

105. E.g., Livy, *History*, 1.58; Valerius Maximus, 6.1. Pref. See *Rape of Lucrece*, 463ff., and cp. Augustine, 1.18–19; see, further, Jan H. Blits, "Redeeming Lost Honor: Shakespeare's *Rape of Lucrece*," *The Review of Politics*, 71 (2009).

106. Plutarch, *Isis and Osiris*, 77 (382c–d).

107. Cicero, *Tully's Offices*, trans. Sr. Roger L'Estrange, 5th ed. (London: Tonson, Knaplock and Hindmarsh, 1699), 116 (translator's italics).

108. Aristotle, *Nicomachean Ethics*, 1124b10–14; see, e.g., Plutarch, *Cato the Younger*, 72.2.

109. See, e.g., Cicero, *Tusculan Disputations*, 5.42.43, *De finibus*, 3.16ff., *Stoic Paradoxes*, 16–19; Seneca, *Letters*, 9.2–22, 85.37, 92.3–7, *On Providence*, 5.7–6.9, *On the Happy Life*; Epictetus, *Discourses*, 1.1, *Manual*, 8, Frag. 8; Marcus Aurelius, *Meditations*, 4.7; Diogenes Laertius, 7.89ff.

110. "Feeders" may also mean "parasites," that is, both those who serve food to the great and those who receive food at the table of the great. In the present context, the senses are hard to distinguish. See Schmidt, s.v. Feeder.

111. For his only previous instance, see 1.2.115–17.

112. Neill, 258.

113. None of her previous six speeches to Antony is more than half a line (3.13.114, 120, 127, 157, 160, 162).

114. For a similar use of the optative imperative as expressing the strongest denial, see 1.1.34–35.

115. Plutarch, *Antony*, 68.1–3.

116. If not this question, the next ("Dost thou hear, lady?" [3.13.177]) marks the first time in the scene that Antony addresses Cleopatra with the intimate pronoun.

117. Blits, *Ancient Republic*, 6–9.

118. Aristotle, *Nicomachean Ethics*, 1116b23–17a1.

Act Four

Act Four, Scene One

Caesar is contemptuous of Antony's words and actions. While Antony insults and rebukes him ("He calls me boy, and chides as he had power / To beat me out of Egypt" [4.1.1–2]), his words serve only to emphasize his own weakness. At least in Caesar's eyes, Antony's attempt to shame Caesar shames Antony himself. What Antony means as an act of defiance appears as an act of desperation. Reporting that Antony has dared him to personal combat as well as whipped his messenger, Caesar dismisses the challenge with derision. "Let the old ruffian know," he states, referring to Antony as a swaggering violent pimp,[1] "I have many other ways to die; meantime / Laugh at his challenge" (4.1.4–6).[2] Antony's challenge, amounting to pure braggadocio, is nothing but ridiculous to Caesar.

Maecenas, addressing Caesar with a newfound deference ("Caesar must think . . ."),[3] sees Antony's actions as offering an important opportunity: "When one so great begins to rage, he's hunted / Even to falling" (4.1.7–9). The more Antony raves against defeat, the closer he is to it. Maecenas therefore urges Caesar to give him no time to recover but, instead, take advantage of his state of mind. "Never anger / Made good guard for itself" (4.1.10–11). Antony's anger may be used against Antony. Caesar, agreeing, says they will fight tomorrow. Regarding the upcoming clash as Antony's final defeat, he describes it as "the last of many battles / We mean to fight" (4.1.12–13). The battle will mark a turning point for Caesar, Rome and the world.

155

Caesar is thinking beyond the next day's battle, as well. Because gener-als have needed to win the support of their troops by satisfying their de-mands,[4] the soldiers' discipline has greatly declined during the decades of Rome's civil wars. With the end of the civil wars now in sight, Caesar needs to establish discipline and loyalty among his troops.[5] He therefore needs to punish Antony's deserters and to spare or reward those who have been loyal to him. He needs a policy that produces both fear and love of him. Under the circumstances, fear and love may be related more as cause and effect than as opposites. Those Caesar spares will love him for fear that he could do to them what he has done to those he did not spare. Fear, properly managed, can produce love rather than hatred.[6] Caesar thus in-structs Maecenas, "Within our files there are, / Of those that served Mark Antony but late, / Enough to fetch him in. See it done" (4.1.13–15). Antony's deserters are to bear the brunt of Caesar's battle with Antony. Caesar, at the same time, will feast his army: "And feast the army. We have store to do't / And they have earned the waste" (4.1.16–17). Like Antony, Caesar will reward his army with a feast. But where Antony spoke of en-joying a grand festive night, Caesar assesses the expense. He calculates, where Antony squanders.

Caesar ends the scene by expressing regret and pity for Antony, though not without some exasperated scorn: "Poor Antony!" (4.1.17). The next time he shows such feelings, Maecenas, at least, will remark that Caesar is thinking not really of Antony, but of himself (5.1.34–35).

Act Four, Scene Two

1.

Antony called for a festive night with his captains (3.13.188ff.). Before the wine and food are brought in, Antony and Enobarbus discuss Caesar's refusal to fight a duel. Antony seems puzzled by the refusal. "Why should he not?" he asks (4.2.2). Enobarbus, answering, explains, "He thinks, being twenty times of better fortune, / He is twenty men to one" (4.2.3–4). Caesar consid-ers himself sure to win. If he thought he had no reason to risk personal com-bat before Actium (3.7.30–34), he certainly thinks so now. Telling Enobar-bus that he will fight tomorrow by sea and land, Antony says that he will "live, / Or bathe [his] dying honour in the blood / Shall make it live again" (4.2.5–7). He will either live or make his honor live again by dying valiantly. His body's death-blood would recover his honor's lifeblood.

Asked whether he will fight well, Enobarbus vows, "I'll strike, and cry 'Take all!'" (4.2.8). While his cry ("Take all!") is that of a gambler staking everything on a final throw of the dice, his vow is deliberately deceptive. "I'll strike" could mean that Enobarbus will fight to the end ("I'll fight to the finish, crying 'Winner take all!'") or that he intends to surrender or defect ("Strike the flag").[7] Although Antony understands him as showing defiant spirit ("Well said!" [4.2.8]), Enobarbus has already decided to desert. His vow, disguising his disloyalty with a quibble, denies what it appears to affirm.

2.

Antony spoke of having a sumptuous feast for his captains, but we see instead his grimly taking leave of his "household servants" (4.2.9). Greeting them, Antony shakes their hands and tells them that "kings have been [their] fellows" (4.2.13). Just as his handshake is a gesture of their equality with him, his reminder that kings have done him a similar service bespeaks their equality with kings. The age of a universal emperor is an age of universal equality, for all men, regardless of rank or position, are the emperor's servants. All are similar and equal.

Antony's greeting ("Thou hast been rightly honest; so hast thou, / Thou, and thou, and thou . . ." [4.2.11–12]), which seems more a valediction than a salutation, appears to anticipate defeat tomorrow. Cleopatra cannot understand why Antony would say such words to his servants at this time ("What means this?" [4.2.13]). Enobarbus attributes Antony's words to his sorrow: "'Tis one of those odd tricks which sorrow shoots / Out of the mind" (4.2.14–15). Carried away by sorrow, the mind blurts out whimsically foolish words without thought or consideration. No less than love or anger, sorrow can disorder the mind.

Antony, praising his servants for their loyalty, says that he wishes to exchange places with them. "I wish I could be made so many men, / And all of you clapped up together in / An Antony, that I might do you service / So good as you have done" (4.2.16–19). The servants would become Antony, and Antony would become the servants. They would be the master; he would be their servant. The exchange would be an inversion of the high and the low as well as of the one and the many. If Antony's servants have been the equals of kings, they would become superior to the man those kings served.

The servants are horrified at the suggestion: "The gods forbid!" (4.2.19). But Antony, apparently oblivious to his effect on them, asks the servants to give him plenty to drink and make as much of him as when both his empire and they were subject to his command (". . . when mine empire was your fellow too / And suffered my command" [4.2.22–23]). Cleopatra, again, cannot understand why Antony would say this ("What does he mean?" [4.2.23]), and Enobarbus, equally at a loss, can only, ironically, describe Antony's effect on his servants as if it had been his purpose ("To make his followers weep" [4.2.24]). Antony asks his tearful servants to tend him tonight, for "May be it is the period of your duty. / Haply you shall not see me more, or if, / A mangled shadow. Perchance tomorrow / You'll serve another master" (4.2.26–28). Although Antony begins each sentence with a conjectural qualifier ("May be," "Haply," "Perchance"), the conjectural quickly becomes the declarative. Explicitly stating that he looks upon them "[a]s one that takes his leave" (4.2.29), Antony, while denying that he is turning them away, asks his servants to "stay till death" and tend him for two hours tonight. "I ask no more— / And the gods yield you for't!" (4.2.31, 32–33). Antony's macabre words make Enobarbus as well as the servants cry. "Look, they weep, / And I, an ass, am onion-eyed. For shame! / Transform us not to women" (4.2.34–36).[8] Besides loving him for his generosity, Antony's most loyal followers love him for his passions and his open display of his passions—a display which serves at once to magnify him and to equalize them with him. It both greatly impresses and greatly flatters them.[9] Antony, by the same token, calls the men "servants" only before they enter (4.2.9). Once they are present, they become "[his] good fellows," "[his] honest friends," "[his] hearty friends" and "[his] hearts" (4.2.20, 29, 38, 41).

When Enobarbus points out the distress he is causing them, Antony, finally catching himself, denies that he meant to make anyone cry or to suggest that he expects to lose tomorrow ("Now the witch take me if I meant it thus" [4.2.37]). Insisting that he "hope[s] well of tomorrow," he assures his followers that he will lead them "[w]here rather I'll expect victorious life / Than death and honour" (4.2.43–44). The reassurance, of course, rings hollow. Claiming that his words were meant to encourage his followers ("I spake to you for your comfort" [4.2.40]), he says that he desires to revel through the night. "Let's to supper, come, / And drown consideration" (4.2.44–45).[10]

Antony will die tomorrow. His last supper echoes Jesus's.[11] Earlier, Antony, comparing himself to the beasts on the hill of Basan (3.13.131–33), alluded to the Psalm whose beginning Jesus quotes when he dies ("My God, my God, why hast thou forsaken me" [Psalm 22:1]).[12] Here, like Jesus, he thrice asks that his followers tend him during what he expects to be his final hours: "Well, my good fellows, wait on me tonight"; "Tend me tonight. . . . Haply you shall not see me more, or if, / A mangled shadow"; "Tend me tonight two hours" (4.2.20, 24, 26–27, 32).[13] Antony, who thanks his men for their loyalty (4.2.11–12, 15), will be betrayed by Enobarbus, whom he, beginning the scene, to emphasize their closeness, calls by his personal name, "Domitius" (4.2.1), as he does nowhere else.[14] Antony finds a better life in death: "Or I will live, / Or bathe my dying honour in the blood / Shall make it live again" (4.2.6–7).[15] He offers his followers communion with one another and with him (4.2.16–19).[16] Inadvertently evoking tears when he means to give comfort, he tries to transform his followers' suffering or despair into hope, speaking specifically of Grace: "Grace grow where those drops fall!" (4.2.38).[17] Calling them his friends, he denies that those who serve him are his servants.[18] And suggesting that his fellows are the equals of kings, he points to the universal equality of all men, emperors and subjects, in the eyes of God.[19] In addition, no one, not even or perhaps especially Antony, understands what is happening ("What means this? . . . What does he mean? . . . What mean you . . . ?" [4.2.13, 23, 33]).[20] Enobarbus, who will in fact repent and die not unlike Judas (4.6.21–40; 4.4.9–26; Matt. 27:3–10), admonishes him, "For shame! / Transform us not into women" (4.2.35–36). Although Enobarbus is surely referring only to Antony's having made the men cry, Shakespeare seems to be referring also to the advent of the new religion, with its emphasis on humility, forgiveness, charity and submission.[21]

Act Four, Scene Three

Where the previous scene points to the beginning of Christianity, the present scene, with a changing of the guard among Antony's soldiers, marks the end of classical paganism. It is the only scene in the play without any major or even named characters. One of Antony's soldiers says that he expects tomorrow's battle to be decisive ("It will determine one way" [4.3.2]). Another is hopeful, providing the navy does well. "And if tomorrow / Our navy thrive, I have an absolute hope / Our landmen will stand up" (4.3.9–10). But the First Soldier no sooner endorses the Second's estimation of the land force ("'Tis a brave army and full of purpose—" [4.3.12]) than the soldiers hear music from below. "'Tis the god Hercules whom Antony loved / Now leaves him" (4.3.21–22). The pagan demigod and hero, Hercules, whose "feats . . . exceedingly surpass[ed] all other that ever were comprised by man's memory" (Diodorus, 4.8.1; Skelton, 360), and whom Antony loved and claimed as his ancestor, forsakes the last hero.[22] The music marks the end of the ancient world. It should not seem strange that Shakespeare presents the emergence of Christianity as preceding the end of paganism. The old and the new religions overlap. The human conditions leading to the disappearance of the pagan world continue beyond, if only for a while, the beginning of the new religion to which they give rise.

Act Four, Scene Four

1.

Antony, who has not mentioned his name before, calls for Eros four times in the first two lines. "Eros! mine armour, Eros! . . . / . . . Eros! Come, mine armour, Eros!" (4.4.1, 2). The felicitously named Eros is Antony's armorer.[23] While Cleopatra wants Antony to return to bed ("Sleep a little" [4.4.1]), Antony is eager for war. In contrast to his mood the night before, his spirits seem high. Urging Eros to dress him in his armor, Antony seems to think that he might lose only because he will deserve to win: "If Fortune be not ours today, it is / Because we brave her" (4.4.4–5). Fortune thwarts those who dare to defy her. She jealously defeats those who are worthy of winning.

Cleopatra, wanting to help put on Antony's armor, shows immediately that she does not know how the pieces fit together ("What's this for?" [4.4.6]). Antony, apparently charmed by her clumsy effort, tacitly distinguishes between her and Eros as his armorer. While Eros is the armorer of his body, Cleopatra is "[t]he armourer of [his] heart" (4.4.7). Eros serves to shield Antony's body and life; Cleopatra serves to stir his spirit and courage. Eros's service is protective or "defen[sive]" (4.4.10). Cleopatra's is combative or defiant ("Well, well! / We shall thrive now" [4.4.8–9]). And so, as soon as Cleopatra figures out how to buckle part of his armor properly, Antony not only compliments her ("Rarely, rarely!" [4.4.11]), but proclaims how fiercely he will fight: "He that unbuckles this, till we do please / To doff't for our repose, shall hear a storm" (4.4.12–13). His heart strengthened by Cleopatra, he will be dauntless in the battle.

Finally dressed in his armor, Antony declares, "O love, / That thou couldst see my wars today and knew'st / The royal occupation, thou shouldst see / A workman in't" (4.4.15–18). Although it is the art of kings ("The royal occupation"), Cleopatra is ignorant of warfare. Before the battle of Actium, Antony expressed no doubt about her knowledge of, or fitness for, war. Now, he says that even if she saw Antony today in battle, she could not appreciate his craft. She could not judge a true warrior. By contrast, when an armed soldier arrives, Antony greets him by saying that he looks like someone who knows warfare: "Thou look'st like him that knows a warlike charge" (4.4.19). Not only the soldier's warlike bearing, but his early arrival and evident delight show his readiness to answer the demands of battle. Accordingly, Antony, having implicitly distinguished between Cleopatra and Eros as his armorer, now implicitly distinguishes between her and a ready soldier. Where Cleopatra, in her first words in the scene, urged Antony to return to bed, Antony associates rising from bed with doing what we love: "To business that we love we rise betime / And go to't with delight" (4.4.20–21). Love's opposites are laziness, lassitude and lethargy. Thus, when more armed soldiers and captains arrive early and in high spirits, Antony happily remarks on the morning's promise: "This morning, like the spirit of a youth / That means to be of note, begins betimes" (4.4.26–27). As we rise "betime" to do what we love, a youth seeking fame begins "betimes" to be of note (see 3.7.25–27).[24] Earliness indicates eagerness.

Antony thus makes light of his parting kiss, saying he would deserve rebuke for anything more than a quick kiss. "Whate'er becomes of me," he tells Cleopatra, "This is a soldier's kiss. [*Kisses her.*] Rebukable / And worthy shameful check it were, to stand / On more mechanic compliment" (4.4.29–32). A more ceremonious farewell may suit the commoners, but "a man of steel" (4.4.33) kisses and leaves quickly and unceremoniously. His mind and heart are on war.

2.

Although eager to help armor Antony, Cleopatra has said very little since the start of the scene—just four short speeches, the longest only eight monosyllabic words (4.4.1, 5–6, 8, 11). Now that Antony and the troops have left, she speaks at greater length. Asking Charmian to lead her back to her chamber, she nearly allows herself to say that she expects Antony to lose. "He goes forth gallantly. That he and Caesar might / Determine this great war in single fight! / Then Antony—but now—" (4.4.36–38). A courageous heart will not win the day.

Act Four, Scene Five

The Soldier who had urged Antony to fight on land at Actium (3.7.60–66) greets him by imploring "[t]he gods [to] make this a happy day to Antony!" (4.5.1). By "a happy day," he means a lucky day.[25] If Antony wins, he would owe his victory to fortune or the gods' favor, not to his own strength. The Soldier's locution is not surprising. The man knows of the recent desertions not only of kings, but of Enobarbus, "[o]ne ever near thee" (4.5.7), this morning. Had Antony listened to him at Actium, he says, "The kings that have revolted and the soldier / That has this morning left thee would have still / Followed thy heels" (4.5.4–6).

Antony is stunned at the news that Enobarbus has left ("What sayest thou? / . . . Is he gone?" [4.5.9, 11]). Though no doubt misled by his deceptive vow (4.2.8), he seems to have taken for granted that Enobarbus would remain loyal, no matter what. Thus, even while openly regretting not having listened to the Soldier at Actium ("Would thou and those thy scars had once prevailed / To make me fight at land!" [4.5.2–3]), Antony initially accepts no responsibility for Enobarbus's flight. On the contrary, as soon as he hears that Enobarbus has left without his treasure, he orders Eros to send it after him, with a letter signed by Antony: "Say that I wish he never find more cause / To change a master" (4.5.15–16). According to Antony's acerbic charge, Enobarbus fled for mercenary and cowardly reasons. He deserted for Caesar's money, but was so cowardly that he ran away too quickly to take his own with him.

Antony, however, appears suddenly to reverse himself: "Oh, my fortunes have / Corrupted honest men" (4.5.16–17). His reversal, however, is equivocal. Antony blames his "fortunes," not himself. He speaks as though his loss of the battle rather than the reason for it has corrupted honest men. One's fortunes determine one's following, as Cleopatra noted in dismay (3.13.39–41). Enobarbus simply sought the victorious side.

Antony thus does not withdraw his angry insult and intended punishment of Enobarbus. Instead of retracting his order to send Enobarbus's treasure after him, he orders Eros to do it right away ("Dispatch" [4.5.17]). Yet, his final word—"Enobarbus!" (4.5.17)—seems to show just how surprised, shocked, shaken and saddened he is.

Act Four, Scene Six

1.

Ordering Agrippa to begin the battle, Caesar says that he wants Antony taken alive ("Our will is Antony be took alive" [4.6.2]). Earlier, he wanted Antony killed (3.12.23; 3.13.17–19), but, now, he seems to wish to capture him as a trophy of war and parade him through Rome in his triumph, as he will later explicitly wish to do with Cleopatra (5.2.62–66). Caesar would thus treat Antony as a non-Roman. No Roman has ever been led as a captive through Rome in triumph. In *Julius Caesar*, Caesar celebrated a Roman triumph for his victory over Pompey's sons in the civil war, but did not parade any of them through Rome (*JC*, 1.1.30–51). Even so, the Romans were outraged.[26] Brutus and Cassius feared that, if they lost at Philippi, Octavius and Antony would lead them "in triumph / Through the streets of Rome" (*JC*, 5.1.108–9). But their own suicides averted that disgrace, if Octavius and Antony had actually intended it. Here, however, Caesar will not only celebrate the victory of a Roman over a Roman, but would presumably be the first Roman to march a Roman captive through Rome in his victory triumph as though a foreigner,[27] stripping him of his legal protections as a Roman.[28]

As Rome becomes universal, the distinction between Roman and non-Roman disappears. While foreigners may now be treated as Romans, Romans may be treated as foreigners. Universal empire obliterates the most basic political distinction.

"The time of universal peace is near" (4.6.5). Caesar's defeat of Antony will mean the end of centuries of Rome's continual foreign wars, culminating in its conquest of the world. "All the countries of the world have been reduced under obedience to the Romans" (Polybius, 3.1.4; Grimeston, 102).[29] Dominating "the three-nooked world" (4.6.6) from Egypt to Gaul, from Iberia to Parthia, from Africa to Armenia, Rome will now have no rival power to seriously threaten it.[30] "The temple of Janus Quirinus, which from the foundation of the City before his days had . . . twice been shut, [Caesar] in a far shorter space of time (having peace both by sea and land) shut a third time" (Suetonius, *Augustus*, 22.1; Holland, 1:97).[31] The whole world "[s]hall bear the olive freely" (4.6.7). The peace, moreover, will be internal as well as external. For the last century, Rome's foreign wars, contributing enormously to its generals' wealth and power, have produced domestic conflicts resulting in betrayals, proscriptions, assassinations and civil wars among rival leaders. Romans have killed one another in the Capitol in Rome and on battlefields abroad. Just as Caesar's victory will leave Rome with no foreign enemy, it will leave Caesar with no domestic rival. The defeat of Antony will put an end to Rome's bloody turmoil.[32]

When he hears that Antony has taken the field, Caesar sends an order to Agrippa to place Antony's deserters in the front line so that "Antony may seem to spend his fury / Upon himself" (4.6.10–11). He wants to punish Antony by having him fight against his former troops. His reason for punishing Antony is different from his reason for punishing Antony's troops. Whereas he wants to punish Antony's deserters in order to help establish discipline and loyalty among his own troops (4.1.13–15), Caesar seems to be prompted by nothing but cruel spite in wanting "Antony [to] seem to spend his fury / Upon himself." His punishment of Antony is to make it seem to Antony that his futile fight against Caesar is nothing but his furious fight against himself—his own self-punishment. We see throughout the play that Caesar's strength lies in waiting for the right moment to act and taking advantage of other people's weaknesses and mistakes. In his vengeful punishment of Antony, we see that this is more than merely a cunning tactic.

2.

Caesar shows no greater gratitude toward Alexas than toward Antony's deserters. Enobarbus, now alone, having heard of his intended treatment of them, tells of his treatment of Alexas. Antony had sent Alexas to Herod to keep Herod from defecting to Caesar. But Alexas, instead, persuaded "Great Herod to incline himself to Caesar / And leave his master Antony" (4.6.14–15), clearing the way for Caesar to enter Egypt from the north.[33] But Caesar "[f]or this pains / . . . hath hanged him" (4.6.15–16).[34] Nor does Caesar think he can trust Canidius, who deserted with his legions and cavalry (3.10.33–35). "Canidius and the rest / That fell away have entertainment but / No honourable trust" (4.6.16–18). Caesar has taken them into his service with pay, but without positions of trust.

His thoughts turning to himself, Enobarbus blames himself for deserting Antony: "I have done ill, / Of which I do accuse myself so sorely / That I will joy no more" (4.6.18–20). In accusing himself, Enobarbus divides himself as both accuser and accused ("I . . . accuse myself"). He distinguishes between his loyal and his disloyal self. Yet, he also seems to attenuate the distinction, referring to himself thrice as "I," once in the past ("I have done ill"), once in the present ("I do accuse myself") and once in the future ("I will joy no more"). Although amounting to guilt, judgment and punishment, Enobarbus's three "I's," like Antony's guilty and judging "I's" ("I followed that I blush to look upon" [3.11.12]), seem to be largely the same self—the same "I"—at different moments. They reduce but do not reject a noble self.

3.

When one of Caesar's soldiers tells him that Antony has sent all of his treasure after him, with generous gifts besides, Enobarbus gives it all to the Soldier ("I give it you" [4.6.25]). The Soldier understands Enobarbus's reply as a sign of his disbelief. "Mock not, Enobarbus. / I tell you true" (4.6.26–27). To Enobarbus, the Soldier thinks, the news is too good to be true. "Your emperor / Continues still a Jove," he assures him (4.6.29–30). But Enobarbus believes the news. Like the Soldier, he sees Antony as a god who bountifully rewards even his betrayers. Thus, when the man leaves, Enobarbus, filled with utter self-contempt and now rejecting his noble self, declares that he is the worst man in the world and that he realizes this more than anyone else ("I am alone the villain of the earth, / And feel I am so most" [4.6.31–32]). Enobarbus sees only Antony's lavish largess, not his intended insult. "O Antony, / Thou mine of bounty, how wouldst thou have paid / My better service, when my turpitude / Thou dost so crown with gold!" (4.6.32–35). Enobarbus's contempt for himself and praise of Antony are reciprocally related. The more Enobarbus admires Antony, the more contempt he has for himself; and the more contempt he has for himself, the more he admires Antony. Enobarbus fails to recognize Antony's gesture as a deliberate affront because he fully accepts its ignominious verdict. He takes Antony's giving at face value because he takes his own contemptibleness for granted. "This blows my heart," he says, describing his melancholic heart as swelling to the bursting point.[35] "If swift thought break it not, a swifter mean / Shall outstrike thought, but thought will do't, I feel" (4.6.35–37). If shame does not quickly break his heart, suicide will do so more quickly, though shame alone, he thinks, will kill him quickly. Enobarbus then refuses to fight against Antony. "I fight against thee?" he asks. "No, I will go seek / Some ditch wherein to die; the foul'st best fits / My latter part of life" (4.6.38–40). Not so much death itself as a shameful death, he thinks, is his fitting self-punishment. A foul death befits his foul final acts.

Act Four, Scene Seven

1.

The battle proves more difficult for Caesar than he (or Cleopatra) had expected. Agrippa calls for a retreat, fearing that his troops have gotten themselves entangled too deeply among Antony's forces. Even "Caesar himself has work" (4.7.2).

2.

Scarus, entering with Antony, confirms Agrippa's report. Addressing Antony as "my brave emperor" (4.7.4), Scarus, who never saw anything more shameful than his flight at Actium (3.10.22–24), praises Antony and his forces for fighting well: "[T]his is fought indeed! / Had we done so at first, we had droven them home / With clouts about their heads" (4.7.4–6). Scarus, proud of his bloody wounds, spiritedly jokes about them. "I had a wound here that was like a T / But now 'tis made an H" (4.7.7–8). Scarus, whose own name is a pertinent pun, makes both an audible and a visible jest. He puns on the pronunciation of H ("ache") and plays on the shapes of the letters T and H: with an additional stroke (wound) at the bottom, H is a T on its side.[36] Scarus's jests point unwittingly past the present fight to the emergence of Christianity, according to which earthly ("terrene" [3.13.158]) rewards and punishments are superseded by those of Heaven and Hell.

3.

Eros further corroborates the news. "They're beaten, sir," he announces, "and our advantage serves / For a fair victory" (4.7.11–12). Caesar's troops are not only retreating; they are being routed. What Antony's forces have already gained favors their winning a complete victory. Scarus therefore wants to continue the drive. "Let us score their backs / And snatch 'em up as we take hares—behind!" he cheerfully suggests. "'Tis sport to maul a runner" (4.7.12–14). Caesar's troops have turned their backs and run. Antony appreciates Scarus's high spirits and valor ("I will reward thee / Once for thy sprightly comfort, and tenfold / For thy good valour" [4.7.14–16]). With Antony urging him on ("Come thee on!" [4.7.16]), Scarus is eager to follow, even though his wounds force him to limp ("I'll halt after" [4.7.17]).

Act Four, Scene Eight

1.

Antony's surprising military success is the first that he wins for himself in the play. Eager to tell Cleopatra, he orders a soldier to run ahead and let her know that his forces "have beat [Caesar] to his camp" (4.8.1). "Tomorrow, / Before the sun shall see's," he confidently tells his men, "we'll spill the blood / That has today escaped" (4.8.2–4). Rather than follow up the rout, as he just seemed ready to do (4.7.16), Antony will wait until tomorrow to pursue a final victory. His delay, caused by his eagerness to "let the Queen know of our gests" (4.8.2), will turn his success into his utter defeat.

Antony thanks his men for being brave fighters ("doughty-handed" [4.8.5]) and praises them for having fought as if they were not merely in service to him, but had been fighting for their own cause as much as for his: "Not as you served the cause, but as't had been / Each man's like mine" (4.8.6–7). Antony's praise is a degraded echo of the cause for which Rome's earlier citizen-soldiers fought. Where they felt their country's fight as their own, Antony's men feel his fight as their own. Their cause is not simply each man's own, but is nonetheless entirely private. "You have shown all Hectors," Antony continues, urging the men to return to "the city" and tell their wives and friends of their feats (4.8.7, 8). But while Hector defended his own city, Antony's men are defending Alexandria, not Rome. At least for Scarus and other Romans among them, "the city" is not their city. Their "cause" is different from Hector's.

2.

When Cleopatra enters, Antony tells Scarus that he will commend his acts "[t]o this great fairy" and "[m]ake her thanks bless thee" (4.8.12–13). As Antony describes her, Cleopatra is a more-than-human enchantress, who wields magical power and whose thanks are a blessing. Before commending Scarus, however, Antony, already celebrating victory, bids Cleopatra, the light or inspiration of the world ("O thou day o'th' world" [4.8.13]), to "[l]eap

. . . , attire and all," to his heart through his impenetrable armor ("proof of harness"), and on his heart "[r]ide on the pants triumphing" (4.8.14–16). Antony's hyperbole, magnifying his triumph by likening it to an impossibility, confounds the material and the immaterial, the animate and the inanimate, the spirited and the erotic. Cleopatra is to penetrate his impenetrable armor and to ride in triumph on his panting breast as if on a triumphal chariot. Cleopatra responds no less hyperbolically. Calling him "Lord of lords" (4.8.16), she attributes to Antony immeasurable manliness ("O infinite virtue" [4.8.17]). Cleopatra describes, however, not Antony's victory, but his escape: "Com'st thou smiling from / The world's great snare uncaught?" (4.8.17–18). Much earlier, expecting victory, she called Antony "[t]he demi-Atlas of this earth, the arm / And burgonet of men!" (1.5.24–25). But now, having expected defeat, she counts an escape as a triumph. Her sights and expectations lowered, she sees glory not in attaining noble victory but in avoiding ignoble defeat. Antony may address Cleopatra as the "day o'th' world," but the world's glory seems already to be dimming for her. It thus seems no mere coincidence that, despite her praising his immeasurable manliness, Cleopatra calls Antony by a New Testament designation for God delivering the Last Judgment ("Lord of Lords" [Rev. 17:14, 19:16; also 1 Tim. 6:15]).

Antony proudly tells "[his] nightingale" (4.8.18) of his military success. Cleopatra is now his "nightingale," a bird, suitably enough, that sings late in the evening. But she is his nightingale not so much because of the beauty of her voice, as Plutarch reports,[37] but because she is now praising rather than taunting him—in fact, praising him for only the second time to his face.[38] Antony can make good her praise with his news. "We have beat them to their beds," he exults (4.8.19). To be beaten to one's bed is not just to be defeated, but to be beaten out of one's standing in the world. It is to be made unmanly.[39] Antony, more particularly, describes himself with a metaphor correcting his debacle at Actium. After Actium, he described his white hairs rebuking his brown hairs for rashness and his brown hairs rebuking his white hairs for fear and infatuation: according to the one, he lacked reason; according to the other, he lacked courage. In the mutual recrimination, his noble self disappeared (3.11.13–15). Now, flushed with the expectation of victory, Antony, using the same metaphor, claims that although he mingles age with youth ("Though grey / Do something mingle with our younger brown"), his reason governs his sinews and he himself can prove the equal of the young ("yet have we / A brain that nourishes our nerves and can / Get goal for goal of youth" [4.8.19–22]). Contrary to Enobarbus's severe indictment (3.13.202–5), reason and prowess together, Antony asserts, form his noble self.

Antony urges Cleopatra to allow Scarus to kiss her hand. When Thidias kissed it, Antony saw the kiss as a sign of her betrayal. With Scarus, he sees it as her honoring the man for his loyalty and courage. "Kiss it, my warrior," he says. "He hath fought today," Antony tells Cleopatra, "As if a god in hate of mankind had / Destroyed in such a shape" (4.8.24–26). Antony's intent to reverse his shame at Actium only increases the irony of Scarus's kiss. Scarus is honored by kissing the queen he cursed at Actium for causing Antony to "kiss . . . away / Kingdoms and provinces" (3.10.7–8). Moreover, his kissing her—part of Antony's impatient interruption of the battle, so that he could boast to Cleopatra of his success—will kiss away what remains of his empire. Not surprisingly, Scarus says not a word throughout the scene.

For Antony, no prize can be too great for Scarus. When Cleopatra rewards him handsomely with "[a]n armour all of gold," which "was a king's," Antony assures her, "He has deserved it, were it carbuncled / Like holy Phoebus' car" (4.8.27–29).[40] As with fire, Scarus's brilliance and destructiveness are one and the same. The man who destroyed Antony's enemies as if he were a god hating mankind deserves the gold armor of a king set with fire-red gems befitting the sun god's chariot. His superlative brilliant reward would match his superlative brilliant deeds.

Although victory is not yet his, Antony wants to celebrate. Taking Cleopatra's hand, he calls upon his men to make a celebratory ("jolly" [4.8.30]) march through Alexandria, bearing their "hacked targets like the men that owe them" (4.8.31). The hacked shields, like the men's wounds, directly reflect their courage. Wishing that his great palace could accommodate all his men, Antony says that, if it did, he would have the entire army feast together and drink heavily "to the next day's fate, / Which promises royal peril" (4.8.34–35). Tomorrow's peril is "royal" in that war is the occupation of kings (4.4.17) and tomorrow's battle holds Antony and Cleopatra's fate. If he could, Antony says, he would have his full army "drink carouses" (4.8.34) to tomorrow's outcome. Then, he calls upon those playing trumpets and drums to make so great a musical din that "heaven and earth" will echo each other and "[a]pplaud . . . [the army's] approach" (4.8.38–39). If Antony's celebration begins with a march through Alexandria resembling a Roman triumph, it quickly becomes an Egyptian revelry.[41]

Act Four, Scene Nine

1.

Antony spoke of fighting before sunrise (4.8.3). But Caesar's sentry expects his forces to take up their positions for battle much earlier. Telling his company that they must return to the guardroom if not relieved within the hour, he reports that "[some] say we shall embattle / By th' second hour i'th' morn" (4.9.3–4). Caesar, whose forces had a terrible day in the battle ("This last day was a shrewd one to's" [4.9.5]), evidently wants to gain the initiative by marshaling his forces early.

2.

Enobarbus, entering in bright ("shiny" [4.9.2]) moonlight, repents to the moon. Previously, he thought or hoped that his loyalty to a defeated Antony would earn him "a place i'th' story" (3.13.47). Now, he expects that his disloyalty to Antony will bring him infamy in history: "Be witness to me, O thou blessed moon, / When men revolted shall upon record / Bear hateful memory, poor Enobarbus did / Before thy face repent" (4.9.9–12). Enobarbus does not expect to be spared a hateful remembrance. He asks only that the "blessed moon" bear witness that he repented. The moon alone will know. But the moon will do more than know. Addressing it now as the "sovereign mistress of true melancholy" (4.9.15), Enobarbus regards the moon as a welcome source of death. "The poisonous damp of night disponge upon me," he bids the moon, "That life, a very rebel to my will, / May hang no longer on me" (4.9.16–18). His life, clinging to him against his will, should leave him, as he left Antony. Enobarbus, however, quickly alters the manner of his sought death. "Throw my heart / Against the flint and hardness of my fault," he implores the moon, "Which, being dried with grief, will break to powder / And finish all foul thoughts" (4.9.18–21). The cause of his death will be internal rather than external. Instead of the dampness of the night poisoning him, the dryness of his heart and the hardness of his deed will destroy him. His heart, dried with grief and thrown against the hardness of his fault, will fall to dust and end his life and all his thoughts of shame. Death, for him, would be both punishment and relief.

Yet, contrary to what he first suggested, Enobarbus finally wants more than the moon to know that he remorsefully repented. He wants Antony's forgiveness.

> O Antony,
> Nobler than my revolt is infamous,
> Forgive me in thine own particular,
> But let the world rank me in register
> A master-leaver and a fugitive.

(4.9.21–25)

The world should remember him for his infamous betrayal, but Antony, the only person he truly cares about, should forgive him. Accordingly, as Enobarbus thinks and dies of heartbreak and shame, his final words are a cry to Antony: "O Antony! O Antony!" (4.9.26). As he divides himself internally between his guilty and his repentant self,[42] he divides himself externally between the infamous Enobarbus the world should know and the repentant Enobarbus Antony should know. Despite thinking the foulest end best fits the latter part of his life (4.6.39–40), he cannot completely renounce his better self.

Although one of Caesar's sentries is certain that Enobarbus is dead ("The hand of death hath raught him" [4.9.36]), others are not so sure: "He may recover yet" (4.9.40). Their doubt or disbelief seems telling. No one in Caesar's world dies for love or shame.[43] Aware that he is a man of some importance, the guards carry Enobarbus off to the guardroom, their hour now up.

Cleopatra, as an oath of love for Antony, cursed herself, her children and all her subjects with their lying "graveless, till the flies and gnats of Nile / Have buried them for prey" (3.13.171–72), if indeed she did not love him. Later, when threatening to kill herself to avoid being paraded through Rome, she will vow, "Rather a ditch in Egypt / Be gentle grave unto me! Rather on Nilus mud / Lay me stark naked, and let the water-flies / Blow me into abhorring!" (5.2.56–59). Like Enobarbus, she speaks of dying foully in a ditch. But however repulsive she intends her end to be, Cleopatra imagines it occurring in Egypt.[44] Her grave or lack of grave is located in the mud of the Nile. In contrast, neither Enobarbus nor any other Roman in the play thinks of Rome when he thinks of death. Just as Enobarbus addresses the moon— the "terrene moon" (3.13.158)—rather than a Roman god, the place where he dies could be anywhere in the world.[45] Universalism has made him, like many other Romans, rootless.

Act Four, Scene Ten

As before Actium, we see the two sides, briefly, in turn. Caesar, having been overmatched on land, prepares to fight at sea as well as on land. "Their preparation is today by sea," Antony reports; "We please them not by land" (4.10.1–2). Despite his advantage on land, Antony lets Caesar determine where they will fight. Indeed, when Antony says that Caesar is preparing for sea, Scarus feels forced to correct him: "For both, my lord" (4.10.2). Antony, answering him, wishes that "they'd fight i'th' fire or i'th' air; / We'd fight there too" (4.10.3–4). He wishes to fight in all four elements. His wish, replacing prudent military strategy with cosmic swagger, not only ignores the urgent tactical issue, but would, yet again, concede the initiative to Caesar.

Antony recognizes, however, that he will fight only on sea and land, as he underscores with an adversative "But": "But this it is: our foot / Upon the hills adjoining to the city / Shall stay with us—order for sea is given" (4.10.4–6). While Antony allows Caesar to begin the battle ("They have put forth the haven" [4.10.7]), his plan is to let the naval forces fight first and, seeing how the sea battle proceeds ("Where their appointment we may best discover / And look on their endeavour" [4.10.8–9]), keep his infantry where he can use them as circumstances develop. This is the plan that failed at Actium (see 3.9.1–4).

Act Four, Scene Eleven

Caesar, outlining his battle plan, points up the importance of Antony's failure to pursue a complete victory, yesterday, and his playing into Caesar's hands, today. He says that his forces will remain quiet on land, unless attacked ("But being charged, we will be still by land" [4.11.1]). And he does not expect to be attacked on land, he adds, because Antony's "best force / Is forth to man his galleys" (4.11.2–3). In addition to fighting from a disadvantage and conceding the initiative, Antony is using his best troops as sailors, as he had at Actium (3.7.61–66). Ironically, he is fighting the sea battle as though it were the land battle it should have been. Not surprisingly, Caesar expects to be able to fight from his most advantageous position (". . . hold our best advantage" [4.11.4]).

Act Four, Scene Twelve

1.

When Antony leaves to observe the imminent sea battle, Scarus, alone, speaks of swallows having built their nests in Cleopatra's ships. The ominous sign, suggesting death and particularly portentous for Isis,[46] evidently frightens or disheartens everyone. Even the soothsayers refuse to say what they think: "The augurs / Say they know not, they cannot tell; look grimly, / And dare not speak their knowledge" (4.12.4–6). The augurs pretend not to understand what they dare not say they know. A reflection of the orientalizing of Roman divination, no Roman interprets the sign favorably, and everyone seems to see it as telling their fate rather than as testing their decision. Antony, for his part, his mood reflecting "[h]is fretted fortunes" (4.12.8), jerks back and forth ("by starts" [4.12.7]) between valor and dejection, between hope because of what he has and fear because of what he lacks.

2.

Antony, returning, announces utter defeat ("All is lost!" [4.12.9]). As at Actium, he loses before the battle even begins, this time because his sailors have abandoned him. "My fleet hath yielded to the foe, and yonder / They cast their caps up and carouse together / Like friends long lost" (4.12.11–13). Antony immediately blames Cleopatra: "This foul Egyptian hath betrayed me" (4.12.10). The fleet has betrayed him because Cleopatra has betrayed him. Their treachery is the result of hers. "Triple-turned whore!" Antony excoriates Cleopatra, "'Tis thou / Hast sold me to this novice, and my heart / Makes only wars on thee" (4.12.13–15).[47] Antony seems to mean that Cleopatra turned from Gnaeus Pompey to Julius Caesar, from Julius Caesar to Antony, and now from Antony to Octavius Caesar, to whom she has sold him. Her political interests determine her allegiance, as the terms "whore" and "sold" seem to stress.[48] Antony, telling Scarus to go and urge his remaining loyal troops to flee, says that he wants to make war only against Cleopatra. "[W]hen I am revenged upon my charm, / I have done all" (4.12.16–17). All Antony has left to live for is to revenge himself upon his beguiling betrayer.

When Scarus leaves, Antony's thoughts turn quickly to suicide. "O sun, thy uprise shall I see no more" (4.12.18). To be alive means to see the light of day. Life, especially a noble life, entails seeing and being seen in full daylight. Yet, despite his real loss and Cleopatra's imagined treachery, Antony finds some basis for pride: "Fortune and Antony part here; even here / Do we shake hands" (4.12.19–20). Fortune and Antony, once enemies (3.11.74–75; 4.4.4–5), now part with mutual respect. In spite of his ignominious defeat, Fortune does not regard Antony with any less respect for having beaten him. But having briefly assuaged his pride, Antony speaks of those who flattered and betrayed him. He is incensed at his former flatterers ("The hearts / That spanieled me at heels" [4.12.20–21]), who now heap their sweet flattery on fortunate Caesar (". . . do discandy, melt their sweets / On blossoming Caesar" [4.12.22–23]). Having been abandoned by them, he now sees their flattery as flattery. Antony is especially enraged at Cleopatra. "Betrayed I am. / O this false soul of Egypt!" (4.12.24–25). As after Actium (3.11.56–61), he angrily acknowledges that Cleopatra ruled him—that he acted in obedience to, and in behalf of, her: "This grave charm / Whose eye becked forth my wars and called them home, / Whose bosom was my crownet, my chief end . . . " (4.12.25–27).[49] Her love was his highest end. But Cleopatra, "[l]ike a right gypsy hath at fast and loose / Beguiled me to the very heart of loss" (4.12.28–29).[50] Antony fought for, and was betrayed by, Cleopatra. As her love was his crowning end, her betrayal is his complete loss.

3.

Antony impatiently calls for Eros ("What, Eros, Eros!" [4.12.30]), and Cleopatra enters, asking, "Why is my lord enraged against his love?" (4.12.31). It is not immediately clear why Antony wants Eros. Nor does he carry out his threat to take revenge upon Cleopatra. "Vanish, or I shall give thee thy deserving / And blemish Caesar's triumph" (4.12.32–33). Antony seems to say that letting Cleopatra live is to spare her. Yet, he threateningly describes what would come of her if she collaborates with Caesar. "Let him take thee," he warns,

> And hoist thee up to the shouting plebeians!
> Follow his chariot like the greatest spot
> Of all thy sex; most monster-like be shown
> For poor'st diminutives, for dolts, and let
> Patient Octavia plough thy visage up
> With her prepared nails!

> (4.12.34–39)

Cleopatra would be punished directly by her own treachery. To join Caesar would mean to ornament his triumphal procession. Losing face figuratively as well as literally, Cleopatra would be exhibited in a cage to the shouting commoners,[51] led in triumph like the most shameful woman, and displayed like a monster in a freak show for the entertainment of the rabble, while long-suffering Octavia would tear up her face with fingernails prepared for the occasion. Life in Rome would be worse for Cleopatra than death in Egypt. This brief exchange, just nine lines, is the only time Antony and Cleopatra, who make their private love public, are alone, together, on the stage.

After Cleopatra leaves, Antony restates his threat to kill her, while repeating his claim to be sparing her. "'Tis well thou'rt gone / If it be well to live. But better 'twere / Thou fell'st into my fury, for one death / Might have prevented many" (4.12.39–42). Antony, in his misery, offers a formal argument. If life is good, he says, it is good that Cleopatra has escaped his fury. But it would be better for her, he concludes, if he had killed her, for her death would forestall the shame and anguish that she is sure to endure, which are as terrible as many deaths.[52] If life is good, death is an evil. But if life entails many miseries as bad as death, then the sooner one dies, the better. Although Antony frequently speaks in generalities, this is the only time he attempts an explicit formal argument, including a conditional major premise ("If . . . "), a minor premise ("for . . . ") and a conclusion by way of contraries ("But better . . . "). Antony, a man with an enormous appetite for life, may be not so much threatening Cleopatra as trying to persuade himself to kill himself.

Calling again for Eros, Antony, likening himself to the dying Hercules, declares that he wears "[t]he shirt of Nessus" (4.12.43). The shirt, poisoned by the Centaur Nessus but believed by Hercules's wife, Deianira, to be a love charm, caused Hercules agony and finally death when he put it on. Hercules in his rage tried to kill the innocent Lichas, who delivered the shirt, and threatened to kill the unwitting Deianira, for conspiring against him.[53] Here, Antony, despite warning Cleopatra of his fury, seems to lack the rage to carry out his threat:

> Teach me
> Alcides, thou mine ancestor, thy rage;
> Let me lodge Lichas on the horns o'th' moon,
> And with those hands that grasped the heaviest club
> Subdue my worthiest self. The witch shall die.
> To the young Roman boy she hath sold me, and I fall
> Under this plot. She dies for't.
>
> (4.12.43–49)

Although at once asserting his heroic worthiness and declaring himself worthiest of death ("Subdue my worthiest self"), Antony needs Hercules to teach him his rage. Notwithstanding his Herculean threats, underscored by his wish to kill, or rekill, [the legendary Lichas, Antony's desire for revenge and wish to die seem insufficient. He needs the god or demigod who has already left him.

Act Four, Scene Thirteen

Cleopatra asks her women for help. Antony is "more mad," she says, "Than Telamon for his shield; the boar of Thessaly / Was never so embossed" (4.13.1–3). Telamon (Ajax) went mad and killed himself when Achilles's arms were awarded to Odysseus, rather than to him, as the bravest of the Greeks at Troy (Homer, *Odyssey*, 11.543ff.). The boar of Thessaly, whose eyes glowed with blood and fire, was sent by a vengeful Diana, showing that wrath can move even the gods, to ravage the fields of Calydon when its king,

Oeneus, neglected to sacrifice to her (Ovid, *Metamorphoses*, 8.271ff.). Cleopatra's comparisons, one human, the other divine, involve suicidal madness and merciless devastation brought on by an enraged sense of deserved honor denied.

Charmian, answering Cleopatra's call for help, thinks of the plan which sets in motion the events that will lead directly to Antony's death. Early in the play, Charmian urged Cleopatra to cross Antony in nothing and give him his way in everything. Even though Cleopatra rejected her advice, saying she spoke "like a fool: the way to lose him" (1.3.7–13), she now follows it. Antony wants her dead, and so Charmian proposes that Cleopatra lock herself in the monument "and send him word you are dead" (4.13.4). Cleopatra's discarding her characteristic contrariness will prove catastrophic.

Charmian explains or defends her drastic proposal by suggesting that Antony is suffering worse than if were he dying. "The soul and the body rive not more in parting / Than greatness going off" (4.13.5–6). As Enobarbus had suggested (3.13.99–100), the loss of greatness is worse than death. Great men can endure the thought of losing their lives more easily than their greatness.

Cleopatra adopts and embellishes the ruse. Mardian is not only to tell Antony that she has killed herself, but to say that her last word was "Antony" and to speak it so as to arouse his pity for her. His pity is to quell his anger. Antony is to think that Cleopatra, grieved by his anger, slew herself out of love for him. Cleopatra also wants to know how Antony takes her death— something she has already suggested a lover can never know (1.3.65–66). She feigns her suicide in order to answer her own doubts about Antony's love in addition to answering his doubt about hers. News of her death, meant as testimony of her love, is at the same time a test of his love.

"To th'monument!" Cleopatra cries twice, echoing Charmian and framing her final speech (4.13.3, 6, 10). The monument is a tomb which Cleopatra has built for herself, dedicated to her immortal fame.[54] Under Charmian's plan, the tomb's secure walls and bolted doors will protect her from Antony's fury. Ironically, Cleopatra in shamming her death seeks protection in a mausoleum which she has built for her death and in which she will in fact soon die. Her false death foreshadowing her true death, her history will imitate her histrionics.

Act Four, Scene Fourteen

1.

Antony, asking whether Eros can still see him ("Eros, thou yet behold'st me?" [4.14.1]), imagines that he is as shapeless on the outside as on the inside, that the shape of his body reflects the state of his soul. Betrayed by Cleopatra, he has no form, no substance. Antony compares himself to the changing shapes of clouds which only resemble solid objects, resemblances which "nod unto the world / And mock our eyes with air" (4.14.6–7). Things that appear large and solid—a dragon, a bear, a lion, a citadel, a rock, a mountain, a promontory—are nothing but airy illusions. "They are black vesper's pageants" (4.14.8)—mere shows, which, dependent, moreover, on the twilight for their illusion, presage the night's full darkness. "That which is now a horse, even with a thought / The rack dislimns and makes it indistinct / As water is in water" (4.14.9–11). No longer even a "vapour" (4.14.3), the apparent object loses all its shape and becomes utterly indistinct.

Antony says that he is such a body. "Here I am Antony, / Yet cannot hold this visible shape" (4.14.13–14). Antony cannot hold his shape because he did not hold Cleopatra's love. He fought his wars for Cleopatra, he says, but she betrayed him. He thought she loved him because he loved her. He gave her not just his heart, but the hearts of a million of his followers. And she "has / Packed cards with Caesar, and false-played my glory / Unto an enemy's triumph" (4.14.18–20). Antony speaks as if his glory had been intact until Cleopatra cheated him of it. Urging Eros not to weep, he indicates that suicide is the one course he has left: "There is left us / Ourselves to end ourselves" (4.14.21–22).

2.

Mardian enters, but before he can say that Cleopatra has killed herself, Antony accuses her—"thy vile lady," he calls her (4.14.22)—of having "robbed [him] of [his] sword" (4.14.23). Cleopatra has robbed him of his manhood and consequently of his sense of being and worth. Mardian replies to the implicit, underlying charge. "No, Antony," he answers, "My mistress loved thee and her fortunes mingled / With thine entirely" (4.14.23–25). Their love was mutual and their fortunes inseparable (see 1.1.38–39). Antony, outraged at being contradicted by a eunuch ("Hence, saucy eunuch! Peace!" [4.14.25]), says that Cleopatra has betrayed him and, speaking in solemn legal language for the imposition of capital punishment,[55] declares that she "shall die the death" (4.14.26). Mardian, shifting to the language of repayment while punning on death/debt,[56] replies, "Death of one person can be paid but once, / And that she has discharged. What thou wouldst do / Is done unto thy hand" (4.14.27–29). What Antony would do has already been done for him. Mardian, suggesting that Cleopatra killed herself because Antony wanted her dead, presumes that Antony, in seeking revenge, cares simply that she is dead, not whether he himself has killed her. What is "done unto [one's] hand" need not be done by one's hand. The eunuch thinks that one can get full revenge without acting. Intention suffices.

Mardian describes Cleopatra's supposed end. He reports her final words— "The last she spake / Was 'Antony! Most noble Antony!'"—and, overplaying the pathos Cleopatra ordered,[57] tells what she was unable to say: "Then, in the midst, a tearing groan did break / The name of Antony; it was divided / Between her heart and lips. She rendered life, / Thy name so buried in her" (4.14.29–34). Antony's name, cut in two, was half-pronounced by her lips and half-retained by her heart. Cleopatra surrendered her life but buried Antony's name in herself.

Antony concludes, as Cleopatra wished, that her death was an act of love for him. "Unarm, Eros. The long day's task is done / And we must sleep" (4.14.35–36). Antony no longer needs his weaponry and armor, the equipment and accoutrement of a warrior, or wants the awakedness of day. Dismissing Mardian quickly and contemptuously, and asking Eros again to unarm him, Antony senses that no protection can keep the grievous news from assaulting his heart. "The sevenfold shield of Ajax cannot keep / The battery from my heart" (4.14.39–40).[58] Nor does he want it to. He wants his heart to swell toward bursting. "O, cleave, my sides! / Heart, once be stronger than thy continent; / Crack thy frail case!" (4.14.40–42). While Cleopatra's putative last word is the same as Enobarbus's actual last word (4.9.26), Antony's wished-for death is the same as Enobarbus's expected death (4.6.35).

After sending Eros away, Antony, no longer angry, now blames himself. Cleopatra's presumed death has extinguished his anger. Whereas Antony sought her death because he suspected she did not return his love, he seeks his own death because he now believes she did. Her death, he thinks, was a selfless act of love, caused by his desire to kill her. Antony, taken in by her ploy, wants to catch up to Cleopatra and weep for her forgiveness in death. "I will o'ertake thee, Cleopatra, and / Weep for my pardon" (4.14.45–46).[59] As she wept for his pardon after Actium (3.11.68–71), he will weep for hers after their deaths.

Death is also a means of escape. "So it must be, for now / All length is torture; since the torch is out . . ." (4.14.46–47). Further life can be nothing but anguish. Cleopatra was for Antony the light ("torch") of the world. Now that the light is out, Antony must "[l]ie down and stray no farther" (4.14.48). All his efforts will turn back upon and destroy themselves. "Now all labour / Mars what it does—yea, very force entangles / Itself with strength" (4.14.48–50). Not only would any act be futile; its strength would strangle its own attempt. Alluding unwittingly to the Day of Judgment, Antony determines to die: "Seal then, and all is done" (4.14.50).[60] The death that ends his life will seal

Cleopatra's pardon. What began with his threat of revenge in life will end with her act of forgiveness in death.

Antony's desolation is relieved only by imagining what will follow in death. Calling at once for his love, the servant whom he wants to kill him and love itself ("Eros!—I come, my queen.—Eros!" [4.14.51]), Antony bids Cleopatra to wait for him in death:

> Stay for me.
> Where souls do couch on flowers we'll hand in hand
> And with our sprightly port make the ghosts gaze.
> Dido and her Aeneas shall want troops,
> And all the haunt be ours.

> (4.14.51–55)

Antony imagines being with Cleopatra in the Elysian fields, the abode of the blessed, where the noble are rewarded with an immortality of bliss.[61] There, they would dwell in love, free of doubts, pain or sorrow. Just as Antony had initially threatened the world with punishment unless it acknowledged them as peerless lovers (1.1.39–41), he envisages ghosts in Elysium thronging to behold them as the greatest lovers ever. As before, noble actions are replaced by love, and lovers enjoy the most glorious distinction. But, unlike before, that love and glory are to be found in death. With the spirit-like ("sprightly") replacing the sensual, death would recover for Antony and Cleopatra the love and glory they lost in the world. While providing what is missing from life, death would not annihilate but rather glorify their superlative distinction. Antony, however, twists the story of Dido and Aeneas in Hades. Dido's ghost refuses not only to answer but even to look at Aeneas when he greets her there. As she wept for him (and killed herself) when he abandoned her in Carthage, he weeps for her as she leaves him behind in Hades.[62] Antony reverses the unhappy story. He wishes to believe that death gave Aeneas, as he hopes it promises him, what he gave up or lost in life.

3.

Antony speaks quite differently once Eros returns. Sounding like a traditional Roman, he says nothing about love and mentions Cleopatra only to emphasize the dishonor of his continued life: "Since Cleopatra died, / I have lived in such dishonour that the gods / Detest my baseness" (4.14.56–58). Antony is shamed by Cleopatra's death. Although he had carved up and ruled the world, he "condemn[s him]self to lack / The courage of a woman" (4.14.60–61). By remaining alive, he shows that he has a "less noble mind / Than she which, by her death, our Caesar tells / 'I am conqueror of myself'" (4.14.61–63). Cleopatra's suicide is her noble self-conquest (see, e.g., 4.14.21–22; 4.15.15–18, 57–60, 90–92). Antony stresses what a Roman would understand.

Antony solemnly reminds Eros that Eros, his freedman, has sworn that, should the extreme need arise and Antony faced "inevitable . . . / Disgrace and horror" (4.14.66–67), he would, upon Antony's command, kill him.[63] By doing so now, he says, Eros would not be striking Antony, but defeating Caesar: "Thou strik'st not me; 'tis Caesar thou defeat'st" (4.14.69). Eros, repelled by the order, says that he cannot bring himself to do what "all the Parthians darts" (4.14.71) could not do. We previously heard that Antony won credit for Ventidius's victory against Parthia (3.1.9ff.). Eros's protest is Shakespeare's only explicit indication that Antony himself fought against the Parthians.[64] His campaign against them, unlike Ventidius's, ended in disaster.[65] It is hard to know whether Eros's words are a correction or a consequence of our earlier impression. Eros, Antony's most loyal officer, may collapse the distinction between who won the victory and who won credit for the victory. In his eyes, Ventidius's victory may truly have been Antony's, his master.

Answering his repugnance, Antony tells Eros the public shame he would witness if Antony lived. "Wouldst thou be windowed in great Rome and see / Thy master," he asks,

> thus with pleached arms, bending down
> His corrigible neck, his face subdued
> To penetrative shame, whilst the wheeled seat
> Of fortunate Caesar, drawn before him, branded
> His baseness that ensued?

> (4.14.73–78)

Antony, emphasizing his helpless passivity by his series of passive past participles and his contrasting Latinate locution,[66] describes the disgrace and horror of his being captured and exhibited by Caesar. While shame seeks concealment, Caesar would shame Antony before all of Rome. Antony's shame would be literally "penetrative." Because it would be public, it would penetrate to the core of his soul. Nothing could affect his heart more strongly; nothing could disgrace him more. Just as celebrating a Roman triumph is a Roman's greatest glory, being led prisoner in a Roman triumph would be the greatest shame. No fate could be worse.

Eros, horrified, can reply only, "I would not see't" (4.14.78). Calling him then to act, Antony says, "[W]ith a wound I must be cured" (4.14.79). A dignified death will heal Antony. The fatal wound will not only forestall his shame, but, as on the battlefield, show his noble courage. Antony will redeem his honor as well as escape his dishonor. Thus, appealing to Eros directly as a soldier, Antony bids, "Draw that thy honest sword which thou hast worn / Most useful for thy country" (4.14.80–81). This is the first time anyone has mentioned the word "country."[67] Since the wars of Marius and Sulla, Roman commanders have granted Roman citizenship along with freedom to slaves they have conscripted into their private armies: "my enfranched bondman" (3.13.154).[68] Eros, a freedman with a Greek name, has consequently come to think not so much of Rome as of Antony's empire as his country. When Eros, however, recoils ("O sir, pardon me!" [4.14.81]), Antony returns to his liberating vow. "When I did make thee free," he repeats,

> swor'st thou not then
> To do this when I bade thee? Do it at once,
> Or thy precedent services are all
> But accidents unpurposed. Draw, and come!
>
> (4.14.82–85)

Antony challenges Eros's loyalty. Loyalty, according to Antony, rests essentially on intention—not simply on the deed, but on the reason for it. Unless Eros now lives up to his sworn vow, nothing that he has ever done in Antony's service would amount to an intentional action ("But accidents unpurposed"). None of his former acts would show loyalty to Antony. Eros's one remaining act gives worth or meaning to all the rest.

Eros, seeming to comply, asks Antony to "[t]urn from [him] then that noble countenance / Wherein the worship of the whole world lies" (4.14.86–87). To Eros, Antony's face possesses everything worthy of honor or worship in the entire world. Eros asks Antony to turn his face away, ostensibly so he will not see it when he kills him, but, in fact, so Antony will not see him kill himself, instead. Eros's loving devotion to Antony—"My dear master, / My captain and my emperor" (4.14.90–91)—causes him to break his sworn word and disobey him. "Thus I do escape the sorrow / of Antony's death" (4.14.95–96). Eros kills himself to avoid the pain of seeing Antony's death. Like Enobarbus, he dies for Antony, his "great chief" (4.14.94). Paradoxically, Eros's love for Antony fails Antony in the end by proving too strong to allow Eros to serve him.

4.

Antony says that he has learned from Eros's noble example. "Thrice nobler than myself! / Thou teachest me, O valiant Eros, what / I should and thou couldst not" (4.14.96–98). Antony sees the suicides of Cleopatra and Eros as both teaching him and winning for themselves a nobler place than himself in history: "My queen and Eros / Have by their brave instruction got upon me / A nobleness in record" (4.14.98–100). As one would expect of a Roman, he considers Eros and Cleopatra as educating him by their brave deeds ("their brave instruction"). Where Greeks learn by noble precepts, Romans learn by noble examples.[69] "[B]y example of himself . . . others he shall bind" (Ovid, *Metamorphoses*, 15.832; Golding, 15.938).[70] And once again Antony finds nobleness in a noble reputation. Just as Cleopatra's and Eros's deeds are noble examples which serve to earn fame and to instruct others—deeds which both are remembered and remind (Varro, *On the Latin Language*, 6.49)—so their glory lies at once in the public recognition of their acts and in the acts that earn it. But, having spoken of his concern for public distinction, Antony, quickly shifting, compares his death to an act of erotic love. "But I will be / A bridegroom in my death and run into't / As to a lover's bed" (4.14.100–102). Antony will lovingly pursue a noble death, because he can be with his love only in death and she will love him only if he dies nobly for love. No longer a bawdy metaphor for sexual pleasure (cp. 1.2.140ff.), dying, for Antony, is a necessary condition to be with his love. It loses its figurative, and takes on a literal, erotic meaning.

Antony, however, bungles his suicide. Although, falling on his sword, he says, "Eros, / Thy master dies thy scholar. To do thus / I learned of thee" (4.14.102–4), he wounds himself severely but does not kill himself. Antony, in what he supposes to be his dying words, intends a paradoxical inversion as a tribute: the master—both lord and teacher—is the student; the former slave and student is the teacher. The high and the low trade places. As Antony's attempt turns out, the inversion is still greater. While the former slave kills himself nobly, the master manages only to wound himself pathetically.[71]

Antony's attempted death points, once more, to the emergence of Christianity. As he had in the play's opening scene ("Then thou must needs find out new heaven, new earth" [1.1.17]), Antony, declaring that he will be "[a] bridegroom in [his] death," alludes to the new heaven of Christianity: "And I, John, saw the holy city, new Jerusalem, . . . prepared as a bride trimmed for her husband" (Rev. 21:2).[72] And, as he had when taking leave of his household servants (4.2.10–25), he suggests his resemblance to Jesus, the bridegroom who will marry the church: "Let us be glad and rejoice, and give glory to him; for the marriage of the Lamb is come, and his wife hath made herself ready" (Rev. 19:7).[73] In addition, reduced to begging the guards to finish what he has badly begun ("Let him that loves me strike me dead" [4.14.109]),

Antony echoes Revelation's description of men wishing to die rather than endure the burden of living in agony: "[I]n those days shall men seek death, and shall not find it, and shall desire to die, and death shall flee from them" (Rev. 9:6). Finally, the guards, similarly echoing Revelation, see his fall as the end of time. "The star is fallen," one guard states (4.14.107; "And the stars of heaven fell unto the earth"; "[A]nd there fell a great star from heaven"; "And the fifth Angel blew the trumpet, and I saw a star fall from heaven unto the earth" [Rev. 6:13, 8:10; 9:1]). "And time is at his period," another guard says (4.14.108; "[T]ime should be no more" [Rev. 10:6]). And the guards call out, "Alas and woe!" (4.1.4–108), echoing what John hears an eagle cry ("Woe, woe, woe to the inhabitants of the earth" [Rev. 8:13]). Where, in *Coriolanus*, the greatest destruction a Roman can imagine is that of his city (e.g., *Cor.*, 3.1.196, 202–5), in *Antony and Cleopatra*, as in Shakespeare's Christian plays, the greatest imaginable destruction is the destruction of the entire temporal world (also 2.7.14–15; 3.13.150–52; 4.15.10–12; 5.2.84–85).

While the others, fleeing, fearfully refuse to kill Antony ("Thy death and fortunes bid thy followers fly" [4.14.112]), one of his guards, Dercetus, thinks he sees an opportunity to benefit himself. Stealing Antony's sword—a weapon so important to Antony (e.g., 1.3.83; 3.11.67; 3.13.27, 180; 4.14.23, 58–59)—, he calculates, "This sword but shown to Caesar with this tidings / Shall enter me with him" (4.14.113–14). Dercetus does not realize that Caesar wants Antony alive, not dead, that he wants his public humiliation, not his bloody sword. Nor does he seem to have any shame about stealing Antony's sword from his wounded body.[74]

5.

Antony, dying, learns that Cleopatra's reported death was a ruse. Instead of killing him, as Antony first asks him to do, Diomedes discloses that Cleopatra is alive. Diomedes explains that Cleopatra, now locked in her monument, was caught between two fears. She was afraid that Antony suspected she had come to terms with Caesar and that nothing would remove his rage, so she sent word that she was dead. But, then, fearing what Antony might do, she sent Diomedes to tell "the truth" (4.14.128)—a word we have not heard from Cleopatra's own mouth and one she will use only to deceive Caesar (5.2.143). Antony, who asks his remaining guards to carry him to Cleopatra, shows not the least surprise at learning of her feigned suicide. Speaking like a Stoic, as on another hopeless occasion (3.11.74–75), he urges the sorrowful guards not to lament: "Nay, good my fellows, do not please sharp fate / To grace it with your sorrows" (4.14.137–38). To deny sorrow is to defy fate. "Bid that welcome / Which comes to punish us, and we punish it, / Seeming to bear it lightly" (4.14.138–40). Seeing his death as a personal contest with fate, Antony says that he can defeat fate by despising it. By welcoming our fate, however unwanted, we can do to fate ("punish it") what fate has come to us to do ("punish us"). We can rise above our suffering by accepting it. No longer thinking of Elysium, Antony seems able to accept death only if he can imagine himself getting the better of it. Particularly in the face of death, spirited victory is everything for the still-Roman Antony.

Act Four, Scene Fifteen

1.

Charmian tries to comfort Cleopatra, who is certain that her worst fear has come true. But Cleopatra adamantly refuses to be comforted. Unlike Antony, Cleopatra denies that death can be defeated by disdain: "All strange and terrible events are welcome, / But comforts we despise. Our size of sorrow, / Proportioned to our cause, must be as great / As that which makes it" (4.15.3–6). Cleopatra's greatness is revealed not by her stoic indifference to death, but by the heroic greatness of her sorrow. While small things like comforts are to be despised, grief must be as great as its cause. Thus, hearing that Antony is close to death ("His death's upon him, but not dead" [4.15.7]) and seeing him below, Cleopatra, matching her words to her loss, implores the sun to consume the cosmos and darken the world. "O sun, / Burn the great sphere thou mov'st in; darkling stand / The varying shore o'th' world!" (4.15.10–12). Cleopatra, sounding like Revelation's description of the Apocalypse,[75] calls upon the sun to burn the sphere it moves in and, wandering endlessly and aimlessly, leave the world in darkness, without the alternation of night and day.

2.

Antony's first words affirm the triumph of his courage. "Not Caesar's valour hath o'erthrown Antony, / But Antony's hath triumphed on itself" (4.15.15–16). As he imagined was true of Cleopatra's death (4.14.62–63), Antony claims that his death is not Caesar's triumph, but his own. Vindicating his courage, it is an honorable Roman death. Cleopatra answers in kind. "So it should be that none but Antony / Should conquer Antony, but woe 'tis so" (4.15.17–18). Antony and Cleopatra both speak in paradoxical *sententia*. Their words are distinctly Roman in manner as well as in matter.[76] In addition, in sharp contrast to him after the recent battles, Antony does not blame Cleopatra in any way for anything.

Announcing "I am dying, Egypt, dying" (4.15.19), Antony importunes death to wait until he gives Cleopatra "the poor last" of "many thousand kisses" (4.15.21). Cleopatra, however, fears that she will be captured if she opens her monument or leaves it. Daring not to come down even for a final kiss, she is afraid of being captured by Caesar and led through Rome in his triumphal display. "Not th'imperious show / Of the full-fortuned Caesar ever shall / Be brooched with me," she avows.

> If knife, drugs, serpents, have
> Edge, sting or operation, I am safe.
> Your wife Octavia, with her modest eyes
> And still conclusion, shall acquire no honour
> Demuring upon me.
>
> (4.15.24–30)

Suicide will save Cleopatra from the disgrace of Caesar's public procession and Octavia's silent judgment, and deprive both Caesar and Octavia—"Your wife," as Cleopatra calls her (see 1.3.21)—of their hoped-for honor. But although she explains her fear of Caesar in the same terms as Antony had threatened her after his final loss (4.12.33–39), she expresses her fear of Octavia differently. Antony spoke of Octavia's plowing nails; Cleopatra speaks of her "modest eyes / And still conclusion." She seems to fear Octavia's silent judgment more than her cutting nails, her loss of face more than the mutilation of her face (see also 5.2.53–54).

Instead of leaving the monument, Cleopatra and her women hoist Antony up.[77] The final events of Antony's life follow the general pattern of Antony and Cleopatra's lives together. From the first, Cleopatra has acted, and Antony has responded, drawn to her. In the end, she pretends to kill herself, he tries to join her by killing himself, she sends a messenger to say she is alive, he goes to the monument to be with her, and she draws him up. The death pattern, with bleak irony, mimics the love pattern. Thus, as she and the other women struggle to raise Antony, Cleopatra repeats bitterly and piteously her much earlier happy diversions.[78] Where she imagined "draw[ing] . . . up" fishes and thinking everyone an Antony whom she had caught (2.5.13), and where Charmian reminded her of her diver's hanging a dried fish on a hook which Antony fervently "drew up" (2.5.18), she and the other women now must "draw [him] up" (4.15.31). Where Antony, proclaiming that not a minute of their lives should be without pleasure, asked, "What sport tonight?" (1.1.48), and where Cleopatra, imagining him on his horse, exclaimed, "O happy horse, to bear the weight of Antony!" (1.5.22), she is now forced to lament,

"Here's sport indeed! How heavy weighs my lord! / Our strength is all gone into heaviness; / That makes the weight" (4.15.33–35). Gravity replacing levity, the dismal replacing the playful, her sorrow ("heaviness") adds to Antony's weight ("heaviness").[79]

Cleopatra wishes she had Juno's power. "Had I great Juno's power, / The strong-winged Mercury should fetch thee up," she tells Antony, "And set thee by Jove's side" (4.15.35–38). Grimly elevating Antony's bloodied, moribund body, Cleopatra alludes to Hercules's apotheosis. "When [Hercules's divine part] is rid from earthly dross, then I will lift it higher, / And take it into heaven," says Ovid's Jove (Ovid, *Metamorphoses*, 9.268–70; Golding, 9.305–6). But recognizing that her wish is impossible ("Yet come a little; / Wishers were ever fools" [4.15.37–38]), Cleopatra, with the others' help, struggles to raise Antony. Antony, she hopes, will not die before she can kiss him. "Die when thou hast lived; / Quicken with kissing. Had my lips that power, / Thus would I wear them out" (4.15.39–41). Antony sought to live long enough to kiss Cleopatra. Cleopatra wishes that her kisses could restore him to life. Cleopatra in her next breath will rail at Fortune for Antony's death (4.15.45–47); and Charmian, bidding the dead Cleopatra farewell, will see her death as dimming Phoebus's visible splendor (5.2.315–17). Apart from these two mentions, both implying the end of noble virtue in the world, Cleopatra's woeful, wishful mention of Juno, Mercury and Jove is the last time any character mentions a pagan god by name.

Antony, repeating that he is dying ("I am dying, Egypt, dying" [4.15.43]), asks to speak, "Give me some wine and let me speak a little—" (4.15.44). But, as when he tried to leave her early in the play (1.3.15ff.), Cleopatra interrupts and contradicts him. "No, let me speak," she insists, "and let me rail so high / That the false huswife Fortune break her wheel, / Provoked by my offence" (4.15.45–47). Cleopatra takes no responsibility for Antony's death, but instead blames Fortune. She blames faithless Fortune—Fortune whose only purpose seems to be to show its power by showing its inconstancy[80]— for treating Antony as Antony believed Cleopatra had treated him. Just as her sorrow must be as great as its cause, her offense must be great enough to enrage Fortune. Incited by her abusive words, Fortune, unable to punish Cleopatra more than she already has, but looking for an object to punish, would turn her anger against her own wheel. Reviled for her inconstancy, she would unintentionally put an end to her mutability. That Cleopatra speaks in the optative imperative ("[L]et me rail so high / That . . ."), however, only stresses her futility.

Antony, trying again ("One word, sweet queen" [4.15.47]), advises Cleopatra to do what he had previously been enraged to think she had done: "Of Caesar seek your honour with your safety" (4.15.48). With his death at hand, Antony thinks chiefly of protecting Cleopatra's life. He is silent about her dishonor in being paraded in Rome. Nor does he hint at their glory in Elysium. When thinking she is dead, he thinks mostly of their love in death. When knowing she is alive and he is near death, he thinks largely of her safety. Cleopatra, however, denies that she can have honor with her safety: "They do not go together" (4.15.49). Honor requires death, while safety entails dishonor. Asking again to be heard ("Gentle, hear me" [4.15.49]), Antony warns Cleopatra not to trust anyone around Caesar except Proculeius. Antony will prove to be mistaken. Proculeius will trap Cleopatra for Caesar.[81] But Cleopatra answers that she will trust no one: "My resolution and my hands I'll trust" (4.15.51). Repeating her earlier vow (4.15.24–30), she seems determined to die.

Cleopatra finally allows Antony to speak. His last speech, contrasting himself now to what he once had been, recalls his political greatness. Instead of speaking of his love or associating nobility and love, he tells Cleopatra how to remember his political triumphs. Exhorting her not to lament or grieve his "miserable change" (4.15.53), he urges her to fill her thoughts with those of his "former fortunes / Wherein [he] lived the greatest prince o'th' world, / The noblest" (4.15.55–57). His dying thoughts remember his good life. And as his life was noble, so is his death. Although his end is "miserable," Antony denies that it is base. "[I] do now not basely die, / Not cowardly put off my helmet to / My countryman; a Roman by a Roman / Valiantly vanquished" (4.15.57–60). Antony, once again, divides himself. But, this time, he finds both parts noble, both parts Roman. Having vanquished himself, he demonstrates Roman virtue, he says, both as vanquished and as victor—vanquished, by bravely enduring his bloody death; victor, by proudly inflicting it.[82] Although forced to declare his noble courage largely in the negative (". . . do . . . not basely die, / Not cowardly put off . . ."), he claims to die like a true Roman. His Roman spirit roused by the imminent prospect of death, Antony's description of his suicide is the only time he uses the word "Roman" as distinguishing a noble action.[83]

"Now my spirit is going; / I can no more," Antony says, in his dying breath (4.15.60–61). Having lived a life of extravagant excess, he dies with not only the word "more," but the phrase "no more," on his lips. His final words speaking against themselves, his endless appetite for more comes to an end only when he is no more.

"Noblest of men, woo't die" (4.15.61). Cleopatra's sorrowful words of love combine the highest praise ("Noblest of men") with the intimate "woo't." Mardian had reported that Cleopatra's last words were "Antony! Most noble

Antony!" (4.14.30). But although she has previously described him in heroic terms, this is the first time Cleopatra explicitly calls Antony "noble." Just as she calls him "[m]y Antony" only in his absence (1.5.6, 40), she calls him noble only in death.

3.

The world becomes repulsive to Cleopatra. "Hast thou no care of me?" she asks the dead Antony. "Shall I abide / In this dull world, which in thy absence is / No better than a sty?" she asks, rhetorically (4.15.62–64). Without Antony, there is no splendor in the world. The world, no better than a pigsty, is wholly lacking. "The crown o'th' earth doth melt" (4.15.65). In Cleopatra's eyes, Antony, the greatest man who ever lived, was the adornment of the world. With his death, human greatness melts and vanishes. Cleopatra describes the world as emasculated and leveled. "O withered is the garland of the war, / The soldier's pole is fallen," she laments, describing Antony as the wreath of victory in war and a soldier's standard. "[Y]oung boys and girls / Are level now with men; the odds is gone / And there is nothing left remarkable / Beneath the visiting moon" (4.15.66–70). Without Antony's extraordinary greatness, there are no distinctions remaining. Men have become indistinguishable from children. The world is left entirely ordinary, dull, empty and flat.

Cleopatra does not exclude herself from her bleak judgment. She is now, she says, no different from a mere maid who does household chores: "No more but e'en a woman, and commanded / By such poor passion as the maid that milks / And does the meanest chares" (4.15.77–79). Without Antony, she is ruled by the same passions as the humblest woman. Nothing ennobles or distinguishes her heart. When he was alive, Cleopatra continues, Antony made the human world rival that of the gods, but the gods punished him jealously for the rivalry.[84] And with him gone, it would be fitting for her to fling her scepter at them to show the gods how little she now esteems the symbol of her royal authority and how much she despises them:[85] "It were for me / To throw my sceptre at the injurious gods / To tell them that this world did equal theirs / Till they had stolen our jewel" (4.15.79–82). The gods inspired Antony to challenge them. But when he succeeded, they destroyed not only him, but the world in which such a man could aspire to do so. Having stripped the world of greatness and nobility, they have left nothing to love or admire. There is no longer any glory in the world.[86] "All's but naught" (4.15.82). To Cleopatra, whose mournful words are a spirited attack on a spiritless world, Antony's death marks the end of a world worthy of love. All that remains deserves nothing but disgust.

Cleopatra says that she has a choice between "[p]atience . . . and impatience" (4.15.83), between calm endurance and open battle. But while the first is doltish ("sottish" [4.15.83]), the second befits only "a dog that's mad" (4.15.84). Where the one is the inaction of a fool, the other is the blind action of a crazed beast. Is suicide, then, a sin? "Then is it sin / To rush into the secret house of death / Ere death dare come to us?" (4.15.84–86). In a moment, Cleopatra will speak of committing suicide in "the high Roman fashion" (4.15.91). But, here, she poses the question of suicide in a Christian rather than a Roman way. While asking whether suicide is a "sin," she is silent about honor or shame.[87] Nevertheless, with suicide in mind, Cleopatra turns her "women" (4.15.86, 88 [twice], 94 [twice]) first into noble women ("noble girls" [4.15.88]) and then into Romans. Exhorting Charmian and Iras to "take heart," while declaring that their "lamp is spent, it's out,"[88] she says they will bury Antony and then do "what's brave, what's noble, / . . . after the high Roman fashion / And make death proud to take [them]" (4.15.90–92). In the meantime, they have no friend, she concludes, but "resolution and the briefest end" (4.15.95).

Notes

1. *OED*, s.v. Ruffian.
2. Plutarch, *Antony*, 75.1.
3. See Suetonius, *Augustus*, 25.1.
4. E.g., Nepos, *On Famous Men*, 18 (Eumenes), 8.2; Sallust, *Catiline Conspiracy*, 11–12; Appian, *Civil Wars*, 5.17; Plutarch, *Marius*, 7.3–4.
5. Suetonius, *Augustus*, 17.3; 24.1–25.1; Dio, 49.13.1–14.5.
6. Machiavelli, *Discourses on Livy*, 3.21, *Prince*, 17, 19; see, e.g., Polybius, 3.60.8–13.
7. Wilson, 208. See *OED*, s.v. Strike *v*. 17c.
8. Enobarbus seems to think that it is unmanly to weep, but not to pretend to (cp. 1.2.176–77; 3.2.51–59).
9. Plutarch, *Antony*, 4.2–4.
10. Plutarch, *Antony*, 75.1.2.
11. John Middleton Murry, *Shakespeare* (New York: Harcourt, Brace, 1936), 302–5; Roy W. Battenhouse, *Shakespearean Tragedy* (Bloomington: Indiana University Press, 1969), 173; Andrew Fichter, "'Antony and Cleopatra': 'The Time of Universal Peace,'" *Shakespeare Survey*, 33 (1980), 99–111.
12. See also Matt. 27:46; Mark 15:34.
13. See Matt. 26:40–45; Mark 14:37–42.
14. See Matt. 26:14–16, 20–25, 45–47; Mark 14:10–11, 41–43; Luke 22:21–23, 47–48; John 13:21–26, 18:2–5.
15. See Matt. 10:39; 16:25; Luke 9:24; 17:33; John 12:25.

16. See Matt. 26:26–29; Mark 14:22–24; Luke 22:19–20; Rom. 12:5; 1 Cor. 11:23–26, 12:12. Also John 6:55–56.

17. "Blessed be God . . . the God of all comforts." 2 Cor. 1:3. "For the grace of God, that bringeth salvation unto all men, hath appeared, And teaches us that we should deny ungodliness. . . . Looking for the blessed hope and appearing of the glory of the mighty God and of our savior Jesus Christ." Titus 2:11–13.

18. "Henceforth, call I you not servants . . . but I have called you friends." John 15:15.

19. "But many that are first shall be last, and the last shall be first." Matt. 19:30. [F]or ye are all one in Christ Jesus." Galatians 3:28.

20. "Many therefore of his disciples (when they heard this) said, 'This is a hard saying. Who can hear it?'" John 6:60.

21. Machiavelli, *Discourses*, 2.2.2.

22. Plutarch, *Antony*, 75.4.

23. Except only for Caesar's name (which he mentions twenty-nine times), Antony mentions Eros's name more often (twenty-six times) than any other noun, proper or common. By contrast, he mentions Cleopatra's name seven times. "Armour," which he mentions, here, thrice (4.4.1, 2, 7), is also a pun on "amor."

24. See Cicero, *De officiis*, 2.45; Polybius, 6.54. Also *Cor.*, 1.3.1–25; 2.2.87–101; Blits, *Spirit, Soul, and City*, 37, 92.

25. *OED*, s.v. Happy *a* 3. See 1.1.63; 1.5.22; 2.2.161; 3.2.64; 3.13.30.

26. "This was the last war that Caesar made. But the triumph he made into Rome for the same did as much offend the Romans, and more, than any thing that ever he had done before: because he had not overcome captains that were strangers, nor barbarous kings, but had destroyed the sons of the noblest man of Rome, whom fortune had overthrown. And because he had plucked up his race by the roots, men did not think it meet for him to triumph so for the calamities of his country, rejoicing at a thing for the which he had but one excuse to allege in his defense unto the gods and men, that he was compelled to do that he did." Plutarch, *Julius Caesar*, 56.4; North, 5:57. See *JC*, 1.1.32ff.

27. Valerius Maximus, 2.8.7.

28. See, e.g., Cicero, *De domo sua*, 33, 43, 77, *Republic*, 3.44; Livy, *History*, 3.13.4, 55.4, 56.1–13.

29. "The achievements of the divine Augustus by which he subjected the world to the power of the Roman people." Augustus, Preface. See also Introduction, n. 3, above.

30. Besides referring to Europe, Asia and Africa, "the three-nooked world" might refer, even more grandly, to "the world [be]tween heaven, and earth, and sea" (Ovid, *Metamorphoses*, 12.40; Golding, 12.42).

31. Augustus, 13; Ovid, *Fasti*, 1.279–78; Virgil, 1.293–96, 7.601–15; Plutarch, *Numa*, 20.1–2, *On the Fortune of the Romans*, 9 (322a–b); Suetonius, *Augustus*, 22; Livy, *History*, 1.19.2–7; Florus, 2.34.64.

32. Velleius Paterculus, 2.48.3; Augustus, 13; Manilius, *Astronomica*, 1.906–21; Tacitus, *Annals*, 1.2; 3.28.1; Horace, *Odes*, 3.14.14; 4.5; 4.14.41–52; 4.15.4–24.

33. Plutarch, *Antony*, 74.1; Josephus, 1.394.

34. Plutarch, *Antony*, 72.3.

35. Bevington, 207.

36. H. Staunton and N. Delius, in Furness, 279.

37. Plutarch, *Antony*, 27.3.

38. For the first, see 3.13.182ff.

39. See 1.2.47–48; 1.5.1–6; 2.1.26; 2.2.187–88, 237–38; 2.5.21–23; 2.6.50; 2.7.30–33; 4.4.1–2; 4.9.36–37; 4.14.35–36.

40. "Among . . . red gems, carbuncles . . . have their name [for] . . . their likeness unto fire." Pliny, 37.92; Holland, 616.

41. Bevington, 210.

42. Enobarbus refers to himself eleven times in the scene, once by name. The references are nearly evenly divided between his guilty (4.9.16, 18 [twice], 19, 22, 24) and his repentant self (4.9.6, 9, 11, 17, 23).

43. M. M. Mahood, *Bit Parts in Shakespeare's Plays* (Cambridge: Cambridge University Press, 1992), 197.

44. Also: "Rather make / My country's high pyramides my gibbet / And hang me up in chains" (5.2.59–61).

45. Cp., e.g., *Cor.*, 5.3.172–73.

46. Plutarch, *Isis and Osiris*, 16 (357c); also Plutarch, *Antony*, 60.3; Dio, 50.15.2.

47. Plutarch, *Antony*, 76.1–2.

48. "Triple-turned whore" could also mean that Cleopatra betrayed Antony at Actium, with Thidias, and now with Caesar. See Marilyn L. Williamson, "Fortune in *Antony and Cleopatra*," *Journal of English and German Philology*, 67 (1968), 427.

49. Antony, emphasizing his submission to even her mute gestures, repeats the word he used in berating Cleopatra after Actium ("Thy beck might . . ." [3.11.60]), which, in turn, closely echoes Caesar's description to Octavia of Cleopatra's power over him ("Cleopatra hath nodded / Him to her" [3.6.66–67]).

50. Antony closely echoes his accusation after Actium: "You have been a boggler ever" (3.13.115).

51. Antony's warning of "the shouting plebeians" and Cleopatra's later reference to "the shouting varletry" and "[m]echanic slaves" (5.2.55, 208) are the only times anyone gives the people the slightest thought after Actium. They have been reduced to mere spectators. Antony's warning is the only time the traditional name for their class, "plebeians," is used. See Cantor, 137.

52. For the gloss of this puzzling sentence, see Kittredge, 1394.

53. Sophocles, *The Women of Trachis*, 572; Ovid, *Metamorphoses*, 9.101ff.; Apollodorus, 2.7.

54. Plutarch, *Antony*, 74.2, 76.2.

55. Johnson, in Johnson-Steevens, 2:70.

56. Walter, 244.

57. Wilson, 227.

58. Homer, *Iliad*, 7.219–20; Ovid, *Metamorphoses*, 13.1–2.

59. Antony has not mentioned Cleopatra's name since he denied that it was still her name ("[W]hat's her name / Since she was Cleopatra?" [3.13.104]).

60. "I heard a voice from Heaven saying unto me, 'Seal up those things which the seven thunders have spoken. . . .'" Rev. 10:4; also 5:1.

61. Hesiod, *The Works and Days*, 167–73; Homer, *Odyssey*, 4.563–69; Virgil, *Aeneid*, 6.637ff.

62. Virgil, *Aeneid*, 6.450ff.

63. Plutarch, *Antony*, 76.4.

64. Shakespeare hints at it when Caesar mentions Antony's conquered lands in Armenia (3.6.14, 36). The Armenian king, Artavasdes, had deserted Antony in a crucial battle against the Parthians. Antony, in revenge, conquered part of Armenia and captured the king. See Plutarch, *Antony*, 39.1, 50.2–4; Dio, 49.25.2ff.

65. Livy, *Periochae*, 130; Plutarch, *Antony*, 37–52; Dio, 49.25ff.

66. Dolores M. Burton, *Shakespeare's Grammatical Style* (Austin: University of Texas Press, 1973), 68–69. For Latinate diction, note also "Th'inevitable prosecution" (4.14.66).

67. Antony will speak of his not having surrendered to "[his] countryman" (4.15.59), and Cleopatra will speak of her "country's" pyramids (5.2.60). Using the word in another sense, one of Caesar's guards will also refer to the Clown as "[a] simple countryman" (5.2.338).

68. Caesar, *Civil War*, 1.57; Livy, *History*, 45.15.3–6; Suetonius, *Divus Julius*, 24.2, *Augustus*, 16.1; 40.4; Appian, *Civil War*, 4.7, 11, 36; Gaius, *The Rules of Ulpian*, 1.6.

69. Quintilian, 12.2.30; see, further, Anonymous, 4.62.

70. Also, e.g., Valerius Maximus, 1. Pref.; Livy, *History*, Pref. 10; Horace, *Letters*, 2.1.130–31; Seneca, *Letters*, 1.6.5; 83.13; Quintilian, 12.2.30, 4; Pliny the Younger, *Letters*, 8.14.5–6, *Panegyricus*, 45–46. See also 3.11.7–8; 4.14.103–4.

71. Plutarch, *Antony*, 76.5.

72. Where, in the immediate sequel, Antony declares, "Come then!" (4.14.102), in the sequel in the Book of Revelation the author writes, "And the Spirit and the bride say, 'Come.' And let him that heareth say, 'Come': and let him that is thirsty come." Rev. 22:17. The word "come" appears with great frequency in the play (more than one hundred times). Among verbs, only "make" and copulative and auxiliary verbs appear more often.

73. Also Matt. 9:15; 2 Cor. 11:2; John 3:29; Ephesians 5:25–32; Rev. 21:9, 17.

74. Plutarch, *Antony*, 78.1.

75. "And I beheld when he had opened the sixth seal, and lo, there was a great earthquake and the sun was as black as sackcloth of hair, and the moon was like blood." Rev. 6:12. "And the fourth Angel blew the trumpet, and the third part of the sun was smitten, and the third part of the moon, and the third part of the stars, so that the third part of them was darkened: and the day was smitten, that the third part of it could not shine, and likewise the night." Rev. 8:12.

76. Quintilian, 8.5.1–8. As suits *sententia*, the four lines contain extensive repetitions. Cleopatra repeats four words in succeeding clauses: "so," "should," "but" and

"Antony." Antony repeats his name, while referring to "valour" by the pronoun "it-self." Cleopatra repeats at the end of her second line the word with which she begins the first: "So . . . so." Each speaker's lines repeat grammatical structures in inverted order. Cleopatra, besides repeating Antony's "But," repeats the word with a new meaning the second time, the first time meaning "except," the second time "how-ever." In addition, she rhymes "woe" and "so." Both *sententia* are also stated as an-titheses. On *sententia*, see, e.g., Aristotle, *Rhetoric*, 1394a19–95b19; Cicero, *Orator*, 39.135; Anonymous, 4.24–25; Seneca, *Letters*, 94.27–29; Quintilian, 9.1.33–34.

77. Plutarch, *Antony*, 77.1–2; Dio, 51.10.9.

78. Staunton, 4:448.

79. For Cleopatra's pun, see Ovid, *Metamorphoses*, 9.270.

80. Machiavelli, *Discourses*, 2.30.5.

81. Plutarch, *Antony*, 77.4–79.3.

82. See Livy, *History*, 2.12.9.

83. Plutarch, *Antony*, 77.4.

84. For such divine jealousy, see, e.g., Herodotus, 1.34; 3.40; Livy, *History*, 5.21.15; Plutarch, *Camillus*, 5. See also Pindar, *Olympian Odes*, 13.24ff., *Pythian Odes*, 8.21ff., 10.10ff., *Isthmian Odes*, 7.35ff.

85. Furness, 324.

86. Augustine, 5.14.

87. This is the play's only mention of "sin." For the "sin" of suicide, see Augustine, 1.17, 20, 27.

88. "And the foolish said to the wife, 'Give us of your oil, for our lamps are out.'" Matt. 25:8.

~

Act Five

Act Five, Scene One

Caesar, appearing with his war council, is seeking to convince Antony to surrender. He wants Dollabella to tell Antony that delaying surrender makes him ridiculous. "Being so frustrate, tell him, he mocks / The pauses that he makes" (5.1.2–3). Although he wants Antony to surrender so that he can humiliate him in a triumph, Caesar pretends to be protecting his pride.

Unannounced and without an escort, Dercetus rushes in with Antony's bloody sword. Caesar, always fearing his namesake's fate,[1] addresses him with a combination of alarm, outrage and the authority of the royal pronoun: "Wherefore is that? And what art thou that dar'st / Appear thus to us?" (5.1.4–5). Although hoping to win Caesar's favor, Dercetus answers with a mixture of high praise for Antony and effrontery toward Caesar. "Mark Antony I served," he replies, "who best was worthy / Best to be served" (5.1.6–7). As is underscored by his chiasmus turning on "worthy" (and sounding like Thidias praising Caesar to Antony as "worthiest" [3.13.91–93]), Dercetus praises Antony as the worthiest man to be served when he was at his best. "Whilst he stood up and spoke," he says, "He was my master, and I wore my life / To spend upon his haters" (5.1.7–9). Then, having praised Antony above Caesar and having declared himself Caesar's former stout enemy, Dercetus, although just rebuffed by Caesar's use of the regal pronoun, addresses Caesar four times in as many lines with the familiar pronoun "thou": "If thou please / To take me to thee, as I was to him / I'll be

193

to Caesar. If thou pleasest not, / I yield thee up my life" (5.1.9–12).[2] Derce-tus's offer of his loyalty or his life obscures the news that he has brought. Cae-sar must ask him what he means, and he must explain, "I say, O Caesar, Antony is dead" (5.1.13).

Caesar's response seems to apply to both the news itself and its manner of disclosure. "The breaking of so great a thing should make / A greater crack" (5.1.14–15). The death of a man as great as Antony should have shaken the entire world, and it should have been announced by someone greater than Dercetus. "The round world / Should have shook lions into civil streets / And citizens to their dens" (5.1.15–17).[3] Antony's death should have forced men and lions—the civil and the bestial—to exchange places or lives. For his death, Caesar continues, is not the death of a single person. "The death of Antony" is the death of "[a] moiety of the world" (5.1.17–19). As Enobarbus joked about the drunk Lepidus (2.7.89–91), with the personal replacing the political, the ruler becomes indistinguishable from the part of the world which he rules. And as two men fight for sole rule of the world, the death of one is the death of half the world.

Dercetus, describing his death, again pays tribute to Antony's singular no-bility. Stressing that he was killed neither by a public minister of justice nor by a hired assassin, he says that Antony was killed by his own hand. The same hand which "writ his honour in the acts it did" has, "with the courage which the heart did lend it, / Splitted the heart" (5.1.23–24). Antony was killed by his own hand and heart—the same hand and heart which brought him courage and honor. Dercetus, however, while silent about Antony's pa-thetic bungling, goes on to add his own low deed to his high praise: "This is his sword; / I robbed his wound of it. Behold it stained / With his most noble blood" (5.1.24–26). Dercetus, at once loyalist and opportunist, has pillaged Antony's most noble bloody wound.

When Caesar sheds tears, Agrippa comments on the curious connection between triumph and lament. "And strange it is / That nature must compel us to lament / Our most persisted deeds" (5.1.28–30). As noted earlier, in ac-cordance with post-Alexandrian sensibility, the victor weeps over the van-quished for fear that he, too, will one day meet a similar end. "When such a spacious mirror's set before him, / [Caesar] needs must see himself" (5.1.34–35]). Whether the result of moderation, superstition or simulation, such tears are intended to show the victor's regard for the power of Fortune in human affairs. No matter how great the victory, the vanquisher may be-come the vanquished, as Antony himself clearly exemplifies. The tears are for the victor, not the vanquished. But whereas Plutarch's Caesar retires into his tent and privately weeps for Antony (Plutarch, *Antony*, 78.2), Shakespeare's openly displays his tears to the men around him: "Caesar is touched" (5.1.33). Caesar's calculating tears seem meant to show, above all, his decorous restraint at the moment of the greatest triumph. Rather than show his pleasure, he publicly mourns.

Maecenas and Agrippa praise Antony, but quite differently. Maecenas goes only so far as to balance Antony's vices and virtues ("His taints and honours / Waged equal with him" [5.1.30–31]). Agrippa, far more generous, and using the same word which he twice used to describe Cleopatra's splendor (2.2.215, 228), sees Antony as having been governed by a singular spirit: "A rarer spirit never / Did steer humanity" (5.1.31–32). Rather than leveling his virtues and vices, Agrippa, sounding not unlike the grief-stricken Cleopatra (4.15.79–82), attributes Antony's faults to the gods' wish to make or keep him human: "[B]ut you gods will give us / Some faults to make us men" (5.1.32–33). Without his faults, Antony would have been more than a man.

Caesar, now sole ruler of the world, is thinking about his reputation in history. Anxious to craft it,[4] he attempts to extenuate or excuse his pursuit of Antony to the death. Acknowledging that he pursued him to this end ("O Antony / I have followed thee to this" [5.1.35–36]), he describes himself as having been compelled by political necessity. "[B]ut," he explains, with a self-exonerating adversative, "we do launch / Diseases in our bodies. I must perforce / Have shown to thee such a declining day / Or look on thine" (5.1.35–39). Antony was a disease in Caesar's body which would have been fatal if not cut out. One imperial rival must have killed the other or would have been killed by him, as Caesar emphasizes with the necessitating imperative "must perforce." In republican Rome, where consuls were elected for a year, the nobles' pursuit of ambition and the people's fear of ambition served to keep honor from resting long with any hero. There was, consequently, frequent turnover in office. Republican rivalry continued for centuries, as Romans, competing among themselves to serve the city and win its honors, ruled one another, in turn. "Rome" always had "room enough" for "more than . . . one man" (JC, 1.2.151–54).[5] But with the start of the civil wars, following assassination of Tiberius Gracchus and the murder of three hundred of his supporters, rivalry in Rome became deadly.[6] Rather than patricians and plebeians contending against each other, with the Senate making concessions through fear of the people and the people out of respect for the Senate,[7] Romans fought against other Romans, and naked power prevailed. The battle produced decades of civil war, proscription, murder and suicide. And as the battle was for sole rule of Rome and the world, one man must have finally destroyed the others. To be "[s]ole sir o'th' world" (5.2.119) is to have no rival. Thus the whole world, Caesar concludes, was not large enough for both of them. "We could not stall together / In the whole world," as Octavia feared and Enobarbus foresaw (5.1.39–40; see 3.4.30–32; 3.5.13–15). The larger Rome became, the less room there was in it for more than one man.[8]

Caesar, however, quickly if tacitly corrects himself. Wanting not only to free himself from moral blame but to elevate himself above political exigencies, he abruptly shifts grounds ("But yet . . .") and blames impersonal destiny rather than personal ambition for Antony's end. Describing Antony as his closest companion and even as the arm and heart of his own body rather than as a disease needing to be lanced, he blames fate for the outcome. "But yet," he says, switching from the necessitating to the optative imperative,

> let me lament
> With tears as sovereign as the blood of hearts
> That thou, my brother, my competitor
> In top of all design, my mate in empire,
> Friend and companion in the front of war,
> The arm of mine own body, and the heart
> Where mine his thoughts did kindle, that our stars,
> Unreconciliable, should divide
> Our equalness to this.
>
> (5.1.40–48)

Where he initially conceded that he sought Antony's defeat but justified his pursuit as politically necessary, he subsequently denies that he sought his defeat and blames the stars for dividing them. Not their ambitions, but their stars, were "[u]nreconciliable." Caesar, always moderate and just, was in no way responsible for the "lament[ed]" outcome.[9]

Caesar wants to say more ("Hear me, good friends—"), but breaks off his self-exoneration and -representation to hear Cleopatra's urgent messenger ("But I will tell you at some meeter season" [5.1.48–49]). Although she appeared resolved upon suicide when we last saw her, Cleopatra no longer seems sure what to do. Her course of action, the Messenger says, depends on Caesar's "intents," for which she "desires instruction" so that she may adapt her actions ("frame herself") "[t]o th' way she's forced to" (5.1.54–56). Caesar tries to reassure her. Without offering anything specific, and while stressing his authority by both repeating the royal pronoun and referring to himself as Caesar ("us . . . ours, / . . . we / . . . Caesar" [5.1.57–59]), he promises to be honorable and kind. "For Caesar cannot live / To be ungentle" (5.1.59–60). But, as soon as the Messenger leaves, Caesar, much as with Thidias after Actium (3.12.26–29), orders Proculeius to hurry to Cleopatra and, assuring her that he intends her no shame, promise her whatever is necessary to capture her alive. Caesar fears that her suicide would "defeat us. For her life in Rome / Would be eternal in our triumph" (5.1.65–66). To exhibit Cleopatra alive in Rome in his triumphal procession would give Caesar's triumph eternal fame.[10]

Resuming his effort to shape his historical reputation, Caesar, urging his war council to go with him into his tent, says he will show them his correspondence with Antony so that they will see how reluctantly ("hardly" [5.1.74]) he was drawn into the war and how moderately ("calm and gentle" [5.1.75]) he constantly proceeded. He wants his council—and the whole world—to know "how fiercely and proudly [Antony] answered him to all just and reasonable matters [Caesar] wrote unto him" (Plutarch, *Antony*, 78.2; North, 6:81). Directing posterity how and what to think of him, he offers evidence (". . . see / What I can show in this" [5.1.76–77]) that he was, even under the pressures of war, always temperate and restrained, as eminent Roman poets and historians—those "with serious gravity and . . . the best" (Suetonius, *Augustus*, 89.3; Holland, 1:155)—will soon record and exaltedly praise. The greatest in power, he is still greater in example.[11]

Act Five, Scene Two

1.

Cleopatra says that her "desolation" has begun to make a "better life" for her (5.1.1, 2). Alone and ruined, she claims to have learned something. The lesson has two parts. The first is to despise the greatest political glory: "'Tis paltry to be Caesar" (5.2.2). Caesar's accomplishment is paltry because it depends not on him but on Fortune. "Not being Fortune, he's but Fortune's knave, / A minister of her will" (5.2.3–4). Fortune, not Caesar, defeated Antony. In one sense, Cleopatra seems correct. Caesar's good fortune, to which he owes his success, is to have had friends and enemies alike who originally raised him up but were then themselves thrown down, leaving him to rule alone. As Plutarch writes, "[I]t was for [Caesar's] sake that Cicero gave counsel, Lepidus led an army, Pansa vanquished the enemy, Hirtius lost his life in the field,[12] and Antony lived riotously in drunkenness, gluttony and lechery." Caesar himself, when sending his grandson to war, will pray that he might prove "as valiant as Scipio, and as well beloved as Pompey, and as fortunate as himself, ascribing the making of himself as great as he was unto Fortune" (Plutarch, *Fortune of the Romans*, 7 [319e–f]; Holland, 632).[13] Cleopatra, however, does not limit her indictment to Caesar. One might have expected her to say, "Not being virtuous, he's but Fortune's knave." But

Cleopatra dismisses the distinction between virtue and fortune. With hero-ism now gone from the world, Fortune, she says, rules human affairs, and so, unless someone is Fortune herself, he is simply her servant. Whatever any-one accomplishes merely carries out Fortune's wishes.

The lesson's second part, a corollary of the first, is the "better life" of death. Death—and only death—defeats Fortune's rule.

> And it is great
> To do that thing that ends all other deeds,
> Which shackles accidents and bolts up change,
> Which sleeps and never palates more the dung,
> The beggar's nurse and Caesar's.

(5.2.4–8)

The one great deed is suicide, because it ends all other deeds. Death is final, preventing all further accidents and change. The woman of continuous in-constancy now seeks immutable constancy. Death is the better life, further-more, because it releases one from the body and hence from the body's lev-eling effect—from the "dung," as Cleopatra puts it, reducing the body's requirements to their most degrading element, which, she adds, nourishes Caesar and a beggar alike (see 1.1.36–37). The woman of sensuality now seeks to be rid of the living body.

2.

Proculeius enters and asks what demands Cleopatra—"the Queen of Egypt," as he unctuously calls her (5.2.9)—makes of Caesar. Cleopatra, telling him that Antony had bade her to trust him, says that Antony's advice does not matter to her because she is not concerned whether or not she is deceived, since she has no need for trust. Presumably, she expects to die soon. Cleopa-tra, nevertheless, makes a demand. "If your master / Would have a queen his beggar," she replies, "you must tell him / That majesty, to keep decorum, must / No less beg than a kingdom" (5.2.15–18). If Cleopatra is to gratify his wish to have a queen beg of him, Caesar must honor her majesty and grant her what is worthy of a queen. Cleopatra then states her regal demand. She asks, as she did after Actium (3.12.16–19), that Caesar give her "conquered Egypt" (5.2.19) for her son.[14] In exchange for her receiving "so much of [her] own," as she bitterly phrases it, she promises to "kneel to [Caesar] with thanks" (5.2.20–21). Proculeius, ignoring the specific request, urges Cleopatra not to fear, but put herself entirely in Caesar's hands. Using a legal term implying mutual benefit, he says Caesar will beg her cooperation in thinking of generous acts that he can do for her (". . . will pray in aid for kindness / Where he for grace is kneeled to" [5.2.27–28]). Her docile submission ("sweet dependence" [5.2.26]) will serve both of their interests. Cleopatra asks Proculeius to tell Caesar that she is "his fortune's vassal" and that she acknowledges "[t]he greatness he has got" (5.2.29, 30). As she did after Actium (3.13.78–82), she submits to Caesar's fortune and recognizes only the greatness he has won. The "doctrine of obedience" (5.2.31) which she says she is learning evidently teaches nothing more than obeying a victorious power. Ironically, Cleopatra acknowledges only what she has just found to be worth no more than dung.

3.

Proculeius no sooner assures Cleopatra that her "plight is pitied / Of him that caused it" (5.2.33–34) than Caesar's soldiers rush in and seize her. Proculeius's mission was not just to sound out Cleopatra (5.1.66–68), but to distract her: "You see how easily she may be surprised. / Guard her till Caesar come" (5.2.35–36). Drawing a dagger ("Quick, quick, good hands" [5.2.38]), Cleopatra immediately tries to kill herself. But Proculeius disarms and once again assures her.[15] Telling her not to do "[her]self such wrong," he protests that his action has "[r]elieved, but not betrayed" her (5.2.39, 40). Proculeius means that he has rescued ("[r]elieved") Cleopatra from death. She takes him to mean that he has deprived ("[r]elieved") her of death: "What, of death too, / That rids our dogs of languish?" (5.2.40–41). Proculeius—or Caesar—has deprived her not only of her kingdom, but of death, which relieves even suffering dogs of their misery. Proculeius, no longer addressing Cleopatra by title or term of respect,[16] reproves rather than reassures her:

> Cleopatra,
> Do not abuse my master's bounty by
> Th'undoing of yourself. Let the world see
> His nobleness well acted, which your death
> Will never let come forth.

> (5.2.41–45)

By taking her life, Cleopatra would cheat Caesar's giving and prevent the world from seeing him act nobly. Unlike earlier, Proculeius is silent about her wronging herself. He also leaves uncertain whether Caesar's nobleness would to be "well acted" in the sense of being generously accomplished or of being theatrically simulated. Like Caesar wanting to show his love for Octavia

(3.6.51–54), he makes clear that Caesar wants to show his nobleness, but not whether it is anything but show.

Imploring death to come and take her, Cleopatra wishes to reverse the high and the low, the strong and the weak: "Where art thou, Death? / Come, hither, come! Come, come, and take a queen / Worth many babes and beggars!" (5.2.45–47). Death comes easily to dogs, babies and beggars, but not to Cleopatra. Defying Proculeius's instruction to be temperate, Cleopatra declares that she will accept any form of death, however slow, abhorrent or shameful, before she will be taken to Rome. If Caesar tries to deny her the means of death, she will go without food, drink or sleep. "This mortal house I'll ruin, / Do Caesar what he can" (5.2.50–51). She would rather die in an Egyptian ditch, lie stark naked in the Nile's mud and become infected with the eggs of flies, or be hanged in chains from one of her country's high pyramids, than face Caesar's court, Octavia's sober eye or the Roman rabble's censuring shouts. Proculeius can do little more than object that she exaggerates: "You do extend / These thoughts of horror further than you shall / Find cause in Caesar" (5.2.61–63). Proculeius, ambiguous again, leaves unclear whether Cleopatra exaggerates what she faces in Rome or what she might do to avoid it.

4.

Dolabella has come to warn Cleopatra of what Caesar intends for her. Dismissing Proculeius so they can be alone, he addresses Cleopatra as "[m]ost noble empress" (5.2.70). The title seems to disregard Octavia and recognize Cleopatra as Antony's widow.[17] Dolabella, hoping for her trust, tries to give Cleopatra confidence that she knows him ("Assuredly you know me" [5.2.71]). But Cleopatra does not care whether she does ("No matter, sir, what I have heard or known" [5.2.72]). Instead, able only to dream and suffer, she wants to describe what she calls her dream of Antony. Although she does not expect a Roman officer to take dreams seriously ("You laugh when boys or women tell their dreams; / Is't not your trick?" [5.2.73–74]), and although Dolabella is at a loss to understand what she is thinking ("I understand not, madam" [5.2.74]), Cleopatra tells her dream. "I dreamt there was an emperor Antony," she says, satisfying Antony's wish to be remembered as the greatest prince of the world. "O, such another sleep, that I might see / But such another man!" (5.2.75–77). A man of such a kind can be found only in a dream of such a kind. Such a man exceeds what exists in life.

Using hyperbolic, heroic comparisons throughout, Cleopatra first describes Antony's body and its qualities. "His face," she begins, "was as the heavens, and therein stuck / A sun and moon which kept their course and lighted / The little O, the earth" (5.2.78–80). Antony's face stood as the heavens to the earth, his eyes lighting the earth with their sight. Cleopatra then describes his legs and arm. "His legs bestrid the ocean; his reared arm / Crested the world" (5.2.81–82). Alluding to the Colossus of Rhodes, Cleopatra likens Antony to the gigantic statue of the sun god, Helios, straddling the entrance to the harbor, one of the seven Wonders of the World, its arm reaching toward Olympus.[18] Next, she describes Antony's voice. It was one thing to friends, another to enemies. "[H]is voice was propertied / As all the tuned spheres, and that to friends; / But when he meant to quail and shake the orb, / He was as rattling thunder" (5.2.82–85). To friends, Antony's voice was like the music of the spheres. It resembled the divine harmony of the motions of the heavenly planets.[19] To enemies, when he wanted to frighten and shake the earth, his voice was like the divine thunder of a punishing god.

Turning to his soul, Cleopatra describes Antony's bounty. "For his bounty," she says, "There was no winter in't; an Anthony it was / That grew the more by reaping" (5.2.85–87). The more Antony gave, the more he had to give. His giving grew on itself. Cleopatra, identifying Antony's boundless bounty as "an Anthony,"[20] puns on his name. *Anthos*, in Greek, means "flower," hence "the height or the pick of something," for example, "[f]lower of warriors" (*Cor.*, 1.6.32). If Caesar's name is the highest political title (3.2.13), Antony's marks the richest munificence. In giving, Antony fully lived up to his superlative name. Cleopatra then describes Antony's pleasures. "His delights," she says, "Were dolphin-like: they showed his back above / The element they lived in" (5.2.87–89). Although his pleasures were coarse, Antony was never dragged down or made vulgar by them. He always rose above the pleasures in which he lived. Concluding, Cleopatra returns to Antony's prodigal giving. "In his livery / Walked crowns and crownets; realms and islands were / As plates dropped from his pocket" (5.2.89–91). While kings and princes were his servants, Antony gave away kingdoms and islands as though they were small change carelessly dropped from his pocket (see 3.6.69–77; 3.11.63–65; 3.12.2–6; 3.13.95–97). In Cleopatra's hyperbolic contrast, the diminution of the royalty who served Antony only magnifies his unrivaled extravagance.

Ignoring Dolabella's attempt to warn her, Cleopatra asks, "Think you there was or might be such a man / As this I dreamt of?" (5.2.92–93). Did such a man, or might such a man, ever live? When Dolabella answers, "Gentle madam, no" (5.2.93), Cleopatra indignantly accuses him of lying loud enough for the gods to hear. But then, at once partly withdrawing and partly enlarging her claim, she insists, "But if there be nor ever were one such, / It's past the size of dreaming" (5.2.95–96). If such a man ever existed, no dream could ever measure up to him. He would exceed the limits even of dreaming.

Enobarbus had described Cleopatra, dressed like Venus on her barge, as surpassing a picture of Venus in which the artist's imagination surpassed nature itself. She was superior to art, which is superior to nature (2.2.208–11). Cleopatra speaks differently of Antony. "Nature wants stuff / To vie strange forms with fancy; yet t'imagine / An Antony were nature's piece 'gainst fancy, / Condemning shadows quite" (5.2.96–99). Nature lacks the material to compete with imagination in producing wondrous forms. But, contrary to what would naturally be expected ("yet . . ."),[21] if one could imagine such a man as Cleopatra's Antony, he would be nature's triumphant masterpiece, discrediting anything that imagination could create. Where Enobarbus spoke of imagination exceeding nature, Cleopatra speaks of nature exceeding imagination. She sees her imagined Antony as perfecting rather than surpassing nature. To imagine him is to make him nature's perfection. Cleopatra thus obscures the distinction between the imaginary and the real. As she presents them, the former perfects the latter. Always an actress, Cleopatra has often elevated the imaginary over the natural or the real, as she did initially with her dream of Antony. But now that he is dead, it is of the greatest importance to her that Antony was real, not merely a dream or imaginary, and that he was superior to anything else found in the world. Cleopatra both poeticizes Antony and insists that her idealized depiction is true. Reflecting the dual and often conflicting tendencies of spiritedness to poeticize or idealize—to elevate, beautify, simplify, and suppress—and to insist that its exaggerated or distorted description is true, Cleopatra is never more concerned with what is actual than when she is most poetic. Antony's death arouses her idealization of what he was and her concern that what he was, was indeed not fanciful or fiction, but real.

Dolabella finally gets a chance to speak. Cleopatra said that her grief should be as great as its cause (4.15.4–6). Dolabella, as though confirming her, says that her loss, like herself, is great and that she bears it in proportion to its grievous weight. Dolabella then imprecates upon himself a conditional curse that he never succeed at what he desires ("Would I might never / O'ertake pursued success" [5.2.101–2]) if he does not feel deep sorrow for her. As she feels the full weight of her loss, he feels a reflected "grief that smites / [His] very heart at root" (5.2.103–4). Cleopatra, thanking him, asks what Caesar intends to do with her. And though initially loath to tell her, he quickly confirms, just before Caesar and his train enter, that Caesar intends to lead her in Rome in triumph.

5.

This is the only time Caesar and Cleopatra are together. His first words—"Which is the Queen of Egypt?" (5.2.111)—are not likely to be a deliberate insult of Cleopatra, but rather to indicate just how much her grief has altered her appearance.[22] Caesar, who knows that Cleopatra has already attempted to take her own life, has no reason to provoke her. When Dolabella returns, he, too, will have difficulty recognizing her (5.2.196).

Throughout their exchange, Caesar and Cleopatra attempt to deceive each other. Caesar, with a mixture of assurances and threats, tries to keep her from killing herself, so he can exhibit her in Rome. Cleopatra, fearing captivity and public shame in Rome, tries to throw him off his guard by indicating that she wants to live, so she will be able to kill herself.[23] Each attempts to lull the other—he, by appearing gracious and kind; she, by appearing covetous and compliant.

The exchange begins with formal courtesy. Cleopatra kneels, but Caesar, calling her by her royal title, implores and then orders her to rise ("I pray you rise. Rise, Egypt" [5.2.114; also 5.2.11, 158, 184]). Cleopatra, however, insists. Saying the gods will have it this way, she declares, "My master and my lord / I must obey" (5.2.115–16). She may be "Egypt," but he is her master and lord. In her final words to Caesar, Cleopatra will address him, again, as "[m]y master and my lord" (5.2.189). Her submissive salutation and valediction frame the exchange.

Reassuring her, while nevertheless emphasizing the injuries she has caused him (and using the regal plural thrice in two lines), Caesar tells Cleopatra that he will forgive the injuries by considering them "[a]s things done by chance" (5.2.119). He will treat them as though she had not intended them, as though they had occurred merely by accident. Fortune's knave will excuse her deliberate acts as acts of fortune. Cleopatra, whether appealing specifically to his patronizing pardon or more generally to his pejorative view of women (3.12.29–31), or to both, blames her sex for her actions. Calling him "[s]ole sir o'th' world" (5.2.119), she says she cannot present herself well enough to make herself look blameless ("clear" [5.2.121]), but "[I] do confess," she adds, "I have / Been laden with like frailties which before / Have often shamed our sex" (5.2.121–23). Where he sees women as weak ("Women are not / In their best fortunes strong" [3.12.29–30]), she pleads the shameful weaknesses of her sex. Caesar, in reply, promises to make light of, rather then stress ("extenuate rather than enforce" [5.2.124]), her offenses, if she follows his "intents" for her, which, he quickly reassures her, are "most gentle" and will "benefit" her (5.2.125, 126, 127). While never specifying those intentions, Caesar expressly warns of the consequences of Cleopatra's taking her own life. If she makes him appear cruel "by taking / Antony's course," she will not only lose the benefits she would otherwise gain ("my good purposes"), but will "put your children / To that destruction which

I'll guard them from," if she cooperates with him (5.2.128–29, 130–31). He will protect her children if she relies on him, but kill them if she kills herself. Cleopatra has stressed her children in asking Caesar for concessions (3.12.16–19; 5.2.19; also 3.6.5–8, 13–16). Caesar, taking his cue from her, attempts to increase her fear by threatening them with death.[24]

The exchange seems concluded, as Caesar begins to leave ("I'll take my leave" [5.2.132]). Cleopatra, however, plays caustically on his farewell ("And may through all the world! 'Tis yours") and on his assurance: "[A]nd we, / Your scutcheons and your signs of conquest, shall / Hang in what place you please" (5.2.133–35). As he may do whatever he wishes ("take [his] leave") throughout the world, he may hang Cleopatra up like a captured trophy or hang her like a captured enemy, anywhere he pleases. Whether or not her wordplay is an aside, Cleopatra aims her next words directly at Caesar. "Here, my good lord," she says, not letting Caesar leave before handing him an inventory of her possessions (5.2.135). Caesar has not asked for such a list and would have left without one. In fact, when handed the inventory, he simply offers another parting general assurance ("You shall advise me in all for Cleopatra" [5.2.136]). Cleopatra, nevertheless, as if forced to vouch for its completeness, insists that the list includes everything: "This is the brief of money, plate and jewels / I am possessed of. 'Tis exactly valued" (5.2.137–38). Then, unprompted by Caesar, she immediately calls her treasurer, Seleucus, to verify the inventory's accuracy. Ordered to "[s]peak the truth" or else face his peril (5.2.143), Seleucus reveals that she has kept back "[e]nough to purchase what [she has] made known" (5.2.147). Cleopatra, who need not have arranged the ploy with Seleucus, seems intent on encouraging Caesar to believe that she has tried unsuccessfully to trick him, because she still wants to live. Her real deception of Caesar is to feign a failed deception of him.[25]

Caesar says he approves Cleopatra's attempt to withhold her possessions. "Nay, blush not, Cleopatra. I approve / Your wisdom in the deed" (5.2.148–49). Caesar may mean just what he says. A man given to guarding his own revenue and expenses (e.g., 3.6.30–31; 4.1.16–17), he may consider such action wise. This is Caesar's sole mention of "wisdom" or of a "deed." To him, a wise deed seems to be an accounting feint.[26]

Just as she feigns her failed deception, Cleopatra feigns her royal outrage at Seleucus's disclosure. She berates and threatens her treasurer, but, unlike her treatment of the Messenger who reported Antony's marriage (2.5.60ff.), she does not attempt to beat him. She limits her abuse to words. Cleopatra, moreover, directs her first response not angrily to Seleucus, but indignantly to Caesar. And the response is a general reflection on the faithless followers of majesty. "See, Caesar!" she warns; "O behold / How pomp is followed!

Mine will now be yours / And, should we shift estates, yours would be mine" (5.2.149–51). Only then does she curse and threaten Seleucus.

Cleopatra decries the "wounding shame" of an impertinent, malicious servant spoiling an emperor's visit—"thou vouchsafing here to visit me, / Doing the honor of thy lordliness / To one so meek" (5.2.158–60), as she says, with the ingratiating combination of an obsequious deference and the familiar pronoun.[27] Next, she confesses to withholding some items but claims that they were meant not for herself, but for Livia (Caesar's wife) and Octavia "to induce / Their mediation" (5.2.168–69). Her confession, seemingly showing a broken spirit,[28] ostensibly acknowledges that she expects to go to Rome. Then, threatening again, she warns Seleucus that her ruin does not prevent her revenge. Finally, she blames his lack of pity for her on his being a eunuch: "Wert thou a man, / Thou wouldst have mercy on me" (5.2.173–74). Seleucus's bitter unmanliness makes him unmerciful. Caesar, who has said very little since he first tried to leave, simply asks Seleucus in a word to have patience and withdraw ("Forbear, Seleucus" [5.2.174]).

Even though she has just admitted trying to hold back more than half of her treasure, Cleopatra now accuses Seleucus of having attempted to embezzle the items from her. And even though she has just emphasized the great disproportion between Caesar ("thy lordliness") and herself ("one so meek"), she now places them on the same level. "[W]e, the greatest," she says, are misjudged for things which others do, "and when we fall, / We answer others' merits in our name" (5.2.175, 176–77).[29] Just as they get the credit when in power for the good things their subordinates accomplish, when monarchs fall they get the blame for their subordinates' misdeeds. When their fortune is good, the credit is theirs; when their fortune is bad, the blame is theirs. Deserts, good and bad, depend not on one's deeds but on one's fortune. We "[a]re therefore to be pitied," Cleopatra concludes (5.2.178). Cleopatra speaks of pity for those blamed rather than of indignation at the blame. She is evidently thinking not of the unjustly misplaced blame, but of the painful fall that caused it. While Cleopatra often speaks of suffering pain, she seldom speaks of justice as anything other than punitive jealousy, human or divine (e.g., 2.5.61–77; 4.15.79–82; 5.2.284–86).

Caesar, resuming legal language and denying his mercenary interest in her treasure, once more tries to assure Cleopatra that all her wealth is safely hers ("Still be't yours" [5.2.180]), that she is not a prisoner ("Make not your thoughts your prisons" [5.2.184]), that she will be treated as she wishes (". . . as / Yourself shall give us counsel" [5.2.185–86]), and that he has a friend's care and pity for her ("Our care and pity is so much upon you / That we remain your friend" [5.2.187–88]). Caesar, evidently pleased with the way the meeting has gone, thinks he has fooled Cleopatra. In his thinking so, she fools him. "I'll seem the fool I am not" (1.1.43). Cleopatra dissembles, and Caesar is deceived. Turning against him his usual strength of taking advantage of other people's weaknesses, she presents herself in accordance with his view that women are no stronger than their fortunes. Deceiving him by pretending to fail to deceive him, she lets him see through her pretense so that, seeing what he thinks is true of all women, he complacently concludes that that is all there is to be seen. He does not see the pretending within or behind her pretending, the deeper level of playacting which conceals even while revealing her playacting.[30] Cleopatra's deception of Caesar, which allows him to leave her unattended ("*Exeunt Caesar and his train*" [s.d. 5.2.189]), is his only major defeat in the play.

6.

Cleopatra recognizes what Caesar was attempting. "He words me, girls, he words me, that I should not / Be noble to myself" (5.2.190–91).[31] To be noble to herself is to kill herself. While the word is used in a sharply diminished sense throughout the play, once Antony, the "[n]oblest of men" (4.15.61) dies, "noble" almost always refers to suicide (4.15.90; 5.2.191, 236, 284, 343), women (4.15.88; 5.2.70, 229) or royal possessions (5.2.167),[32] and is most often spoken by a woman. In the darkened world of Imperial Rome, nobility becomes divorced from manliness and associated instead with private action directed against oneself.[33] In Caesar's telling phrase "noble weakness" (5.2.343), it now goes together with deficiency, not strength. It makes "defect perfection" (2.2.241). Charmian, replying to Cleopatra's whispers, encourages her, "Finish, good lady" (5.2.192). This is the time to die. Antony had told Eros, "The long day's task is done" (4.14.35). Charmian, closely echoing him, tells Cleopatra, "The bright day is done / And we are for the dark" (5.2.192–93).[34] Imploring Charmian to act quickly, Cleopatra refers cryptically to her secret preparation for suicide: "I have spoke already and it is provided. / Go put it to the haste" (5.2.194–95). Whether to spare herself or her companions, Cleopatra avoids the word "death."

7.

Having been deeply touched by her, Dolabella, who does not take the danger to himself lightly (see 5.2.101–4), returns at his peril with the urgent warning that Caesar intends to leave very soon with Cleopatra and her children. He says he has returned because he has "thereto sworn by [Cleopatra's] command" to tell her what he can, which "[his] love makes religion to obey" (5.2.197, 198). Nothing we have seen showed Cleopatra commanding Dolabella or Dolabella swearing to obey. Cleopatra entreated him to say what he knew, and Dolabella, cursing himself conditionally if he did not feel deeply for her, confirmed Caesar's plans (5.2.101–9). Now, however, his heartfelt grief having turned into love, and love having the power to command, Dolabella says that he tells her because his love makes a religion to obey her commands. A harbinger of Christianity, he obeys a new religion whose commandment is love:

> Jesus said to him, "Thou shalt love the Lord thy God with all thine heart, with all thy soul, and with all thy mind. This is the first and the great commandment. And the second is like unto this: Thou shalt love thy neighbor as thyself."
>
> (Matt. 22:37–39)[35]

Dolabella, a Roman officer, personifies the transformation of Rome's principle of war, which teaches men to love their fellow citizens and hate their country's enemies. By following the principle, Rome conquered the world. But Rome's universal conquests have turned the principle of war into the commandment of love. For Rome's former enemies are now Romans, and, with no enemies left to hate, all of mankind are now fellow citizens or fellow subjects. Mirroring the pagan world in general, the principle of war destroys itself by fulfilling itself. It turns itself into its opposite. Paradoxically, the principle of war now requires all of mankind to be loved.

8.

Cleopatra, who appears to think that Iras's resolve (unlike Charmian's) needs strengthening, describes the repulsive disgrace awaiting them in Rome. Despite—or perhaps because—Iras is one of the queen's maids, Cleopatra, largely repeating Antony's taunt of her (4.12.33–37; also 5.2.54–56), appeals to the servant's adopted royal pride. She first emphasizes the horror of their being paraded past the filthy, stinking artisans, who will take rude liberties with them as they handle them,[36] and their being grabbed at by insolent and lascivious minor officials who punish strumpets ("[s]aucy lictors" [5.2.213]). Then she emphasizes the horror of their being mocked and ridiculed in songs and on the stage: "[S]cald rhymers [will] / Ballad us out o'tune. The quick comedians / Extemporally will stage us and present / Our Alexandrian revels" (5.2.214–17). Contemptible singers and actors will judge them as though they were their moral superiors. And the dishonor will be compounded by their having to witness the spectacle themselves. "I shall see / Some squeaking Cleopatra boy my greatness / I'th' posture of a whore"

(5.2.218–20).[37] The insult will be to their faces. Iras thus vows, "I'll never see't, for I am sure my nails / Are stronger than mine eyes" (5.2.222–23). Although Iras speaks of blinding, not of killing, herself, Cleopatra appears satisfied. "Why, that's the way / To fool their preparation and to conquer / Their most absurd intents" (5.2.223–25). Cleopatra seems to have increased Iras's resolve. Yet, although addressing Iras, Cleopatra, who is often willful but seldom brave, may be trying to strengthen her own resolve.

9.

Cleopatra wants to die looking like a queen. "Show me, my women, like a queen. Go fetch / My best attires. I am again for Cydnus / To meet Mark Antony" (5.2.226–28). Rather than be staged by Caesar as a captive in Rome, Cleopatra will stage her own royal death in Egypt. Her death, a repeated stage play, will be another grand theatrical performance.[38] As magnificent as her most magnificent moment in life, it will not only avoid Caesar's mortifying public pageantry, but will replace it with the full splendor of the Egyptian monarchy: "Bring our crown and all" (5.2.231). Cleopatra's death is to be a royal performance, staged in full costume. Urging the women to act quickly, Cleopatra promises Charmian that once she has completed this chore, she will give her "leave / To play till doomsday" (5.2.230–31). She will allow Charmian an eternity of "play" in both the theatrical and the sexual sense. She will permit Charmian an everlasting life in death resembling Cleopatra's own life in this world.

10.

Suicide is a quintessentially Stoic act, and Cleopatra, wanting to die "after the high Roman fashion" (4.15.91), sees hers in a characteristically Stoic way. "What poor an instrument / May do a noble deed. He brings me liberty" (5.2.236–37). The Clown and the asp are poor instruments, which will free the Egyptian queen by allowing her to die nobly. Death is liberty. Suicide is an escape from, and hence protection against, servitude and disgrace.[39] It is a noble deed which can be achieved privately, even stealthfully. Although a victory over one's conqueror, it is a reflexive action, carried out by, and directed toward, oneself. Moreover, like Stoicism in general, it lends itself to theatrical display.[40]

Suicide cannot be achieved by a woman, however. Announcing that her resolution is fixed ("My resolution's placed" [5.2.237]), Cleopatra unsexes herself. "I have nothing / Of woman in me," she declares. "Now from head to foot / I am marble-constant. Now the fleeting moon / No planet is of mine"

(5.2.237–40). Women, like the moon, are ever-changing, never constant. They lack the constancy and resolution that Cleopatra now claims to have (see 3.13.158). Cleopatra, furthermore, undeifies herself. The Egyptians identify Cleopatra with Isis (3.6.16–19; 3.13.158) and Isis with the moon.[41] In claiming to be marble-constant, Cleopatra denies her identification with Isis. Her unsexing and undeifying herself are related. Isis, Plutarch writes, is "the female part of nature, apt to receive all generation. . . . [C]apable of all, she receives all forms and shapes."[42] It thus seems no accident that Cleopatra, relinquishing natural generation, appears to ignore Caesar's threat to kill her children (5.2.128–32). Unlike earlier, her children now seem very far from her mind. After Caesar's threat, she in fact never mentions them again. When she dies, she will speak of "[her] baby at [her] breast" (5.2.308), but it will not be any of her children.

When the Clown enters, Cleopatra, whom Antony used to call "my serpent of old Nile" (1.5.26), asks whether he has "the pretty worm of Nilus" (5.2.243). The serpent of the Nile will kill the serpent of the Nile. Cleopatra asks the man whether the worm "kills and pains not" (5.2.243). Caesar will report that her physician said Cleopatra pursued innumerable experiments ("conclusions infinite") to find "easy ways to die" (5.2.354, 355). Physically timorous, she is particularly afraid of bodily pain. For her, the pain of achieving death conflicts with desirability of death.[43] Cleopatra fears what she most desires.[44]

The Clown, disposed to malapropisms, answers, "Truly, I have him; but I would not be the party that should desire you to touch him, for his biting is immortal. Those that do die of it do seldom or never recover" (5.2.244–47). The Clown appears to confuse "mortal" and "immortal." What brings death, he says, avoids death. Despite himself, however, the Clown speaks "[t]ruly." His malapropism correctly anticipates Cleopatra's wishful declaration, "I have / Immortal longings in me" (5.2.279–80). The Clown promises the death containing deathless life that Cleopatra longs for.

Cleopatra, still uncertain or wary, asks, "Remember'st thou any that have died on't?" (5.2.248). Although she means "die" literally, the Clown, echoing Enobarbus's bawdy pun (1.2.140–51), tells of a woman he heard of only yesterday who died of it, "a very honest woman, but something given to lie, as a woman should not do but in the way of honesty" (5.2.250–52). With triple wordplay, the man quibbles on "lie" (tells lies and lies with men), "honesty" (tells the truth and is chaste) and "die," leaving altogether unclear whether the woman told the truth but was unchaste, did not tell the truth but was chaste, neither told the truth nor was chaste, or even whether she is now dead or alive.

The Clown reports what he has heard that the woman said about how she died from the worm's biting and of the pain she felt. "Truly, she makes a very good report o'th' worm," he tells. But then he immediately casts doubt on her word: "[B]ut he that will believe all that they say shall never be saved by half that they do. But this is most fallible, the worm's an odd worm" (5.2.252–57). The Clown, in his characteristic manner, alludes to man's Fall in the Garden of Eden. In addition to his malaprop pun on Fall ("fallible"),[45] he points directly to Adam and Eve. While death results from the man's belief in what the woman said of the serpent ("th' worm"), the man who believed what she said, but could not be saved by what she had done, is Adam (Genesis 3:1–19).[46] Thus a guard will soon speak of "fig leaves" in connection with the outcome of the serpent's work (5.2.350). The Clown also alludes to the Christian (specifically, Protestant) doctrine of Salvation: "[H]e that will believe all that they say shall never be saved by half that they do."[47] While pointing on the one hand to the Biblical account of the origin of death, the Clown points on the other hand to the Christian account of what comes with death. The new heaven of Christianity offers a new understanding of death. As sin brings death into the world, men can share eternal life with God after death: "Jesus said unto her, 'I am the resurrection and the life. He that believeth in me, though he were dead, yet shall he live. And whosoever liveth, and believeth in me, shall never die'" (John 11:25–26). If sin brings worldly death, death can bring eternal life through salvation. "For as in Adam all die, even so in Christ shall all be made alive" (1 Cor. 15:22).[48] No longer distinguishing man from the gods, death links man to God.

Cleopatra tells the man to go, but he does not leave and, instead, wishes her "all the joy of the worm" (5.2.259). When she tells him again to go, the Clown, continuing his wordplay, assures her that the worm "will do his kind" (5.2.262). The serpent will act according to his nature: He will copulate with and kill his mate.[49] And when Cleopatra once more impatiently tells him to go, the man, still lingering, warns that "the worm is not to be trusted but in the keeping of wise people, for, indeed, there is no goodness in the worm" (5.2.264–66). The malevolent worm, bringing both pleasure and death, is not to be trusted.

After the Clown advises her not to feed the worm because it is not worth the feeding, Cleopatra asks, "Will it eat me?" (5.2.270). She seems to be wondering whether the serpent can be counted on to bite her. The Clown, however, puns on "eat." Echoing Enobarbus, Antony and Cleopatra herself (1.5.31–32; 2.6.128; 3.13.121–23), he answers, "I know the devil himself will not eat a woman. I know that a woman is a dish for the gods if the devil dress her not" (5.2.272–74). The Clown quibbles on "dress" as well as on "eat." As "eat" has both a sexual and a literal sense, to "dress" a woman can mean either to put her in clothes or to prepare her for cooking (in Hell).[50] Thus, a woman is a dish for the gods if the devil leaves her (perhaps) naked or (perhaps) uncorrupted. "But truly," the Clown observes, repeating his first and one of his favorite words,[51] "these same whoreson devils do the gods great harm in their women, for in every ten that they make, the devils mar five" (5.2.274–76). The Clown, speaking obscenely and obscurely, may mean that the devils excite the gods' sexual desires ("make") but then interfere with their performance by impairing their potency ("mar") half the time[52] or that the devil leads half the women God has created ("make") away from God by leading them into sin ("mar").[53] On the Clown's lips, the sexual and the spiritual are not so much contrasted as conflated. Told, yet again, to go, the Clown finally leaves, wishing Cleopatra, again, "joy o'th' worm" (5.2.278).

11.

Cleopatra dresses for death. Always artfully attired, she put on the trappings and symbols of her royalty. "Give me my robe. Put on my crown. I have / Immortal longings in me" (5.2.279–80). Cleopatra longs for immortality. In death, she expects or hopes to find immortal life. Echoing the words of Jesus at the Last Supper, she gives up the taste of wine: "Now no more / The juice of Egypt's grape shall moist this lip" (5.2.280–81).[54] Afraid of Caesar's degrading procession, she urged Charmian to act quickly in summoning the Clown (5.2.192–94). Now, she urges Iras to act quickly ("Yare, yare, good Iras! Quick!" [5.2.282]), not from fear of Caesar, but because "Methinks I hear / Antony call. I see him rouse himself / To praise my noble act" (5.2.282–84). Cleopatra's death will be her final act in both senses of the word. It will be her last deed and her last theatrical performance—a noble deed performed in order to win the praise of an admiring Antony.

When Antony died, Cleopatra blamed the gods' jealousy for his death (4.15.79–82). She now sees the same divine jealousy as his revenge: "I hear [Antony] mock / The luck of Caesar, which the gods give men / To excuse their after wrath" (5.2.284–86). Where she said the gods inspired Antony to rival them, but then punished him for doing so, she says they gave Caesar extraordinary good fortune in order to justify their jealous punishment of him. With both men, the gods' wrath is their jealousy in disguise. But while Antony was "[the] jewel" of the world (4.15.82) and deserved to rival the gods, Caesar owes everything to his good luck, which the gods have given him only to excuse their angry punishment for it afterward. Caesar's undeserved victory over Antony will become Antony's vengeful victory over Caesar.

"Husband, I come! / Now to that name my courage prove my title!" (5.2.286–87). Hoping to rejoin Cleopatra in death, Antony, thinking she had killed herself, sought to be "[a] bridegroom in [his] death and run into't / As to a lover's bed" (4.14.101–2). He pursued death as a lover because only in death, he thought, he could be with his love and she would love him in death only if he died as nobly as she. Cleopatra, also seeing death as her marriage to Antony, similarly thinks that her courage in killing herself entitles her to be his wife. Both finally see courage as uniting them in death as husband and wife.[55] For both, spiritedness supplants sensuality. A spirited death will earn for each the other's undying love.

Yet, while Cleopatra's sensuality transforms itself into spiritedness, her spiritedness, in turn, transforms itself into spirituality. With the world stripped of possible noble achievements, spirit, turning against the world— and, indeed, against itself—spiritualizes itself. "I am fire and air; my other elements / I give to baser life" (5.2.288–89; see 4.10.3–4). Cleopatra repudiates her bodily elements. In the end, she rejects the living world in its entirety. Where spirit tends generally to resist the degrading effects of mortality,[56] with Cleopatra it ultimately denies life itself. Rather than rising above death, she finds a "better life" in death. Claiming to be composed only of the higher elements, Cleopatra leaves to baser life her baser elements. Formerly the incarnation of bodily pleasure, she now sees herself as the decarnation of bodily life. Desiring and finding meaning in death, she, like Antony, unwittingly alludes to the vision of the new Jerusalem—he as the groom, she as the bride or as the holy city itself ("And I, John, saw the holy city, new Jerusalem, . . . prepared as a bride trimmed for her husband" [Rev. 21:2]).[57] Death is not only a release or even a refuge, but a reward, for them.

Bidding them "[f]arewell . . . long farewell" (5.2.291), Cleopatra kisses Charmian and Iras with "the last warmth of [her] lips" (5.2.290). Iras immediately falls and dies. Cleopatra wonders whether she has killed Iras with her kiss: "Have I the aspic in my lips?" (5.2.292). In an unintended sense, her parting kiss may have killed Iras. Iras may have died, not from the venom of the asp, but from the grief of taking her mistress's leave. Like Enobarbus, she seems to die of a grievous, broken heart. From the start, Cleopatra has been surrounded by a female court. In the end, her only loyal friends are her serving women.

Iras's death reassures Cleopatra. "If thou and nature can so gently part, / The stroke of death is as a lover's pinch / Which hurts and is desired" (5.2.293–95). Death, resembling an amorous embrace, is not painless, but its pain is not to be feared, for it is a mild pain that gives pleasure. Cleopatra need not fear her greatest desire. Cleopatra then adds a second meaning to

Iras's swift, silent death. She understands it as reflecting on the merit of the world. "If thus thou vanishest, thou tell'st the world / It is not worth leave-taking" (5.2.296–97). While identifying Iras entirely with her soul ("thou vanishest"), Cleopatra concludes that Iras's lack of ceremony at her parting indicates the lack of worthiness of what she leaves. Just as it involves no fearful pain, death entails no fearful loss.

Charmian, however, wants the gods to weep. "Dissolve, thick clouds, and rain, that I may say / The gods themselves do weep!" (5.2.298–99). Charmian wants to be able to believe that the gods themselves find Cleopatra's death heartbreaking. Like Cleopatra, who wanted the cosmos to match her sorrow and darken the world at the approach of Antony's death (4.15.10–12), she wants the gods to share her sorrow at Cleopatra's death. Their grief would be her consolation.

Cleopatra suddenly fears what might follow death. A moment ago, she bid Iras to act quickly because she thought Antony roused himself to praise her noble act (5.2.282ff.). Now, just as she thought her courage in dying proved her title as Antony's wife, she fears that Iras's dying first "proves me base" (5.2.299). She is afraid that the handsome ("curled" [5.2.300]) Antony will meet Iras first, ask her about Cleopatra ("make demand of her" [5.2.301]), fall in love with Iras for being nobler, and then "spend that kiss / Which is my heaven to have" (5.2.301–02). Her jealous fear carries over even beyond the grave.

Cleopatra applies the deadly asp to her breast. "With thy sharp teeth this knot intrinsicate / Of life at once untie" (5.2.303–4). Cleopatra sees life as an intricate and intrinsic union ("knot intrinsicate") of body and soul. Death does not so much end life as untie the soul from its mortal combination with the body. The asp, however, fails to respond to her command, and so Cleopatra must provoke it.[58] "Poor venomous fool, / Be angry and dispatch," she says, punning on "dispatch" (5.2.304–5). She must anger the snake so that it strikes her swiftly and fatally. Believing that she is defeating Caesar by dying, Cleopatra, at once personifying the snake and seeing it as her ally, wishes it could speak so that she might "hear [it] call great Caesar ass / Unpolicied!" (5.2.306–7). The asp will make an ass of Caesar by thwarting his plan to exhibit her in Rome. It would proclaim that great Caesar has been politically outwitted ("[u]npolicied") by a "[p]oor venomous fool." Cleopatra's victory over Caesar consists not simply in her escaping from him, but in her getting the better of him, and doing so by using as "poor an instrument" as an asp. Her spirited, spiteful victory lies in Caesar's public humiliation, just as her being led in his procession would have been her great public disgrace.

Charmian exclaims in dismay, "O eastern star!" (5.2.307). The eastern star is Venus, the morning star. Enobarbus had compared Cleopatra to Venus (2.2.210), and Antony had said that his pleasure lies "[i]'th'East" and the beds "i'th' East" are soft (2.3.39; 2.6.50). In more than one regard, Cleopatra, whom "[a]ll the East" (1.5.48) was to consider its mistress, has been queen of the East. She has embodied as well as ruled the voluptuous excesses of the East. The eastern star also signifies the birth of Jesus:

> When Jesus then was born at Bethlethem in Judea in the days of Herod the King, behold, there came Wisemen from the East to Jerusalem, saying, "Where is the King of the Jews that is born? For we have seen his star in the East and are come to worship him."
>
> (Matt. 2:1–2)[59]

In one respect the eastern star falls ("The star is fallen" [4.14.107]), but in another it rises. Eastern sensuality gives rise to Eastern spirituality. The star's double nature, while capturing the sensuality and spirituality of the East, reflects, in particular, Christianity's double treatment of the body. Christianity incarnates God as a man ("And the word was made flesh" [John 1:14]) and at the same time decarnalizes man's body. While the son of God not only lives but dies, man is promised an eternal life in death ("[T]he gift of God is eternal life" [Rom. 6:23]). While Jesus accepts all the sufferings of death in the flesh, man's life becomes wholly spiritualized. Thus, Cleopatra, applying the serpent to her breast, calls it "my baby . . . / That sucks the nurse asleep" (5.2.308–9). The baby kills the mother, nursing it. The baby gives death to the mother giving it nourishment and life. Yet, by killing her, the baby, whose mortal bite is "sweet," "soft" and "gentle" (5.2.310), nourishes the mother's new life, her life in death. No longer railing at or rising above it, Cleopatra, at her end, assumes death while giving it meaning.

"What should I stay—" (5.2.312). Cleopatra's final words, asking why she should remain, are an unfinished question, though with an implicit answer. "What" has the sense of "why" when the expected answer has the force of a negative.[60] The rhetorical question answers itself. The irony of Cleopatra's dying words is akin to that of Antony's. While Antony had a passion for "more" which ended only when he was "no more" (4.15.61), Cleopatra ends her life of constant change with the word "stay," while implicitly denying there is reason to stay. Her last words, like his, speaking against themselves, at once epitomize and contradict her life.

Charmian completes Cleopatra's question: "In this vile world?" (5.2.313). Charmian is speaking for both herself and Cleopatra. The world is now empty and worthless. For Cleopatra, it was empty and worthless without Antony; for Charmian, without Cleopatra. Death, on the other hand, has been enriched. "Now boast thee, Death, in thy possession lies / A lass unparalleled" (5.2.314–15). When Antony died, Cleopatra said that she was now no different from a milkmaid (4.15.77–79). Now that Cleopatra is dead, Charmian speaks similarly of her. Cleopatra is an ordinary woman ("lass") in death, although she was "unparalleled" in life. Her death, like Antony's, levels the high and the low, the noble and the common. "Downy windows, close," Charmian continues, "And golden Phoebus, never be beheld / Of eyes again so royal!" (5.2.315–17). Cleopatra's death lessens the sun's visible splendor (see 4.8.27–29). It darkens the world by closing the most magnificent eyes.

Charmian says she will straighten Cleopatra's crown, the last emblem of her royalty, "and then play" (5.2.318). Once she completes her final act of duty, she will accept the queen's permission and "play till doomsday" (5.2.230–31). She will choose to die. Suitably enough, just as she echoes Cleopatra's "ass / Unpolicied" with her "lass unparalleled" (5.2.306–7, 315), and will soon repeat Cleopatra's "dispatch" with her own (5.2.305, 321), Charmian rhymes Cleopatra's last word "stay" with her own intended last word "play."

Charmian's dying is briefly delayed by Caesar's guard, entering rapidly and noisily ("*rustling in*" [s.d. 5.2.318]). Caesar, who feared that Cleopatra would, after all, take her own life, has sent, as Charmian pointedly remarks, "[t]oo slow a messenger" (5.2.320). Despite Caesar's usual quickness, Cleopatra outpaced him. "[S]he hath . . . celerity in dying" (1.2.151). The guard, afraid that Caesar has been deceived ("All's not well. Caesar's beguiled"), reprovingly demands, "Is this well done?" (5.2.322, 324). And Charmian, shifting the sense of his word, replies with proud simplicity, "It is done well, and fitting for a princess / Descended of so many royal kings" (5.2.325–26). The end not only of a queen or even of the three-centuries-old Ptolemaic line but of three millennia of Egyptian pharaohs, Cleopatra's death was noble and fitting for monarch descended from countless generations of royal monarchs. Her action befits her ancestry.[61] As Eros could not bear to live without Antony and killed himself in the same way as his master (4.14.90–96), so, too, Charmian does not for a moment think of living without Cleopatra and kills herself in the same way as her mistress ("O come apace! Dispatch! I partly feel thee" [5.2.321]).[62] Outliving the queen whom she served by barely a dozen lines (see 1.2.32), she applies the asp, falls and dies.

12.

Dolabella, describing Cleopatra's suicide in the language of the theater, says that Caesar's fears have been realized: "Thyself art coming / To see performed the dreaded act which thou / So sought'st to hinder" (5.2.329–31). Caesar, however, is surprisingly generous. After Dolabella flatters him for having feared what in fact occurred ("O sir, you are too sure an augurer: / That you did fear is done" [5.2.333–34]), Caesar praises Cleopatra's courage and cunning: "Bravest at the last, / She levelled at our purposes and, being royal, / Took her own way" (5.2.334–36). Most impressive at her end, she was shrewd enough to realize what Caesar had intended, and brave and dignified enough to take her own life to avoid it. Caesar, seeing none of them bleeding, tries to determine how the women died. Supposing that they could not have been poisoned since they have no external swelling,[63] and describing their suicides—or their willingness to die—as "noble weakness," he praises Cleopatra's beauty in death: "[S]he looks . . . / As she would catch another Antony / In her strong toil of grace" (5.2.343, 345–47). Death takes nothing from her grace, a beauty or grace that Caesar never acknowledged when she and Antony were alive.

Cleopatra wished to kill herself "after the high Roman fashion" (5.1.91), but she sought an easy, painless death. "[H]er physician tells me," Caesar reports, "She hath pursued conclusions infinite / Of easy ways to die" (5.2.353–55). Like Antony's final celebratory march through Alexandria (4.8.30–39), Cleopatra's suicide combines the Roman and the Egyptian—a stern Roman act and a soft Egyptian means.

Caesar allows Cleopatra to be buried with Antony.[64] "She shall be buried by her Antony," he announces. "No grave upon the earth shall clip in it / A pair so famous" (5.2.357–59). Antony and Cleopatra will be buried in the tomb in which they both died.[65] Perhaps unsurprisingly, Caesar forgets his "dearest sister." Like Dolabella (5.2.70), he speaks as though Cleopatra, not Octavia, had been Antony's wife. While burying him as a lover rather than as a Roman, Caesar gives Antony and Cleopatra the distinction which Antony had sought (1.1.37–41; 4.14.52–55). Where the play began in Egypt with a Roman soldier criticizing Antony and Cleopatra, it ends in Egypt with the Roman emperor praising them. Caesar praises them as superlative lovers. Yet, however magnanimous it may seem, his praise becomes a testimonial to himself:[66] "High events as these / Strike those that make them, and their story is / No less in pity than his glory which / Brought them to be lamented" (5.2.359–62). The account of these great events brings no less glory to Caesar than pity for Antony and Cleopatra. Indeed, the greater the pity for them, the greater the glory for him, for the pity is a measure of the conqueror's achievement. Caesar thus praises himself in praising his defeated enemies. He may forget his sister in paying tribute to Antony and Cleopatra, but he does not forget himself.

Caesar concludes by looking to the future. He will have his army attend Antony and Cleopatra's funeral "[i]n solemn show . . . / And then [go] to Rome" (5.2.363–64). Instead of degrading Antony and Cleopatra in Rome, he commands "[h]igh order in this great solemnity" for them in Egypt (5.2.365). Caesar stresses formal dignity, gravity and stateliness. His final words anticipate his return to Rome, where his title or designation as "Augustus," identifying him as an object of reverence or worship, will rest largely on his preeminent dignity and authority. "Afterwards, he assumed the surname . . . of Augustus . . . , because religious and holy places, wherein also anything [that] is consecrated . . . [are] called Augusta" (Suetonius, *Augustus*, 7.2; Holland, 1:85). "[T]he boy Caesar" not only becomes "[s]ole sir o'th' world," but will assume a name that ranks with Jove: "With Jove himself Augustus name doth share" (Ovid, *Fasti*, 1.608; Gower, 18).[67]

13.

Caesar's victory brings universal peace. But the end of Rome's foreign and civil wars also brings slavery to Rome. "The Romans had no hope of safety other than retreating into slavery" (Florus, 2.14.4–5). With peace come submission and humility, contempt for one's present existence, and hope, even confidence, in a better life in death. The age of politics is over. Taught to "seek . . . first the kingdom of God and his righteousness" (Matt. 6:33), followers of the new religion become indifferent to political affairs. "There is nothing more alien to us than public matters" (Tertullian, 38.3). The world thus becomes dimmer with Caesar's victory. "The bright day is done / And we are for the dark" (5.2.192–93).[68]

One might suppose that Shakespeare exaggerates Antony's nobility and Caesar's calculating cold-bloodedness in order to underscore the world's loss in Antony's defeat. Efficient administration replaces political, even heroic, action. Yet, however much he presents Caesar as less noble-hearted or noble-minded than Antony, Shakespeare also indicates that Antony's victory would have passed to Cleopatra, and the East would have triumphed over the West. Antony's victory would have been the triumph of Orientalism. With Caesar's victory, however, Rome, not Alexandria, remains the capital of the Roman empire and will become the capital of Christendom. And notwithstanding the eventual relocations of their capitols to Constantinople, both the Roman empire and the Christian church will remain—or at least claim to remain—Western.[69] Even latter-day Byzantine emperors, while denying the term to any other potentate, will profess the name of "Romans." "Whatsoever changes had been introduced by the lapse of ages," Gibbon writes of those emperors,

> they alleged a lineal and unbroken succession from Augustus and Constantine; and, in the lowest period of degeneracy and decay, the name of ROMANS adhered to the last fragments of the empire of Constantinople. (Gibbon, 53, 3:296)

Particularly important, the Latin and Greek languages are retained. "While the government of the East was transacted in Latin, the Greek was the language of literature and philosophy."[70] Thus, the history of Rome and Greece will manage largely to escape the injuries of time. Although the Christian religion will try to eliminate every vestige of paganism,[71] it will fail because it will be forced to retain the Latin and Greek languages, the former particularly for the law,[72] and hence willy-nilly retain much of pagan literature.[73] The indigenous languages will preserve the offensive history.

Caesar's victory over Antony is thus crucial to the political development of the modern West. It helps to preserve the example of classical republicanism—the very regime which, ironically, Caesarism defeated. And the example will inspire and instruct medieval and modern republicanism—a republicanism, which, freed from the killing, conquest and plunder that were the constant practice of ancient republics, will become softened by centuries of Christianity. It may be true that the new religion will eliminate ancient virtue.[74] But it is no less true that the replacement of the fierce by the gentler virtues will allow republicanism eventually to return to the West without the warlike spirit of the ancient model. The worldliness of modern republicanism will be commercial rather than combative, humane rather than heroic. Finance and industry will replace nobility and honor.

Notes

1. "The death of Caesar was ever before his eyes." Gibbon, 1:63. See, e.g., Suetonius, *Augustus*, 35.1–2.
2. Neill, 298.
3. See Jeremiah 4:7.
4. On the difficulty of writing history under the Caesars, see Dio, 53.19.
5. See, further, Blits, *Spirit, Soul, and City*, 32–33.
6. "This was the first sedition among the citizens of Rome that fell out with murder and bloodshed, since the expulsion of the kings." Plutarch, *Tiberius Gracchus*, 20.1; North, 5:225.
7. See, e.g., *Cor.*, 3.1.141–48.
8. Cantor, 130.

9. See, e.g., Dio, 56.38ff.

10. Suetonius, *Augustus*, 17.4; Plutarch, *Antony*, 78.3.

11. Velleius Paterculus, 2.126.4. See also *Augustus*, 8; Ovid, *Metamorphoses*, 15.832.

12. For Pansa and Hirtius, see 1.4.58–59.

13. Also Plutarch, *Sayings of Romans*, Augustus Caesar, 10 (207e).

14. Plutarch, *Antony*, 78.4.

15. Plutarch, *Antony*, 79.1–2.

16. Previously, she was "Queen of Egypt," "dear lady" and "worthy lady" (5.2.9, 32, 38).

17. Granville-Barker, 2:157. Only Iras has called her by the title before (3.11.33; 4.15.75).

18. Pliny, 34.41.

19. Cicero, *Republic*, 6.18; Pliny, 2.84.

20. The Folio reads "an Anthony," which nearly all editors, following L. Theobald (1733), change to "an autumn."

21. *OED*, s.v. Yet *adv*. 3.9.

22. Plutarch, *Antony*, 82.1.

23. This intention seems to explain why Cleopatra, telling Proculeius that she "would gladly / Look [Caesar] i'th' face" (5.2.31–32), seemed to invite the exchange.

24. Plutarch, *Antony*, 82.2.

25. By contrast, in Plutarch Seleucus is present "by chance" and corrects Cleopatra of his own accord (Plutarch, *Antony*, 83.3; North, 6:84).

26. Caesar speaks of "acts" and of "action" once each. By the former he means the general tendency or effect of one's character (2.2.121); by the latter, the gestures indicating one's frame of mind (3.12.35).

27. This is the only time she uses the familiar pronoun in speaking to Caesar.

28. Plutarch, *Antony*, 83.5; Dio, 51.13.3.

29. "Merits," here, means "demerits" or "faults." "*Merits* formerly meant 'what one deserves, whether good or ill.' See *deserts* in modern usage." Kittredge, 1401.

30. Plutarch, *Antony*, 83.5.

31. Cleopatra used the same verb ("word") to order Mardian to deceive Antony with her reported death (4.13.9).

32. The sole exceptions are Antony's sword stained with "his most noble blood" (5.1.26) and Caesar's reported wish to let the world see "his nobleness well acted" toward Cleopatra (5.2.44).

33. In Cleopatra's phrase "Be noble to myself," "The heavy stress falling on *self* after three unstressed syllables indicates a stronger meaning than that normally conveyed by the reflexive pronoun *myself*." Neill, 314.

34. Also, e.g., 3.11.3–4; 3.13.158; 4.14.1–14, 47, 86–87; 4.15.89; 5.2.78–80, 315–17. The past participle "done" appears more often in *Antony and Cleopatra* (thirty-seven times) than in any Shakespeare play, except *Macbeth* (thirty-eight times).

35. "A new commandment give I unto you, that ye love one another; as I have loved you, that ye also love one another." John 13:34–35.

36. Wilson, 239.

37. For the pornographic allusion of "posture," ostensibly a theatrical term, see Partridge, s.v. Posture.

38. "Cleopatra's death scene . . . is the most self-consciously *performed*, the most elaborately gestural dying in all Shakespearian tragedy." Neill, 78 (his italics).

39. See, e.g., Seneca, *On Anger*, 3.15, *Letters*, 12.10, 65.22, 70.5, 14–16, 77.15, 117.21–22; Epictetus, *Discourses*, 1.24.20, *Manual*, 21; Marcus Aurelius, *Meditations*, 5.29, 8.47, 10.8; Diogenes Laertius, *The Lives and Opinions of Eminent Philosophers*, 7.130.

40. See, e.g., Cicero, *On Old Age*, 70; Seneca, *Letters*, 7.11–12, 29.12, 74.7, 76.31, 77.20, 80.7, 84.9–10, 85.37, 108.6–8, 115.14ff., 120.22; Epictetus, *Discourses*, 1.2.16, 1.29.42, 3.22.26, *Manual*, 17; Marcus Aurelius, 3.8, 10.27, 12.36; Diogenes Laertius, 7.160. See, further, Blits, *Deadly Thought*, 39, 163. Caesar, although he does not kill himself, pointedly turns his death into a theatrical display; see Suetonius, *Augustus*, 99.1.

41. Diodorus, 1.11.1; Plutarch, *Antony*, 54.6, *Isis and Osiris*, 52 (372d–e); Dio, 50.5.3; Diogenes Laertius, 1.10.

42. Plutarch, *Isis and Osiris*, 53 (372e); Holland, 1309; also 43 (368c–d). See also Macrobius, *Saturnalia*, 1.21.11.

43. Plutarch, *Antony*, 71.4–5.

44. Anna B. Jameson, *Shakespeare's Heroines: Charactersitics of Women, Moral, Poetical, and Historical* (London: George Bell and Sons, 1879), 274.

45. Neill, 318.

46. Fisch, 64.

47. "He seems to have been listening to sermons on Salvation by Faith, not Works." Wilson, 241. See, e.g., Martin Luther, *The Freedom of a Christian*, in Harold J. Grimm, ed., *Luther's Works*, 55 vols. (Philadelphia: Muhlenberg, 1957), 31:348.

48. Also, e.g., John 3:16; 6:40; 10:28; 17:2; Rev. 21:4.

49. For the sexual puns, see Partridge, s.vv. Do, Kind.

50. Wilson, 241.

51. 5.2.244, 253, 274; also "forsooth" (5.2.278).

52. *OED*, s.v. Make, 69b; Partridge, s.v. Mar.

53. E.g., Matt. 4:1ff., 13:39; Luke 4:1ff., 8:12; John 13:2.

54. "I will not drink hence forth of this fruit of the vine until that day when I shall drink it new with you in my Father's kingdom." Matt. 26:29.

55. In Plutarch, Cleopatra hopes only, with the help of the gods, to be buried with Antony (Plutarch, *Antony*, 84.2–4).

56. See Blits, *Spirit, Soul, and City*, 2.

57. Note, in this context, 5.2.341–42.

58. Plutarch, *Antony*, 86.1–3.

59. Also Matt. 2:9; Rev. 2:28; 22:16; see 1.2.27–31.

60. Schmidt, s.v. What 1.b.

61. Plutarch, *Antony*, 85.3–4.

62. Ernest Schanzer, "Plot-Echoes in Shakespeare's Plays," *Shakespeare Jahrbuch* (1969), 110.

63. On the absence of swelling and the painless, slumberous death, see Nicander, *Theriaca*, 187–89; Philumenus, *On Poisonous Animals*, 16.3; also Lucan, *Pharsalia*, 9.815ff.

64. Plutarch, *Antony*, 86.4.

65. Suetonius, *Augustus*, 17.4.

66. MacCallum, 389.

67. Also *Augustus*, 34; Dio, 53.16.7–8.

68. Augustine, 5.14.

69. Gibbon, 17, 1:520ff.

70. Gibbon, 53, 3:296. "There are three sacred languages—Hebrew, Greek and Latin—which are preeminent throughout the world." Isidore of Seville, *Etymologies*, trans. Stephen A. Barney, et al., (Cambridge: Cambridge University Press, 2006), 9.1.3.

71. See, e.g., John of Salisbury, *Policraticus*, 8.19.

72. E.g., Justinian, *Corpus Juris Civilis*, 527–65.

73. Machiavelli, *Discourses*, 2.5.1.

74. Machiavelli, *Discourses*, 1, Pref., 2.

~

Index

Abbott, E. A., 102n48, 152n85
Achilles, 174
"act" (term), 11n25
action: and inability, 41, 45, 62, 77, 141; and intention, 63, 77, 142, 176–77; moralizing in place of, 145; and nobility, 5. *See also* "act"; honor; noble; suicide
Adam and Eve, 210
Aemilius Paulus, 111
Aeneas and Dido, 34–35, 178
Alexander the Great, 15, 49n3, 111
anger, 28, 80, 174–75. *See also* indignation; punishment
Antigonus, 111
Antonius, Lucius, 61
Apis, 103n74
Appian, 87, 96
Augustus (*Res Gestae*), 189n29

Bible: 1 Corinthians, 210; Galatians, 189n19; Genesis, 210; John, 9, 189n18, 189n20, 210, 212, 214, 220n35; Matthew, 8, 51n48, 159, 192n88, 207, 214, 217, 220n54;

Psalms, 146, 158; Revelation, 8, 9, 18, 167, 181–82, 183, 191n60, 191n72, 191n75; Romans, 9, 214; Titus, 189n17
Brutus, Junius, 133
Brutus, Marcus, 6, 68, 78, 84, 85, 111, 133, 162
Burton, Robert, 102n51

Caesar, Julius, 4, 29, 33, 46, 48, 51n46, 67, 72–73, 84–85, 86, 88–89, 100–101nn21–22, 111, 143–44, 117, 118, 125, 172, 193
Caesarion, 73, 88, 101n22, 118–19, 137
Calpurnia, 100n21
Capell, Edward, 10n16
Carrhae, battle of, 68
Cassius, 11n26, 15, 29, 51n46, 85, 133. *See also* Brutus, Marcus
Christianity: decarnalizes life, 214; emergence of, 8–9, 18, 25, 158–59, 165, 181–82, 206–7, 217–18; and hymns, 98; and incarnation, 9, 214; and Latin and Greek languages, 218; new heaven of, 8, 181, 210;

223

Rome: versus Alexandria, 119, 217–18; augury and divination in, 24, 74; Augustan Principate, 129, 217; and Christendom, 217–18; citizenship, 180; as city, 10n6; civil strife in, 4, 195; civil wars of, 3–4, 32–33, 36, 67–68, 84–85, 90, 156, 163, 195–96; destruction of, 182; and *exempla*, 181; first triumvirate, 117; foreign luxury in, its source, 101n28; gods of, 2, 8, 24; leaders, depended on for valor, 127; lieutenancy, victory through, 106–8, 133, 138–39, 179; marriages in, 67, 100nn20–21; not mentioned, 15, 60, 115; military discipline in, 3–4, 156; military service in, 3–4, 42; orientalizing of, 74, 171; plebeians in, 4–5, 190n51; political oratory, now absent from, 4–5, 11n20; and the principle of war, 8, 207; private replaces public in, 2–3, 6–8, 20, 69, 74, 84, 85–86, 90, 92, 97, 114–15, 142–43, 194; republican regime, 1–3, 7, 20, 61, 85, 107, 114–15, 133, 134, 195; second triumvirate, 53–54n87, 61, 67–68, 84, 117; senate, 2, 84–85; slavery of, 217; sole rule in, 195–96; triumphs in, 118–19, 162, 173, 179, 197, 207–8; universal empire of, 1, 4, 7–8, 84, 142–43, 157, 163, 207; and universal peace, 163, 207, 217. *See also* Christianity; Egypt; Greece; Romans
Romulus, 24

Sallust: *Catiline's Conspiracy*, 20; *Histories*, 85
Scipio Aemilianus, 111
Scipio Africanus, 111
sententia, 183, 191–92n76
Sethos (Egyptian king), 49n14
Shakespeare, other works: *Coriolanus*, 2, 4, 7, 15, 42, 114–15, 182, 201; *King John*, 10n14; *Julius Caesar*, 3, 4, 11n26, 14, 15, 20, 33, 51n46, 67, 85, 111, 133, 152n87, 153n95, 162, 195; *Macbeth*, 219n34; *The Merchant of Venice*, 11n25; *The Rape of Lucrece*, 10n15
shame: and action, 29–30; of defeat replaced by scorn of victory, 135–36; and the face, 19, 134, 184; and fearless fury, 149; and fear of infamy, 29; public view, seeks to avoid, 19, 131, 134, 179, 184; and self-dissolution, 132, 133; and self-division, 23, 130, 131–32, 140, 152n82, 164, 169–70, 190n42; and self-punishment, 165; self-reflexive, 131; shaming those who shame one, 147. *See also* death; love; noble; pride; revenge; "shame"
"shame" (term), 50n28
Sicily and Sardinia, 86, 89
"sin" (term), 188, 192n87
soliloquy, Cleopatra without one, 142
speech, Asiatic, 16
spiritedness, 9, 20, 106, 130, 183, 202, 212. *See also* honor; Romans; shame
Stoicism, 6, 143, 208. *See also* suicide
Suetonius: *Augustus*, 43, 163, 197, 217; *Divus Julius*, 86
suicide, 178–81, 198, 208–9, 216. *See also* Christianity; glory, political; noble; women
Sulla, 85, 100n21, 180

Tacitus: *Annals*, 134; *Dialogue on Oratory*, 5; *History*, 49n16
Tarn, W. W., 151n42
tears, in victory, 111–12, 194–95
Telamon (Ajax), 174
Tertullian, 8, 150n19, 217
Thetis and Peleus, 126

~

About the Author

Jan H. Blits is a professor in the University Honors Faculty at the University of Delaware. He received his B.A. from St. John's College, Annapolis, Maryland, and his Ph.D. from the New School for Social Research in New York City. He has served as Secretary of the Navy Distinguished Fellow at the U.S. Naval Academy and has won the University of Delaware's Excellence in Teaching Award. He is the author of *The End of the Ancient Republic: Shakespeare's* Julius Caesar, *The Insufficiency of Virtue:* Macbeth *and the Natural Order, Deadly Thought:* Hamlet *and the Human Soul, The Soul of Athens: Shakespeare's* A Midsummer Night's Dream, and, most recently, *Spirit, Soul, and City: Shakespeare's* Coriolanus. His articles have appeared in *The Review of Politics, The Journal of Politics, Interpretation, Apeiron, The Southern Journal of Philosophy, Educational Theory,* as well as other journals.